The Gourmet's Tour of
GREAT BRITAIN
and IRELAND

The Gourmet's Tour of GREAT BRITAIN and IRELAND

Thirty Great Restaurants and Their Favourite Recipes

Text by	Sir Clement Freud
Photographs by	Claude Pataut

A Bulfinch Press Book • Little, Brown and Company
Boston • Toronto • London

First English Language Edition

The recipes are produced by kind permission of the Chefs concerned. One of the recipes from the Waterside Inn, "Pêches Rôties au Caramel Noisettine", is reprinted from the Roux Brothers' book on "Pâtisserie", published by Macdonald & Co Ltd.

International Standard Book Number
0-8212-1727-5

Library of Congress Catalog Card Number
89-61064

Bulfinch Press is an imprint and trademark of Little, Brown and Company (Inc.)

Published simultaneously in Canada by Little, Brown & Company (Canada) Limited

Printed in Italy

Note to Readers

All quantities in this book have been given in imperial (British Standard) and metric measures (in this order), except for butter and margarine quantities, which have also been given in American measures. When following the recipes, use one set of measures throughout, since imperial and metric have been calculated separately and are not necessarily direct equivalents.

Imperial measures (cups, tablespoons, etc.) are not always equivalent to American and Canadian Standard measures.

The most notable discrepancy is that British Standard pints, cups, and tablespoons are slightly larger in capacity than American and Canadian Standard pints, cups, and tablespoons. The British Standard fluid pint measure has a capacity of 20 fluid ounces; the American and Canadian Standard fluid pint measure has a capacity of 16 fluid ounces. Correspondingly, the British Standard ½ – pint measuring cup has a capacity of 10 fluid ounces; the American and Canadian Standard ½ – pint measuring cup has a capacity of 8 fluid ounces. And the British Standard tablespoon measures 1 fluid ounce; the American and Canadian Standard tablespoon measures ¾ fluid ounce. Pints and cups are rarely used as liquid measures in this volume. Most of the liquid measures are given in fluid ounces.

In addition, the British Standard fluid ounce and the American and Canadian Standard fluid ounce, while nearly equivalent, do differ slightly: 1 fluid British ounce = .96 fluid U.S. ounce. This discrepancy is not enough to make a difference in measurement for most recipes, but it should be kept in mind when the liquid quantities involved are large; subtract one ounce when the quantity is over 25 ounces, subtract two ounces when the quantity is over 50 ounces, and so on.

Finally, in Britain, as in most other parts of the world, dry ingredients are measured by weight rather than volume, so for many of these recipes the American cook will need a gram/ounce scale. Please remember that American cooks will run into trouble trying to measure ounces of flour, sugar, or other dry ingredients in their measuring cups, for an American fluid ounce is not the same as an American ounce in weight.

Conversion Table for Liquid Measures

Metric	British	American
1 ml.	.035 oz.	.034 oz.
28.4 ml.	1 oz.	.96 oz.
29.56 ml.	1.035 oz.	1 oz.
236 ml.	8.26 oz.	1 cup (8 oz.)
284 ml.	1 cup (10 oz.)	9.66 oz.
473 ml.	16.55 oz.	1 pint (16 oz)
½ litre	17.5 oz.	17 oz.
568 ml.	1 pint (20 oz.)	19.31 oz.
946 ml.	33.11 oz.	1 qt (32 oz.)
1 litre	35.19 oz.	33.81 oz.
1136 ml.	1 qt (40 oz.)	38.62 oz.

Contents

The history of British and Irish gastronomy embraces a profusion of fine ingredients assembled by practitioners who have skill – rather than passion or cunning. The French did amazing things with tripe, the Italians achieved world-wide fame by macerating breasts of peacock which were larded and flamed and I don't know what else. We conceived the cutlet frill; our butchers invented the crown of lamb, married pastry to fruit and meat to create pies and puddings.

The charcutiers of Paris blended choice cuts of pork with game to make terrines and pâtés; our people quietly fed scraps of pork into large amounts of bread to produce the sausage, loved by Britons even if most other nations think ill of it and the EEC have legislated for a minimum meat content which would have disqualified much of what our forefathers ate with enjoyment: Saveloys, Cumberland Rings, Lincolnshire Bangers, et al.

In the restaurant trade our grill cook was The Man; elsewhere in the world, fame and fortune were accorded the one who made sauces... and as our nation's restaurants tended to serve pretty much what was eaten in our nation's homes, going out for dinner did not catch on the way it did across the Channel. All has changed, but there are still those who believe that "le goût anglais" is overcooked cabbage; it is for them that I am particularly proud of presenting a selection of marvellous restaurants that grace our land. You can now eat as well in Britain as anywhere in the world and, while a bit of work still has to be done on the lower end of the market, "going to Britain for its good food" no longer gives rise to incredulity.
There are a number of questions that deserve discussion : why thirty restaurants? Well, why not, is the first answer that comes to mind. Thirty is a good number, the average month has 30 days and if you wanted to ruin your waistline as well as your pocket, you could use April, June, September or November to visit each of the listed places, though care should be taken for some are closed on Sundays, others on Mondays.

Why these 30 restaurants is an altogether better question. The answer is that they are among the best in the land, bearing in mind the need for diversity and regional representation. (We did not think there would be a very wide interest in a book of "The 30 best Chinese restaurants in Kensington".)

This is a companion volume to similar ventures undertaken in France and Italy and there is one great difference: in Britain, with a few notable exceptions, the restaurants are run as businesses; are bought and sold; have staff who can be enticed away by promises of a brighter future or simply a higher salary.

On the continent of Europe the majority of restaurants are vocational; families own them and pass them on to their children and their childrens' children, who are bred into the trade. In France there are gastro-dynasties whose names are bigger than the establishment or the town or village in which they are located. Go to Bocuse or Troisgros or Vergé or Georges Blanc, the guides tell you... never having to add "and do make sure that the eponymous proprietor is still there". In Britain, while this book was being written, five restaurants changed ownership, six had different chefs from the ones promised by the current year's Food Guides. In an effort to make this book as useful as possible in the long term, we have given assessments that will remain relevant – even if the chef is "transferred" or the manager has decided to hang up his VAT returns and retire. It is important to bear in mind that when a famed restaurant is run as a business it tends to retain much of the quality that made it great. The new purchaser will have paid substantially for "goodwill" and will do everything in his power to retain the old clientele. A talented chef who wants to set up on his own can create goodwill, has no need to buy someone else's reputation.

The book is an appreciation, not a critique. I have in my time "reviewed" restaurants all over the world; written about them from the standpoint of the customer and sniped at the burnt pigeon, the oversalted soup, the unoriginality of the salad – which are matters of only passing interest. Everyone will occasionally get things wrong; if they get them wrong too often they do not win awards, nor obtain Michelin stars and are not fully booked when all about them are forced to advertise or promise special "deals" to potential clients.

When people ask me who is the most important person in a restaurant, I tend to ask "from whose point of view?". For the customers, it is a close run between chef and waiter – for the best food is spoilt when served by clumsy, churlish, abusive or arrogant staff. From the proprietor's point of view, the most important person is the controller, without whom there would be no profit. I do not believe that good food in isolation merits more than a cool nod in the direction of the kitchen. Good food in a rotten atmosphere ruins an evening. There is a tendency with the new prestige in which successful chefs wallow to make restaurants the locations for ego-trips. We have excluded those from this book in the belief that however wrong a customer may be, the job of a waiter is not to point this out. Cooking brilliantly must not be part of a grim drive for recognition as a genius but a component (OK, an important component) of a happy occasion.

There is another cardinal difference between the catering trade in Britain and in the rest of Europe. In the United Kingdom there is a gut feeling that working in a restaurant is sort of demeaning; people confuse "being of service", which is honourable, with "being servile", which is despicable. As a consequence, putative waiters and waitresses in Britain become shop assistants, in which calling they know they can give customers a hard time with impunity.

Elsewhere a waiter is an important person in the community: waiters become Mayors of towns and in the South of France, where I worked in a hotel, I helped the wine-butler win election to the district council. Such a thing is inconceivable in this country where restaurant staff are looked at askance when they ask for a mortgage. Nevertheless, when you get a good British waiter he tends to outperform all others. If I wanted English-speaking staff, I should recruit from Devon and Cornwall, Scotland or the North East – in each of which locations they still seem to produce people who find the acceptable stance between aloofness and grovel.

The reader will note that there is nothing jingoistic about the selection of places in this book: French is the language of the restaurant kitchen, which does not give that nation a monopoly of skill, though it does give them about a century's start when it comes to running successful catering establishments. As we become increasingly European, there will be more and more places where you can mix the cuisines of the world at a single meal: start with a Bird's Nest Soup, move from Smoked Scotch Salmon via Poulet de Bresse to Rhubarb Fool with Cornish Cream. In ten years from now restaurant menus will have changed beyond recognition – but the approach to public gastronomy is likely to remain. It is about making good ingredients look attractive, taste delicious, and getting caring people to serve them at the right time and at the right temperature which, with the exception of clear soup, must never be too hot; then when the customer wants his or her bill, that should not take too long nor be too hot either.

As a cook there is a slightly uncomfortable feeling about writing a book in which two and a half dozen of one's fellow practitioners give recipes and I give none. Here is a long-forgotten far-off soup, which they used to serve to returning revellers, when the market of Paris was in Les Halles in the centre of the city.

In two ounces of clarified butter you simmer twelve ounces of thinly-sliced white onion until soft and slightly golden. Add one bottle of Champagne and bring to simmering point. Decant the hot, buttery, oniony Champagne into a soup tureen that can withstand heat and make for it a lid of a scraped camembert cheese topped with toasted breadcrumbs. Bake in a medium oven and when the top is golden and bubbling, remove the "lid", cut it into quarters and place these over the ladle of soup that is served in each of four marmites.

Sir Clement Freud

RUE ST JACQUES

The northern end of Soho, really only Soho if you live there and want to be part of the cosmopolitan restaurant scene, is known as Fitzrovia, runs from Fitzroy Square to Oxford Street and is just a couple of streets wide. Charlotte Street is the principal thoroughfare; a few east-to-west streets are in with a shout and Whitfield Street, parallel and to the east of Charlotte Street, qualifies.

During the Second World War and in the 1950s 'The Fitzroy Tavern' became a popular meeting place for artists; "Schmidt's", across the road from the Fitzroy, was a German restaurant famed for its excellent Frankfurters and unobliging staff, which finally closed its doors in the 1970s. At the end of the street stands "The White Tower" restaurant, opened by the charismatic Mr Stais, now run by his daughter and son-in-law, and which is loved for the consistency of its moussaka, the fine language of its menu and also the niceness of its carriage attendant, who will park your car. The Belle Meunière' was the favourite eating place of the young Princess Margaret; Bertorelli's was cheap and Italian and once denied access to a black couple, whereafter it lost its liberal clientele. Nearly every house in Charlotte Street was, or is, or will one day be a restaurant and the parking is easy; the adjacent advertising agencies and independent television offices make for a young, well-heeled clientele to whom proximity matters nearly as much as quality.

The Rue St Jacques is at No 5 Charlotte Street – third house on the left hand side if you are going north – and is an oasis of formal professionalism in an area which is primarily casual. Across the road Greek restaurants pour yoghourt onto their braziers and barbecue garlicky chickens; an oriental greengrocer arranges his exotic fruit; the odd drunk lurches by looking for the "Four Chairmen", open all afternoon, but inside Rue St Jacques the staff are dressed in black and white and might intimidate, were they not so effortlessly efficient and knowledgeable and on hand to check that things are going as they should. For customers, jackets and ties are de rigeur and the place is a haven not only for highly sophisticated food but for people mourning the decline of standards, who take along their young nieces to show them the way it used to be.

The chef, who has created this establishment of excellence, is Gunther Schlender, one of the great sauce cooks of the world; his intense sauces and glazes are set in small pools and complement – never overpower or drown – the food with which they arrive. This is a very mature restaurant for grown-up people and above all an establishment in which you find it rewarding to let them do it their way; quite apart from the fact that they do know best, to take on the staff in gastro-combat is never conducive to a happy evening out.

Rue St Jacques has, to my mind, the best wine list in the country: not the longest, and not quite the most expensive but 18 pages of really well-chosen vintages and shippers; compendious countries of origin – maps to show whither the wine that you drink emanates (which is a useful conversation piece), a good supply of half bottles, some stunning magnums, a genuinely comprehensive choice of dessert wines and a fine selection of classified clarets and upmarket Burgundies from distinguished vintners like Bernard Grivelet and Doudet-Naudin. There is also a wide range of champagnes – from half-bottles of house to magnums of Cuvée Sir Winston Churchill Pol Roger 1975 and Roederer Cristal Brut 1981. If you can only manage the 75 cl red house wine, for £10 a throw there is a Château de Terrefort-Quencard 1984, a medal-winning Bordeaux Supérieur.

A recent change of proprietor and decorative work to mark this event mean that there are now six small interlinking dining rooms each containing up to five tables where you can be at peace with the world and also get a serious, executive-type waiter to control your meal. If he wants to keep your bottle on his sideboard, out of your reach, this is only aggravating if he is not around when you want to refill your glass: he is.

There is a daily menu – with eight choices at each course and an *à la carte* with a similar range – no dish being duplicated on the two menus. Why the table d'hôte diner should be deprived of *Boudin de canard sauvage à la vinaigrette de poivrons doux* and forced to eat the *Terrine de ris de veau et de foie gras* which the *à la carte* consumer cannot have, is just one of those things. Schlender is very into making *saucissons* of things: monkfish, smoked lamb, langoustines, and, as a master saucier, his crab mousse with cream and lobster sauce, and his home-made seafood can-

nelloni show both imagination and real artistry. For vegetables he buys and immaculately undercooks the very best, youngest, tenderest carrots and broad beans. Among the puddings there is an unusual confection: *Pyramide de chocolat amer*, which has wafer thin slices of dark chocolate divided by a white chocolate mousse. As you would suppose in a cosmopolitan restaurant which is French by inclination, there are cheeses which have been selected with expertise and are presented with a flourish – goat cheeses are especially admirable – and freshly baked bread.

At lunchtime there is a set menu costing about the same as a single course at night. This is a bargain, makes you decide to come back when you have more time to eat and drink and concentrate on the pleasures of the table.

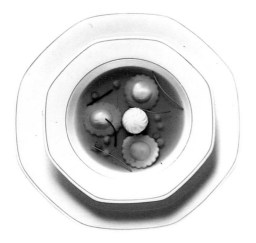

Consommé de champignons sauvages aux raviolis

(Wild mushroom consommé with ravioli)

Serves 12
For the consommé:
1 ½ lb (680 g) wild mushrooms, finely chopped
1 ½ lb (680 g) button mushrooms, finely chopped
8 pints (4.5 litres) well-flavoured chicken stock
5 fl oz (140 ml) Madeira
pinch of powdered saffron
8 oz (225 g) finely-chopped onions
8 oz (225 g) finely-chopped carrots
8 oz (225 g) finely-chopped celeriac or celery
6 egg whites
salt and freshly-ground pepper
For the ravioli:
3 eggs
2 egg yolks
12 oz (340 g) strong white flour
olive oil
1 lb (455 g) mushrooms, finely diced and seasoned well, then cooked out in butter until all liquid is evaporated and allowed to cool
egg wash
chicken stock
For the garnish:
12 nice white poached, turned button mushrooms
36 pearls each of carrot, celeriac and courgette (use a pearl vegetable cutter or cut into julienne)
12 slices of truffle (optional but nice)
fresh chives

To make the consommé, place all the ingredients except the seasoning in a large, heavy-bottomed pot, stir well and season if necessary. Bring to a gentle simmer, stirring the bottom of the pan occasionally. Once at a gentle boil, leave to simmer for 30 minutes, then strain through a muslin cloth.

To make the ravioli, mix the eggs and egg yolks into the flour with salt and pepper and a little olive oil. Knead well, occasionally dusting with flour to prevent sticking. When thoroughly mixed, leave to rest in the refrigerator, then roll out as thinly as possible into 2 rectangles. Place teaspoons of the mushroom mixture at 1 ½ in (4 cm) intervals on one of the rectangles and brush with egg wash in between. Cover with the second layer of pastry and use a round cutter to cut into ravioli. Poach in chicken stock until they begin to float.
Place the piping hot consommé into soup plates, add 3 ravioli per serving and garnish with the vegetables evenly divided and a few strands of chive.

Symphonie de poissons à la betterave

(A medley of fish with beetroot sauce)

Serves 4
2 large scallops, cut in half horizontally or 4 whole small ones
4 rounds monkfish
4 thick slices sea bass, about 2 in (5 cm) in length
4 thick slices salmon, about 2 in (5 cm) in length
4 thick slices brill, about 2 in (5 cm) in length
For the sauce:
2 tablespoons finely-chopped shallots
4 oz (1 stick/110 g) butter
5 fl oz (140 ml) dry white wine
5 fl oz (140 ml) well-flavoured fish stock
salt and freshly-ground pepper
2 tablespoons beetroot puree (liquidize cooked beetroot, pass through a fine sieve and season well)

To make the sauce, simmer the shallots in 2 oz (55 g) of the butter until transparent, then add the wine and fish stock. Reduce by half, then season and beat in the remaining butter until frothy. Keep warm.
Season the fish and steam for 3-4 minutes (do not overcook). Arrange neatly onto very hot serving plates. Beat the beetroot purée into the sauce and pour carefully around the fish, being careful not to drop any on top of the fish. Garnish the spaces between the fish with neatly-picked chervil leaves or strips of truffles or turned courgettes.

Chef's hints
You may change the variety of fish according to taste but make sure the fish is not cut too thinly and is of approximately the same size. Do not boil the sauce after the beetroot puree has been added or it will lose its colour.

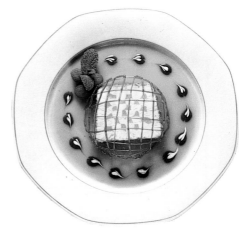

Noix de coquilles St Jacques fumées en petite salade

(Smoked slices of scallop with a vegetable assortment)

Serves 4
8 large scallops
salt and freshly-ground pepper
cayenne pepper
olive oil
8 tablespoons thin mayonnaise
16 leaves of chicory (Belgian endive)
3 tablespoons blanched matchsticks
   of carrot
3 tablespoons blanched matchsticks of
   celeriac
3 tablespoons matchsticks of
   cucumber, skin on but seeds removed
3 tomatoes, skinned and sliced
<u>For the dressing:</u>
2 tablespoons tarragon vinegar
6 tablespoons olive oil
fresh chopped herbs

Season the scallops with salt, pepper and a little cayenne pepper. Brush with olive oil. Cook in a smoking oven for 5 minutes at 160°C/320°F. Alternatively, if you have no smoking oven available, gently sauté with butter in a frying pan until golden brown. To serve, mix together the dressing ingredients with salt and pepper to taste. Pour enough thin mayonnaise on each of the serving plates to make a nice circle, then arrange the chicory leaves, with the tips pointing outwards, on top. Toss the carrots, celeriac and cucumber in the dressing and place in the middle of the plates. Sprinkle with the tomato slices. Slice the still warm scallops very thinly (without breaking) and arrange slightly overlapping on the vegetables. Sprinkle over a little more of the herb dressing.

Rosette d'agneau au pistou et petits légumes

(Rosette of lamb with pistou and baby vegetables)

Serves 4
1 oz (30 g) chopped shallots
3 oz (¾ stick/85 g) butter
5 fl oz (140 ml) well-flavoured lamb stock
2 tablespoons lamb jus
4 pieces of lamb fillet, 4 oz (110 g) each,
   taken from a pair of trimmed best ends
salt and freshly-ground pepper
<u>For the sauce:</u>
2 tablespoons fresh basil
2 tablespoons fresh curly-leaved
   parsley
2 cloves garlic, sliced
½ teaspoon fresh thyme
1 tablespoon pine nuts
<u>For the garnish:</u>
12 each neatly turned carrots, turnips
   and courgettes, cooked al dente,
   warmed in a little butter and seasoned

To make the sauce, blanch the basil, parsley and garlic for 15 seconds in boiling water, refresh in iced water and drain. Chop very finely, adding the thyme and pine nuts, until a purée-like consistency. Push through a fine sieve and set aside.
Simmer the shallots in 1 oz (2 tablespoons/ 30 g) of the butter until transparent, add the lamb stock and jus and reduce by half. Beat in the rest of the butter and all of the purée. Bring to a simmer and keep warm.
Season the lamb fillets and sauté in a hot pan with a little oil and butter on all sides for about 5 minutes in total. Remove and rest for 5 minutes, keeping warm.
To serve, slice the lamb fillets thinly and arrange in a circle in the middle of the plates, surround with the sauce, garnish with the baby vegetables and accompany with green noodles if liked.

Chef's note
The green noodles can be made by following the recipe for the ravioli and mixing 1 good tablespoon of spinach purée into the dough.

Parfait de mangue au coulis de mangue

(Mango parfait with mango coulis)

Serves 6-10
8 fl oz (225 ml) milk
5 oz (1 stick plus 2 tablespoons/140 g)
butter
4 oz (110 g) sugar
1 ½ oz (40 g) egg yolks
2 eggs
pinch of salt
1 teaspoon Cointreau
5 ripe mangoes
white wine

Planning ahead
Make the custard base 1 day in advance.

Place the milk, butter and sugar in a pan and bring to the boil. Place the yolks, eggs and salt in a bowl, mix together, then pour the boiling milk on top, whisking until smooth. Transfer the mixture to a blender and process for 2 minutes. Allow to cool, then place in an airtight container and leave for 24 hours in the refrigerator.
Whisk the mixture with the Cointreau to soft peaks, then store again in a cool place.
Peel the mangoes and cut the flesh from the stones. Liquidize until smooth, divide in half and cool in the refrigerator.
Fill one piping bag with the parfait mixture and another with half the puréed mango. Fill the base of a terrine mould, 12 x 3 x 3 in (30 x 8 x 8 cm), with the parfait mixture, then pipe alternate strips of the mango and the parfait mixture until the terrine is nearly full. Add a final layer of the parfait mixture and freeze the terrine for 6 hours. Thin the remaining mango purée to a pouring consistency with a little white wine. Pour a circle of this coulis onto each plate. Unmould the parfait and place a slice on top of the coulis.
For a more elaborate presentation, make a caramel cage to enclose each serving and decorate with fresh fruits.

ALASTAIR LITTLE

49 Frith Street, London W1V 5TE. In the centre of Soho. Open Monday to Friday; closed on Bank Holidays. (Children's helpings; no dogs.) To visit nearby: Oxford Street shopping; Piccadilly Circus; Shaftesbury Avenue theatres. No credit cards. Tel.: (01) 734 5183

Alastair Little read archaeology at Downing College, Cambridge – which led in a roundabout sort of way to his becoming the cook at "Les Routiers" in Wrentham, a village of only small merit on the A12, south of Lowestoft in Suffolk. (My father once bought a house there, sat on it for three years and managed to sell it at a loss.) The owner of the Wrentham premise moved on to London and Mr Little, after working in Richmond, then widening his experience via a job at "L'Escargot", decided to become his own man and took premises in Frith Street.

Soho, the rectangle of central London bounded by Charing Cross Road, Coventry Street, Oxford Street and Regent Street, has throughout the century been a haven for cosmopolitan eating-houses. In Old Compton Street, the main drag, was the shop where every chef bought his whites (professional term for blue-check trousers, double-breasted chef's jacket and tall white hat) and his knives. A pâtisserie, now called Valerie's, was the rallying point for coffee and croissants and gossip about jobs in the catering trade. All around, Italian, French, Greek and later Indian, Chinese and Thai restaurants opened and flourished. The undesirables moved in, as they do in cosmopolitan areas of cities and the carriage trade stayed away. Then came the "Beveridge Report" and the ensuing legislation, which caused hookers to beckon from first floor windows when they had previously propositioned on the pavements; more recently the Westminster City Council's admirable clean-up campaign restored the district to its former eminence: people walk the streets with heads held high and Soho is once more a gastronomic wonderland in which sex-shops, strip-joints and basement bars with nude dancers and undrinkable champagne are the exception rather than the rule.

The main arteries are Wardour, Dean, Frith and Greek Streets, which intersect Old Compton Street. The principal industry – apart from car-clamping – is feeding the passing multitudes and there are great names who started here and moved on. Some – like "Mario and Franco" and "Wheelers" – began here and branched out; others – like "The Gay Hussar", meeting place of Labour politicians – are permanent fixtures and will remain so. Onto this geographical scenario did the archaeologist Bachelor of Arts open his doors. He found a thin, office-like, ground-floor room in Frith Street and turned it into an upmarket café: white Venetian blinds in the windows, wooden floor, such pictures as were around on the walls, black slatted chairs, black Formica tables on silver bases, proper silver, paper napkins, glasses which you could break in depth without feeling even a tinge of remorse and lighting which was trendy in the early 1980s but never caught on. In a word, there was nothing to distract anyone from the food. He presents a different menu for every meal – giving a choice of a dozen starters, up to ten main courses and puddings. The food is international: a Chinese dish here, an Italian smoked meat there, Swedish gravlax, Japanese teriyaki – menus depend on what the owner bought in the market that morning and how he decides to prepare what he has found.

You may get a home-made ravioli filled with slices of black truffle in a sauce of cream and basil; or fresh oysters from Cork; chicken satay with soy and coriander and Japanese mustard; terrine of pheasant with onion marma-

lade; cabbage and bacon soup with sour cream and chives. Main courses might be the freshest fish in a rocket and butter sauce; a pot au feu with gherkin sauce; chicken stuffed with chanterelles; partridge with Savoy cabbage. There is bread on the table; it is bread of no great quality – perhaps so that it does not deter people from ordering a pudding. Puddings are of substantial appeal: caramelized apple tart; dark and white chocolate truffle cake with ginger sauce; Pavlova.

There are three staff for the thirty customers, they are dressed in ultra casual clo-

thes; they are entirely perfect: allow you to sit where you want to sit and move (if there is room) when the people at the next table light cigars, let people take their time, accept orders, bring the right food, find more delicious vegetables, like a mousse of potatoes and baby turnips, and salsify in a cheese sauce, and smile when you catch their eye. As they bring the bill – which is *not* a café-priced bill – their faces fall a bit as you offer a credit card: "we don't take credit cards, do you have a cheque, or cash?" No Visa or Access signs on the door. It is a café, albeit with the best food in the square mile of tightly-packed restaurants, determinedly doing its own thing.

Alastair Little is a tiger of a chef, attracting a clientèle that is predominantly young, discriminating and comprises many women eating with other women, probably because elsewhere such customers are given a hard time. No-one

gets a hard time at 49 Frith Street.

The wine list is written on an A4 card: 41 wines include four champagnes led by Adnams' excellent special cuvée at £18; people who began their catering careers in East Anglia tend to stay loyal to Adnams. A brace of dessert wines are a premier cru sauternes and a Californian moscato which is delicious and served by the glass. There are 19 whites and 16 reds, listed higgledy-piggledy in order of price: a Napa Valley Sauvignon beside a Rioja next to a Florentin AC beside a marvellous Spanish Tinto Pesquara. The whites range from £8 to £26, for which you get a Chassagne Montrachet 1986 Bernard Morey, which would cost more elsewhere.

Here, then, is an establishment that must be taken for what it is: friendly, casual, unpretentious to the highest degree, and gastronomically brilliant. Whether you enjoy yourself will depend substantially on whether you are, as they say, after the steak or the sizzle.

Roast red mullet with salsa and sautéed fennel

Serves 2
2 baby fennel
olive oil
2 red mullet, 8 – 10 oz (225 – 285 g)
  each and preferably with livers,
  cleaned and scaled (or use steaks
  from a larger fish)
seasoned flour
fresh coriander sprigs to garnish
For the salsa :
1 tomato, skinned, seeds removed and
  diced
1 red chilli pepper, seeds removed and
  finely chopped
1 red pepper, skinned and finely
  chopped
1 red onion, finely chopped
1 clove garlic, finely chopped
2 tablespoons tomato passata
2 teaspoons vinegar or juice of
  ½ lemon
2 tablespoons extra virgin olive oil
6 olives, stoned and chopped
a little salt
handful of picked coriander leaves,
  chopped

To make the salsa the ingredients may be chopped in a food processor but hand cutting and mixing makes a better sauce. Place all the ingredients together in a bowl and mix well. Set aside.
Preheat the oven to maximum. Cut the fennel in half and place in a frying pan just big enough to hold them with a little olive oil. Sauté them gently until tender and very brown, especially on the cut face.
Coat the fish in seasoned flour. Lightly oil a roasting dish and heat in the preheated oven for 10 minutes, then put in the fish and roast in the oven for 3 minutes, turn and roast for 3-5 minutes more. Check that the fish is cooked, then transfer to serving plates. Add the hot fennel and a tablespoonful of cold salsa. Garnish with fresh coriander.

Tataki of tuna with spinach, soy and strong, Japanese mustard

Serves 4
17 oz (500 g) tuna, very fresh and cut
  from a middle section in one piece
salt and freshly-ground pepper
1 lb (455 g) spinach or 1 packet of
  dehydrated 'wakame' seaweed
light soy sauce
juice of 1 lemon
2 spring onions or a little flaked dried
  bonito
Japanese mustard (substitute English
  mustard if unavailable)

Planning ahead
All the Japanese ingredients should be available in oriental supermarkets : many Chinese and Indonesian shops have a small Japanese section.

Season the tuna thoroughly with salt and pepper and heat a ribbed grill pan as hot as possible. (Open the kitchen window as there will be lots of smoke.) Prepare a container holding enough iced water to immerse the tuna.
Grill the tuna on all faces for 1 minute per face. Immediately plunge into the iced water to arrest the cooking process. Remove from the water as soon as it is cold, pat dry and refrigerate.
Blanch the spinach in boiling water until just cooked and plunge into the iced water. Drain and squeeze dry. (Rehydrate the seaweed if using.)
Mix the soy sauce with the lemon juice in the proportion 4 parts soy to one lemon juice. Slice the spring onions very finely. Make up the Japanese mustard with a little water (as for English mustard).
To serve, arrange a mound of spinach on each plate and spoon over a little of the soy mix. Slice the tuna into 24 neat slices across the grain and arrange domino fashion next to the spinach. Place a mound of mustard on one corner of the plate. Sprinkle with the spring onion or dried bonito. Provide chopsticks and more of the soy mixture in dipping plates.

Warm salad of wild duck breast, artichoke hearts and French beans

Serves 4
1 mallard, breasts removed (use the legs and carcase for other recipes e.g. salmis)
salt and freshly-ground pepper
4 oz (110 g) mixed salad, e.g. radicchio, lollo rosso, oak leaf, frisée
2 oz (55 g) French beans, blanched
4 – 6 artichoke hearts preserved in oil, drained and cut into quarters
vinegar
For the vinaigrette:
1 tablespoon good wine vinegar
1 tablespoon good strong mustard
3 tablespoons peanut oil
2 tablespoons extra virgin olive oil

Heat a sauté pan very thoroughly. Remove the skins from the mallard breasts and season heavily with salt and pepper. Sauté the breasts for 2 minutes on each side, remove and allow to rest.
Beat all the ingredients for the vinaigrette together with seasoning to taste, then dress the salad, French beans and artichoke hearts. Slice the duck breasts and arrange in circles on warm serving plates. Place the salad, beans and artichoke hearts on top. Deglaze the sauté pan with a little vinegar, then pour over the salad.

Breast of chicken wrapped in savoy cabbage and pancetta

Serves 4
8 outer leaves of Savoy cabbage (not the tough outermost leaves)
8 thin slices pancetta, 4 oz (110 g) approx.
4 oz (1 stick/110 g) butter
4 large chicken breasts (from free-range or corn-fed birds)
salt and freshly-ground pepper
10 fl oz (285 ml) chicken stock (water will do)
a little double cream

Preheat the oven to maximum. Blanch the cabbage leaves for 1 minute in boiling water, drain, cool and remove any major stalks. Butter four 10 in (28 cm) square sheets of foil. Spread the cabbage leaves out, two to each sheet, then cover with the pancetta slices. Spread a knob of the butter over each, then place the chicken breast centrally, one to each piece. Season lightly with salt and more heavily with pepper. Wrap up, so that the foil loosely encloses the chicken.
Take a good baking tray or cast iron frying pan large enough to hold the chicken parcels. Add the stock or water to the pan, then the parcels, followed by any remaining butter. Bake in the preheated oven for 25 minutes. Remove the parcels, open carefully and tip any juices into the roasting pan. Place the pan over a medium heat, add the cream and simmer until thickened to a sauce. Meanwhile, slice the chicken and arrange on serving plates. Pour the sauce over and serve straightaway.

Variation
This recipe works well with pheasant or guinea fowl breasts.

Prune and almond tart

Serves 8-10
1 lb (455 g) best prunes
a little armagnac
1 x 10 in (28 cm) flan tin lined with thin puff pastry, frozen
For the almond paste:
4 eggs
4 oz (110 g) ground almonds
4 oz (110 g) caster sugar
2 oz (55 g) flour
2 oz (½ stick/55 g) butter

Soak the prunes in a little water and a little brandy overnight, then poach for 10 minutes. Leave to cool, then remove the prunes and stone them. Preheat the oven to maximum.
To make the almond paste, put all the ingredients in a blender or food processor to a paste.
Take the pastry case out of the freezer at the last minute. Spoon the almond paste in the case, then gently push the prunes half info the mixture. Bake in the preheated oven for 10 minutes until the pastry rim shows signs of cooking and firming up, then turn the oven down to 200°C/400°F/Gas Mark 6 and bake for a further 20 minutes. Finally turn down to 120°C/250°F/Gas Mark ½ and cook until the almond paste in the centre is done.
Serve with crème fraîche, Jersey cream or ice cream.

Variation
Ripe raw figs, quartered, may be substituted for the prunes. We use new season's pruneaux d'Agen and only serve it in winter.

NINETY PARK LANE

Grosvenor House, 90 Park Lane, London W1A 3AA. In central Mayfair on the edge of Hyde Park. Open Monday to Saturday except Saturday lunch, all year round. (Vegetarian meals; children welcome; air-conditioned.) Private parties: 100 in main room. Guest accommodation: 468 rooms all with bath/shower. (Swimming pool; sauna; pets welcome.) To visit nearby: Hyde Park; Marble Arch. Credit cards accepted: Access, AE, Carte Blanche, Diners, THF Gold Card, Visa.
Tel.: (01) 409 1290

This is the flagship of the Trusthouse Forte chain; Lord Forte, were you to give him the Savoy Hotel A shares he has set his heart upon, would take you to dinner at Ninety Park Lane by way of thanks. For a THF employee to land a job at this prestigious restaurant is akin to a diplomat getting the embassy at Washington or Paris.

Hardly any expense is spared on the place: as you enter by a walkway at the northern end of Grosvenor House, you pass through a pair of genuine panelled doors, arrive in a lounge bedecked in greys and creams and gold, paintings by real painters, upholstery by firms that advertise in glossy magazines. It is no easy task to manifest excellence within the confines of a corporate structure, yet Sergio Rebecchi, arguably (in my view unarguably) the most talented maître d'hôtel in Britain, does a tremendous job. Unlike the majority of egocentrics who pursue this calling, Mr Rebecchi delegates and has a sharp eye for charismatic young people to join his team.

The restaurant retains Louis Outhier, "patron" of the three star "L'Oasis" at La Napoule on the Côte d'Azure, to mastermind the cuisine. And there are times when he is there, cooking and treading the carpets in his tall white hat, making gestures of Gallic welcome to the customers; Stephen Goodlad, the indigenous chef des cuisines, carries out his instructions during the master's long sojourns in his native land. Goodlad is a chef of substantial ability.

You arrive and are met by a young man of immaculate manners, who will doubtless become a captain of industry in the 21st century – even Robert Maxwell had to start somewhere. He enquires whether you would like a drink in the lounge, to sit and sip some champagne at your table, to telephone New Zealand... you get the overall impression that they want you to have a happy time. The whole pace is leisurely. You are going to be there for a long time; they will not insult you by giving the sort of service you might require at a station buffet. No-one races up with a menu or a wine list; they amble over with the appetisers "with our compliments" (now so *de* rigeur that people would complain if they were not 'given') and in the background, always in the background even if you are seated by the side of his Baby Grand, a man plays tunes by Noel Coward or ones that the master did not get round to writing – nothing since 1950, to make people like me feel trendy.

You sink into a banquette, the table slides towards you effortlessly, there is a thick bolster-like cushion on which to rest your elbow and the pianist plays "Dancing Cheek to Cheek"; it is a shade early for "A Nightingale Sang in Berkeley Square".

The menu is the size of a tabloid newspaper but in better taste and glossier. Items are expensive – £3.50 for a cup of coffee – but look around the clientèle and the need for stringent economy is not a trait you are likely to encounter. The appetiser is a sliver of truffled breast of guineafowl that has somehow attained the texture of tongue. There is a five-tier sweet trolley in a corner bearing a raspberry-flavoured bombe in pride of place – at the top. A liqueur trolley shows armagnacs and cognacs, calvados and vintage ports and a silver duck press hovers, lest you should decide to indulge in the essence of a canard sauvage. The maître d. suggests a fresh langoustine ravioli, which is perfect: the pasta, the filling and the deeply-flavoured sauce on which they perch and for the consumption of which they provide the best silver cutlery. Glasses still reflect the "we are part of a great chain" approach but insist and you get real claret and burgundy balloons. Bread is freshly baked, brown or white, makes frequent appearances; salt and pepper come in mills; a profusion of waiters dressed unprovocatively as high-class penguins move around smoothly, glancing this way and that as they go. When the food arrives, it is plated, beneath the shiniest silver cloches, to disclose, well, what you ordered. Perhaps a pot-roast meadow partridge in Provence wine with turnip purée, the pianist plays "The Pride of London Town" and a sickle plate of nouvelle cuisine vegetables is placed by your side: small château celeriac, a julienne of carrots, mousse of Brussels sprouts and another dish bearing *Pommes Maxim*, a dozen rounds of golden potato slices artistically formed into a circle. The production is stylish, the service serious, the food carefully prepared, on the light side of classical, because current trends demand that and Outhier is into lightness as well as into oriental flavours, so you will find slivers of ginger unexpectedly draped over a poached

fillet of monkfish. And yet despite all the gravitas, you get the feeling that if you said "let's have egg and chips and a bottle of brown sauce", they would take it in their stride, and ask whether you preferred "Flag" to "Daddy's". Great credit goes to Mr Rebecchi for retaining individualism in this ocean of tradition. Gershwin follows Coward, and the man behind the sweet trolley tells you all: passionfruit tart; rich chocolate cake with Tia Maria; walnut gâteau and then he lowers his voice an octave, like a host introducing the home help's aunt at a party, "lemon meringue pie?" The selection of cheeses is miniscule and faultless. If you stock the Appleby family's Hawkstone from Cheshire, there is no urgent need to look further. The wine list is frankly disappointing: huge, expensive; has too much of what everyone knows and far too little of what people might want to try; barely a bottle from the New World. Perhaps when Lord Forte buys New Zealand...

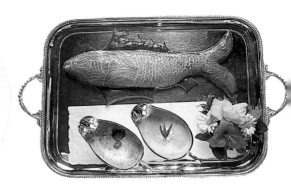

Langoustine ravioli with tomato and a cordon of saffron butter

Serves 2
For the ravioli:
4 ½ oz (125 g) strong white flour
1 egg
1 egg yolk
½ teaspoon virgin olive oil
½ teaspoon water to bind
10 large cooked langoustines
salt and freshly-ground pepper
For the sauce:
4 fl oz (110 ml) langoustine stock
4 fl oz (110 ml) fish stock
1 tablespoon crème fleurette or
   whipping cream
2 oz (½ stick/55 g) unsalted butter
8 strands of fresh saffron
2 oz (55 g) brunoise of carrot,
   courgette skin, shallot (chop or
   finely shred and cook in 1 oz/
   2 tablespoons/30 g unsalted butter)
cayenne pepper
juice of ½ lemon
For the garnish:
6 fresh chives
4 thin strips of tomato

Blend the flour, egg, egg yolk, oil and water together in a food processor, then leave to rest in the refrigerator for approximately 2 hours. Peel the langoustine and season. Roll out the ravioli dough as thinly as possible, then cut into circles about 2 in (5 cm) in diameter, allowing about 5 per person. (Use the remaining dough another time.) Overlap 2 pieces of whole langoustine if small, 1 piece if medium to large in the middle of each circle and fold the pasta over. Seal with a cutter and use the fingertips to shape.
To make the sauce, boil the langoustine and fish stocks together to reduce a little, then stir in the cream to bind. Whisk in the butter, piece by piece, then add the saffron and allow to infuse for about 5 minutes. Pass the sauce through a fine chinois. Add the brunoise of carrot, courgette skin and shallot to the sauce. Season with salt and cayenne pepper as needed, then stir in the lemon juice.

Quickly cook the ravioli in boiling, salted water for 1 minute. Remove and drain. Set the ravioli in the bottom of a warm soup plate, spoon the sauce over each ravioli, then arrange the tomato strips in the middle of each plate with the chive strands in between. Serve straightaway.

Sea bass filled with lobster mousseline in a vinegar pastry

Serves 2
1 sea bass, about 1 1/2 lb (680 g),
   cleaned and filleted, head reserved
melted butter
salt and freshly-ground white pepper
cayenne pepper
1 fresh Scottish lobster, about 2 lb
   (900 g), tail meat intact and claws
   cleaned
sprigs of lemon thyme
egg yolk and milk mix, to glaze
For the butter-vinegar pastry:
13 oz (370 g) strong white flour
4 ½ oz (1 stick plus 1 tablespoon/125 g)
   unsalted butter
2 ½ egg yolks
1 tablespoon white wine vinegar
For the lobster mousseline:
11 oz (310 g) lobster meat (blanch the
   lobster in water for a few minutes to
   ease removal of meat)
2 oz (½ stick/55 g) butter, melted and
   cooled
2 egg whites
14 oz (400 g) double cream
1 teaspoon lobster glaze
For the sauce béarnaise:
8 oz (2 sticks/225 g) butter
2 ½ oz (70 g) chopped shallots
1 ¾ fl oz (50 ml) tarragon vinegar
¼ oz (7 g) freshly-ground black pepper
4 egg yolks
1 ½ tablespoons chopped fresh
   tarragon
1 ½ teaspoons chopped fresh chervil
For the sauce portugaise:
5 oz (140 g) finely-chopped onions and
   shallots

a little crushed garlic
2 fl oz (55 ml) olive oil
2 lb (900 g) roughly-chopped skinned
   tomato
1 bay leaf
pinch of sugar
3 fl oz (85 ml) tomato juice
3 ½ fl oz (100 ml) tomato essence
   (reduction from tomato coulis)
3 ½ fl oz (100 ml) veal glaze
dash of Worcestershire sauce
1 tablespoon finely-chopped fresh
   coriander

To make the pastry, mix the flour, butter, egg yolks and vinegar together in a food processor, adding a little water to bind. Blend until smooth, then rest in the refrigerator for 2 hours. To make the lobster mousseline, purée the lobster meat in a liquidizer or blender, then add the melted butter and season with salt and cayenne pepper. Transfer the mixture to a bowl and beat in the egg whites. Place the bowl on ice and beat in the cream, a little at a time, then stir in the lobster glaze. Poach a little of the mixture in order to taste and adjust the seasoning. Set aside in the refrigerator.

Dry the fish fillets thoroughly, then brush the outsides with melted butter. Season well with salt, white pepper and cayenne pepper. Spread an even layer of the lobster mousseline over the 2 fillets. Slice the lobster tail meat and stud down one of the fillets interspersed with the claw meat. Sandwich the 2 fillets together and fill in any gaps with the remaining lobster mousseline. Pick the leaves from the lemon thyme and scatter over the fish, top and bottom.

Preheat the oven to 180°C/350°F/Gas Mark 4. Roll out the pastry to ¼ in (0.5 cm) thickness and large enough to wrap round the fish. Place the fish in the middle and use the head to give a good fish shape. Fold over the pastry, mark the pastry in a fish pattern and glaze with the egg wash. Bake in the preheated oven for 35-40 minutes.

To make the sauce béarnaise, clarify the butter by melting it slowly and skimming the surface. When melted pour off the clear butter and discard the whey. Combine the shallots, vinegar and pepper in a saucepan, bring to the boil and reduce to one-third of the volume. Add a little water and allow to cool until lukewarm. Place the saucepan in a bain marie and briskly whisk in the egg yolks, until the sauce is creamy and forms ribbons from the whisk. Transfer to a stainless steel bowl and stir in the clarified butter off the heat. If the sauce is too thick, add a few drops of water. Season with salt and a little cayenne pepper, then strain through a piece of muslin and add the chopped herbs. Keep warm while making the sauce portugaise.

Sweat the onions and garlic in the oil in a flame and ovenproof casserole, then add the chopped tomato, bayleaf, salt, pepper and a pinch of sugar, cover and cook out in a preheated oven at 200°C/400°F/Gas Mark 4 for 20-30 minutes. Remove from the oven and stir in the tomato juice, essence and veal glaze. At the last minute, stir in the Worcestershire sauce and coriander, then fold into half of the sauce béarnaise.

Arrange the fish on serving plates and serve the sauces separately.

Eminсé of Bresse pigeon with wild mushrooms, foie gras and maize

Serves 1
1 Bresse or Norfolk pigeon, about 14 oz
   (400 g), cleaned with liver reserved
4 oz (110 g) assorted wild mushrooms
1 oz (2 tablespoons/30 g) butter
1 oz (30 g) corn niblets
2 oz (55 g) escalope of foie gras
2 oz (55 g) mache (lamb's lettuce)
vinaigrette made with walnut oil
1 oz (30 g) grated walnut
3 turned apple barrels, glazed in sugar
   butter

For the port wine sauce:
1 oz (30 g) finely-chopped shallots
4 oz (110 g) chopped celery, leek,
   mushroom and carrot
8 fl oz (225 ml) chicken stock
4 fl oz (110 ml) port wine
1 oz (2 tablespoons/30 g) unsalted
   butter
For the roesti: 1 large potato, clarified
butter, cumin seeds
Planning ahead
The potato for the roesti should be cooked a day before it is required.

Wash the potato for the roesti carefully and cook in salted water with a handful of cumin seeds, making sure that it does not break up during the cooking. Drain off the water and leave the potato to cool completely.

Preheat the oven to 200°C/400°F/Gas Mark 6. Roast the pigeon for 20-25 minutes until still rosy inside. Remove from the oven. Remove the legs and carve the breast meat. Keep warm.

Chop up the pigeon carcase and place in a saucepan with all the other port wine sauce ingredients except for the port and the butter. Cook for 30 minutes, then pass through a piece of muslin and keep warm.

Peel the cooled potato and rub through a coarse grater, making sure the mixture is not squashed. Season with salt and pepper. Heat a frying pan, add some clarified butter, then add the grated potato formed into 2 rounds. Cook until golden brown on both sides. Set aside and keep warm.

Quickly wash the wild mushrooms and slice. Sauté them in half the butter with the sweetcorn until all their liquid has evaporated, then arrange in a circle on a serving plate. Fry the foie gras and the pigeon liver in the remaining butter, then place on top of the mushrooms.

Arrange the reserved breast meat in the middle of the mushrooms. Remove the thigh bones from the pigeon legs and arrange on a side plate together with the mache tossed in vinaigrette.

Scatter the grated walnut over the salad. Finish the port wine sauce with the port and butter. Spoon over and around the mushrooms. Arrange the apples around the plate and serve with the hot potato roesti.

LE GAVROCHE

43 Upper Brook Street, London, W1Y 1PF. In the heart of Mayfair. Open Monday to Friday; closed over Christmas holiday. (No children under 8; no pipe smoking; air-conditioned; no dogs.) Private parties: 8-20 in private room. To visit nearby: Bond Street galleries and Oxford Street shopping districts. Credit cards accepted: Access, AE, Carte Blanche, Diners, Visa. Tel: (01) 408 0881

Last year I sat on a judging panel to determine the "Best Restaurant in London" for a glossy magazine and one of our number said "How about Le Gavroche?" The immediate reaction was "not the Gavroche AGAIN, *they* don't need us to vote for them." It was Oscar Wilde who wrote that "approval of what is approved of is as false as a well-kept vow" and of course Oscar Wilde was wrong. The only thing against "approval of what is approved of" is that it doesn't get the headlines; most competitions want to come up with a newsworthy winner: someone who, but for their careful research, would have continued unnoticed in a suburban back-street. (Le Gavroche still won.)

This restaurant is actually in a class of its own. Nowhere is the mix of brilliant food, caring service, total professionalism of approach, stunning silver, glass, china and napery and a wine list as thick as a telephone directory so steadily, immaculately available. I accept that in each sub-section of award categories there will be a place that shines like a beacon, that deserves the highest praise for this chef, that headwaiter, such and such a wine list... but on aggregate Le Gavroche wins. There is something about success bringing success: a restaurant that has been awarded three Michelin stars – as has this elegant Upper Brook Street basement – causes the chefs to bask in recognition, to perform with a deep awareness of the honours bestowed. What is admirable is that they don't rest on laurels; frequently surprising their most regular clients with innovative additions to their *carte*. These are often based on the simplest of ingredients, like a pot au feu, a choux braisée aux gibiers, a sauté of lamb with haricot beans and garlic. And the waiters are relaxed and attentive, knowing that when they lift the silver cover from a plate, happiness will descend upon the beneficiary.

The Roux Brothers – Meilleur Maître chef de cuisine, Albert, and Meilleur Ouvrier de France, Michel – began their public catering life in London's Lower Sloane Street (they had previously been in private service – Embassies, Rothschilds, Astors, Clores) then spread their wings AND encouraged the men and women who worked for them to set up on their own. The Rouxs branched out – bought a butchery, a charcuterie, a transport company to bring daily supplies from the market at Rungis in Paris – and they developed vacuum cooking, advise airlines on first-class in-flight meals, host a successful TV show... But Le Gavroche is their flagship, their centre of excellence, the nucleus of their Empire from which the other ventures draw their oxygen and their kudos.

Some years ago I was served in that Mayfair eating-house a parcel of smoked salmon filled with a mousse of smoked trout. It was one of the very best starters I have eaten and I – in common with many others – sought to emulate this at home; best smoked salmon, immaculate trout, minced, sieved, with and without horseradish, double cream, zest of lime... all in vain. It is as inimitable as their *Soufflé Suissesse* for which men would kill.

Each day there is a set lunch and a set dinner – the lunch one of the great bargains of London – and there is also a menu of the day's specialities: a noisette of venison with wild mushrooms; a panache de poissons à la creme d'herbes, plus the awesome *à la carte* menu listing some 30 charismatic dishes – also a Menu Exceptionel – and if you feel as I do that "exceptionel" is a word that should come from the consumer, not the supplier, an *Escalope de foie gras aux topinambours, Petites bourses de langoustines aux deux sauces, Granité aux pommes, Poulette de Bresse* with wild mushrooms and corn salad, then cheese, then *Millefeuille de poires avec son coulis de framboise* might persuade you to accept the appellation. The price of this is £40, including tax

and service. It is quite remarkably good value.

As you come into the restaurant from the street there is a ground floor bar where you may drink champagne by the glass and they will bring you appetisers of appeal; like so many outstanding chefs, Albert rose through the pâtisserie and his tartelettes and millefeuilles are outstanding. In the restaurant below there is an aura of contented plushness, and the service, under the command of Silvano Geraldin, copes brilliantly with the steady capacity clientèle of 70 – each of whom is given a careful expla-

and the richness of the main courses is born in mind when the sweet trolley arrives, laden with light, fruity, original puddings *and* there is a refrigerated trolley of home-made sorbets.

If the British Embassy in Paris, the French Embassy in London and the Rothschilds, Astors, Clores and Cazalets miss their former chef: their loss is our gain.

nation – and in the case of cold starters, a sight – of what there is on the menu. The wine list is predominantly French, with a few bottles from other lands and not enough half bottles of anything. But if you wanted to accompany your Daube de bœuf à la crebillon with half a dozen different vintages of first growth clarets (all are there, for all the great years), then you should go nowhere else and they do take credit cards, for it would do terrible harm to your suit to carry the money required for these wines.

Few people go to Le Gavroche in order to economise; they go to eat the very best food in the world and in passing they might notice that the vegetables which are brought with the main courses are quite especially fine: half a dozen different varieties, perfectly cooked, each having its own separate taste. The salads, also, are very beautiful

Gâteaux aux deux mousses de légumes

(Mousses of carrot and leek with salad and scampi)

Serves 12
9 oz (255 g) leeks
9 oz (255 g) carrots
butter
18 fl oz (510 ml) double cream
salt and freshly-ground pepper
4 leaves gelatine
9 fl oz (250 ml) gelle Jurançon (aspic flavoured with Jurançon wine)
pinch chopped fresh parsley
pinch chopped fresh chives
pinch chopped truffles (optional)
For the garnish:
mixed salad
very small turned and cooked vegetables
20 fl oz (565 ml) tomato coulis flavoured with basil
24 scampi tails, lightly steamed

Slice the leek and carrot finely. Sweat in butter in separate pans until soft, then add half the cream to each pan. Boil to reduce, then allow to cool slightly and season with salt and pepper. Put 2 leaves of gelatine in each pan. When dissolved, puree the vegetable mixtures separately in a liquidizer, then season to taste.
Pour a thin layer of jelly in the bottom of 12 small dariole moulds, allow to set, then sprinkle with the mixed herbs and truffle (if using). Carefully divide the carrot mixture between the moulds and allow to set, then add a layer of the leek mixture to each mould. Leave until set.
To serve, unmould the mousses onto serving plates and garnish each with a little mixed salad, a bouquet of vegetables, a spoonful or two of tomato coulis and 2 scampi tails.

Assiette du boucher

(A meat assortment)

Serves 6
veal: 6 slices cut from the fillet, each 2 ¼ oz (60 g)
beef: 6 mignonettes cut from the fillet, each 2 ¼ oz (60 g)
lamb: 6 noisettes cut from the saddle, each 2 ¼ oz (60 g)
For the sauces:
5 shallots, chopped
butter
14 fl oz (400 ml) dry white wine
40 fl oz (1.1 litres) double cream
salt
1 teaspoon Dijon mustard
¾ oz (25 g) finely-chopped chives
¾ oz (25 g) finely-chopped fresh parsley
¾ oz (25 g) finely-chopped fresh chervil
11 fl oz (310 ml) Madeira
¾ oz (25 g) fresh basil leaves, cut into julienne, stalks reserved
18 fl oz (510 ml) lamb stock
For the pommes de terre duchesse:
11 oz (310 g) potatoes
1 oz (2 tablespoons/30 g) butter
salt
2 egg yolks
For the garnish:
60 French beans, cut to approx. 1 ¼ in (3 cm) in length from the centre
12 small potatoes
1 oz (2 tablespoons/30 g) butter
12 turned carrots
8 oz (225 g) tagliatelle
tomato concassé

To make a herb sauce for the beef, sweat the shallots in a little butter without allowing to colour, then deglaze with the white wine. Bring to the boil and reduce by three-quarters. Add the cream, season lightly with salt and reduce again. Divide the liquid into 2 pans. Put the first pan to one side and to the second add the mustard and chopped herbs. Keep warm.
To make a basil sauce for the veal, place the Madeira and reserved basil stalks in a pan, bring to the boil and reduce by three-quarters. Add the reserved cream sauce and reduce again. Pass through a fine sieve, then stir in the julienne of basil.
Bring the lamb stock to the boil and reduce by three-quarters.
To make the pommes de terre duchesse, boil the potatoes until tender, drain and dry off. Sieve them, then add the butter and season with salt. Blend with the egg yolks and keep warm.
Cook the French beans in boiling, salted water, refresh, then toss in melted butter. To make pommes de terre fondantes, cut the small potatoes into even shapes. Melt the butter in a sauté pan, add the potatoes and cook over a gentle heat until golden brown and tender, turning once during cooking. Cook the turned carrots and the tagliatelle.
Pan-fry the meats separately.
To serve, place the sieved potato into a piping bag and pipe 3 lines on each serving plate to divide it into 3 equal segments. Spoon a little of the lamb stock into the top segment and arrange 1 slice of lamb and 2 pommes de terre fondantes on top. In the next segment place a slice of beef, spoon over some of the herb sauce and garnish with 2 carrots. In the final segment place a nest of tagliatelle, then a slice of veal on top. Spoon over some basil sauce, then add a little tomato concassé. Finish by placing some French beans in the middle of the plate.

Flan de poireaux
(Leek flan)

Serves 6
11 oz (310 g) leeks, finely sliced
butter
14 oz (400 g) white fish
1 egg white
18 fl oz (510 ml) cream
salt and freshly-ground pepper
12 fresh scallops
30 very thin slices of cucumber
Champagne butter sauce
tomato concassé
chopped fresh chervil
chopped fresh chives

Take 6 ring moulds, 3 in (7.5 cm) in diameter, and cover the bottoms with buttered paper. Cook the leeks in butter until soft but not coloured, then leave to cool. Place the fish and egg white in a food processor and process until smooth, then pass through a fine sieve. Place over a basin of ice and fold in the cream. Season with salt and pepper. Mix the fish mousse into the cold leeks and divide the mixture between the 6 ring moulds. Wrap in cling film.
Cover the bottoms of 6 more ring moulds of the same diameter with buttered paper. Slice the scallops horizontally and arrange alternate slices of scallop and cucumber in the bottom of the moulds in a flower shape using 5 slices of each.
Cook the mousses in a steamer for approximately 8 minutes, then place on serving plates and carefully unmould. Quickly steam the scallops, then, using a kitchen slice, carefully place on top of the mousses. Serve with a Champagne butter sauce garnished with tomato concassé and fresh herbs.

Sablés aux fraises
(Shortbread with strawberries)

Serves 6
1 lb 12 oz (800 g) fresh strawberries
For the sablés:
9 oz (255 g) flour
7 oz (1 ¾ sticks/200 g) unsalted butter
4 oz (110 g) icing sugar
salt
2 egg yolks
1 drop vanilla or lemon essence
egg wash
For the coulis:
1 lb (455 g) fresh strawberries
juice of ½ lemon
4 fl oz (110 ml) sorbet syrup (30°
  density)

Planning ahead
The sablé dough can be made up to 1 week in advance, wrapped in cling film and stored in the refrigerator.

To make the shortbread rounds, sift the flour onto a work surface and make a well in the centre. Dice the butter into the middle and work the butter until very soft. Sift the icing sugar onto the butter, add a pinch of salt and work together. Add the yolks and mix well. Gradually draw in the flour and mix until completely amalgamated. Add the vanilla or lemon essence and rub into the dough. Place to rest in the refrigerator for at least 1 hour.
Preheat the oven to 200°C/400°F/Gas Mark 6. Roll out the dough on a floured marble surface to a thickness of 1/8 in (2 mm). Cut out 18 circles with a round 4 in (10 cm) pastry cutter and arrange on a baking tray. Brush 6 rounds with egg wash and decorate as desired or mark with the back of a knife. Bake in the preheated oven for 6 – 8 minutes, until lightly coloured. Leave to cool a little, then transfer to a cooling rack.

To make the strawberry coulis, wash, drain and hull the fruit, then place in a food processor or liquidizer with the lemon juice and sorbet syrup and purée. Pass through a chinois (conical sieve) and reserve in the refrigerator.
Wash the remaining strawberries, reserve 6 and hull and halve the remainder. Mix them in the coulis.
To serve, place 1 of the undecorated sablés on each serving plate, cover with strawberries, place another round on top and add another layer of strawberries. Top with the decorated round. Spoon on a little coulis and decorate with the reserved strawberries. Alternatively, the top sablé round can be dusted with icing sugar.

Auberge de Provence

St James Court Hotel, Buckingham Gate, London SW1E 6AF. In the middle of Westminster. Open all year round lunch and dinner. Guest accomodation : 480 rooms all with bath/shower. To visit nearby : Buckingham Palace ; St James Park ; Westminster Cathedral ; Houses of Parliament. Credit cards accepted : Access, AE, Diners, Visa.   Tel : (01) 834 6655

St James' Court is a turn-of-the-century apartment block, upon which the TAJ company spent £40m to transform it into a luxury hotel boasting an elegant courtyard and fountain, a foyer/lounge with the second largest expanse of marble in SW1 ; also round the clock service in the public area... which is rare among hostelries.

The Auberge de Provence – recently moved from one part of the building to another – is franchised to the folk who run the "Oustau de Beaumanière" in Les Baux, an eatery that has retained three Michelin stars since 1955 – a rare achievement. It was here that Her Majesty (Queen Elizabeth II of Great Britain) – on holiday with Prince Philip – received Salvador Dali. When the audience ended, the veteran surrealist attempted to leave the room walking backwards, colliding with furniture, sending vases and the contents of sideboards crashing to the floor. Dali always claimed that this was the accident-strewn progress of a fervent royalist. The Queen is believed to have thought it was a deliberate "happening".

To my mind an "auberge" is homely, unpretentious, with check tablecloths ; auberges serve cassoulet and wine by the jug. I looked up the word in a French/English dictionary which seemed to share my view : "Inn. auberge de jeunesse – Youth Hostel". Well now : THIS auberge has carpets in which a small man could disappear completely ; décor to high standards of luxury ; flowers that would not disgrace Buckingham Palace (where they have the largest expanse of marble) and gleaming silver ; bespoke china and staff who speak English, with the sort of accent that manifests their determination to remain uninvolved. Their rapport with the clientèle is that of the missionary to the cannibal. "We have come", they seem to suggest, "at considerable inconvenience to ourselves, to give you glimpses of our superior way of life which you will appreciate. And appreciate it is what you are likely to do in this outstation of the Provençal motherhouse, whence they send staff to spread the word.

The term "sérieux" is very much more meaningful in French and they are "sérieux" alright. You arrive and they acknowledge you with an inclination of the head and just a suspicion of a smile. You are escorted into the bar when it has been properly established that you are who you said you are and the name corresponds with that in their reservation book. A headwaiter comes to take you to your table, makes exactly the right amount of extra fuss of ladies than gentlemen, gives an ounce more weight to the courtesy shown the host than his guests and stands by to recommend a "specialité".

Once through this theatricality, you will have a marvellous meal cooked by chefs who are deeply, uniquely dedicated to excellence, and who, perish the thought though it does keep recurring, might just go out in the evenings and eat le fish-and-chips.

In France, Raymond Thuilier, founder of the impeccably-formal, handsomely-gardened Oustau (the nearest gastro-oasis to the culinary void of the Camargue) has handed control to his grandson – Jean-André Charial ; it is he who masterminds the London operation also, seeming to translate his philosophy to SW1 rather than hanging around to see what it is the chaps around Buckingham Gate are after. That is courageous in a caterer and one welcomes such courage, especially when it eschews the pretentiousness of nouvelle cuisine mini-portions and comes up with real plates filled with full-flavoured food. As befits an establishment that bears the name "Provence", there is the aroma of best olive oil about the dishes, there is fish cooked with basil and garlic and garnished with black olives ; their navarin of lamb is the real traditional navarin – classic dishes require interpretation not innovation ; the ratatouille has about it the perfect balance of experience.

Charial (why don't we have third gene-

ration chefs in Britain?) had the theoretical experience to which he added practical education both with his grandfather and the Brothers Troisgros. His cuisine is simpler than those currently encountered in this league: when it comes to garnishes he keeps them in their place, monkfish tastes of monkfish, not as you might find in the cuisines of his rivals, slivers of the fish intertwined with salmon and John Dory, served on a mousse of langoustines beside a lobster coral sauce. His food is also lighter, uses cream only in moderation and, uniquely among French three star restaurants, he has a vegetarian menu – within which you find the most brilliant *Feuilleté de champignons* containing all the most rare and desirable wild mushrooms.

It is admirable in this complicated profession to come across men who are content to be judged by dishes of simple quality: like the Auberge's steamed sea bass served on a bed of diced tomato and basil; the salmon is presented with a chive and butter sauce, the scallops with melted chicory. There is a breast of duck garnished with lime and a fresh mint sauce, which makes you retrospectively angry about all the cherries and sweet oranges that have disguised the goodness of other ducks. The cheese tray is impressive, the bread freshly baked and there is much variety – like olive, onion, herb – and among the puddings you will discover the *Tarte Tatin*, the famed, hot, caramelized,

apple tart for which the "Oustau" became renowned.

If I have been less than enthusiastic about the French approach to service in foreign lands, I want to salute the decency of the author of the wine list... and the woman wine butler who is knowledgeable, authoritative and has an ideal table-side manner. More women should enter this profession. Among the well-chosen red wines on the list, nothing costs over £40; in each section there is good choice below £20 and I write this not because there is sound argument against listing really expensive wines but because their presence is inhibiting if you are unable to afford them. At the Auberge you can lord it with a Gevrey Chambertin 1979 from Etienne Morillon and no-one can upstage you by drinking La Tàche or Romanée. A white Châteauneuf du Pape 1986 might be the best buy.

At the end of the meal, to celebrate that you have taken on the very sérieux French and emerged with a powerful feeling of well-being, you can mark your enjoyment with cognacs, armagnacs, Calvadoses and Marcs de Bourgogne, watch them "welcoming" the new arrivals and wonder what you were worrying about when you came in. Perhaps this is a place to which we should go frequently, dispensing a little Britannic charm to moderate their Gallic dedication, or, learn French and make them feel at home.

Salade de coquilles St Jacques

(A scallop salad with honey sauce)

Serves 2
1 ½ oz (40 g) honey
juice of 2 lemons
salt and freshly-ground pepper
4 fl oz (110 ml) olive oil
2 fl oz (55 ml) sherry vinegar
12 chicory leaves
2 oz (55 g) red lettuce
2 oz (55 g) frisée
1 large tomato, skinned
12 fresh scallops
sprigs of fresh chervil to garnish

To make the honey sauce, place the honey in a pan and bring to the boil. Add the lemon juice and bring back to the boil, then season with salt and pepper and pour in 3 fl oz (80 ml) of the olive oil. Set aside and keep warm. Mix together the sherry vinegar, ½ − 1 fl oz (15 − 30 ml) of the remaining olive oil, salt and pepper. Toss the salad leaves in this dressing. Place the tomato in boiling water for 40 seconds, then plunge into iced water − this will make it easy to skin. Cut the tomato in two and squeeze out the seeds. Cut the flesh into small cubes.
Pan-fry the scallops in a little butter. Arrange on serving plates with the mixed salad. Pour over some honey sauce and garnish with the tomato and chervil.

Filets de St Pierre à la badiane et à l'orange

(John Dory fillets with star anise ans orange)

Serves 2
1 John Dory, about 1 lb 5 oz (600 g)
juice of 4 oranges
8 star anise
2 fl oz (55 ml) single cream
salt and freshly-ground pepper
3 oz (¾ stick/85 g) butter
For the garnish:
orange segments
star anise

Gut the fish, then wash, fillet and skin. Bring the orange juice and star anise to the boil and continue cooking until reduced by half. Add the cream, bring back to the boil and reduce again by half. Whisk in the butter a knob at a time.
Season the fish and steam for 5-8 minutes, depending on thickness, then place on serving plates and pour the sauce around. Garnish with orange segments and a star anise.

Rouget au basilic

(Red mullet with basil)

Serves 2
⅓ oz (10 g) fresh parsley
2 oz (55 g) fresh basil
⅔ oz (20 g) chopped shallot
¼ oz (7 g) chopped garlic
3 fl oz (85 ml) sherry vinegar
salt and freshly-ground pepper
7 fl oz (200 ml) olive oil
2 large tomatoes, weighing about 12 oz (340 g), skinned
2 red mullet, each 11 oz (310 g)
For the garnish:
⅔ oz (20 g) pitted and sliced black olives
fresh basil leaves, cut in julienne

Roughly chop the parsley and basil and mix with the shallot and garlic. Stir in the vinegar and season with salt and pepper. Heat the olive oil gently, then pour it over the herb and vinegar mixture. Keep at a tepid temperature.
Cut the tomatoes in half and squeeze out the seeds. Cut the flesh into small cubes. Gut and wash the fish, then fillet carefully removing all the bones. Cook the fish in a little olive oil, skin side down for 1-2 minutes, then turn over and cook again for 1-2 minutes. Spoon some of the sauce onto serving plates and arrange the fish on top. Garnish with the diced tomato, olive slices and basil leaves.

Noisettes d'agneau à la crème de persil et beignets d'ail

(Lamb fillet with a parsley cream sauce and garlic fritters)

Serves 2
4 lb (1.8 kg) rack of lamb
10 cloves garlic
18 fl oz (510 ml) milk
4 oz (110 g) plain flour
3 ½ fl oz (100 ml) lager
salt and freshly-ground pepper
2 courgettes
2 oz (½ stick/50 g) butter
2 fl oz (55 ml) whipping cream
¾ oz (25 g) basil
2 small potatoes
9 oz (255 g) carrots, chopped
4 oz (110 g) onions, chopped
3 oz (85 g) celery, chopped
3 ½ fl oz (100 ml) white wine
1 egg yolk
oil for deep frying
For the parsley cream sauce:
7 oz (200 g) parsley
1 fl oz (30 ml) double cream
butter

Remove the bones from the rack of lamb and reserve. Trim all the fat from the meat. Peel the garlic, cover with some of the milk and bring to the boil, then drain and repeat 4 or 5 times, using fresh milk each time. The final time continue cooking the garlic until tender, then drain and pan-fry the garlic in very hot butter until golden. Drain on kitchen paper and set aside.
To make the fritter mixture, combine the flour and beer with a spoonful of water and salt and pepper. Set aside.
Slice the courgettes thinly. Melt 1 oz (2 tablespoons/25 g) of the butter in a frying pan and add the courgettes, then season and pour over the cream and half the basil. Bring to the boil and cook until tender. Remove the courgettes with a slotted spoon and reserve the cream. Slice the potatoes thinly and cook the same way as the cour-

gettes, using fresh butter and the remainder of the basil but pouring over the reserved cream. Remove the potatoes and reserve the cream.
Roast the lamb bones in a flame and oven-proof dish in a preheated oven at 230°C/450°F/Gas Mark 8 until nicely browned, then add the chopped vegetables and cook until browned. Transfer to the top of the stove and add half the wine and just enough water to cover. Bring to the boil and cook until the liquid is a good clear brown. Strain and set aside.
To make the parsley cream, wash the parsley and remove the stalks. Cook briefly in a large pan of boiling, salted water, then refresh in iced water. Drain and dry on kitchen paper. Bring the cream to the boil and stir in the parsley. Season and whisk in a little butter to finish.
Arrange alternate slices of courgette and potato in a tight circle in the middle of the serving plates. Mix the egg yolk with the cream in which the vegetables were cooked and spoon it over the vegetables. Cook in the oven at a very low temperature until set. Meanwhile, pan-fry the lamb in a little olive oil and butter. Set aside and keep warm. Bring the lamb stock and the remainder of the wine to the boil and reduce. Coat the garlic in the fritter mixture and deep-fry until golden brown.
To serve, slice the lamb and arrange round the circle of vegetables, placing each slice on top of a mound of parsley cream. Finish the reduced sauce with a little unsalted butter and season to taste. Spoon the sauce over the lamb and add the garlic fritters.

Figues chaudes aux pignons et au miel de Baux

(Hot figs with pine nuts and honey sauce)

Serves 1
4 figs
2 oz (55 g) honey
juice of 1 lime
20 fresh raspberries
⅔ oz (not quite 2 tablespoons/20 g) butter
¾ oz (25 g) pine nuts
1 egg white, lightly beaten
2 oz (55 g) sugar
fresh mint leaves to decorate

Preheat the oven to 160-180°C/325 – 350°F/Gas Mark 3 – 4. With the tip of a knife, cut a cross through the top of each fig and pull the skin downwards in 4 quarters. Place the figs onto a piece of foil and pour over the honey and lime juice. Add the raspberries and dot with 2 or 3 knobs of butter. Draw up the foil to make a parcel and place in the preheated oven. Cook for 4 – 5 minutes.
Mix the pine nuts first in the egg white, then in the sugar. Heat up a little butter in a non-stick pan and fry the nuts until golden.
Remove the figs from the parcel and arrange on serving plates. Pour over the juices and add the pine nuts. Decorate with mint leaves.

LE SOUFFLÉ

Inter-Continental Hotel, 1 Hamilton Place, London W1V 0QY. Near Hyde Park Corner. Open all week except Saturday lunch, all year except 26 Dec & 1 Jan: adjusted each year. Private parties: 1400 main room, 10 in private room. To visit nearby: Buckingham Palace; The Cabinet War Rooms; Hyde Park; Speakers' Corner. Credit cards accepted: Access, AE, Diners, Visa.   Tel: (01) 409 3131.

In the board game "Monopoly", Park Lane is second only to Mayfair on the property totem pole and one forgets that there used to be an unfashionable part. Yet at the northern end by Marble Arch stood Tyburn's Tree, scene of public hangings as recently as the second half of the last century ... and "trade" began at Grosvenor House, crept down to the Dorchester, on to The Hilton and the Inn on the Park.

The Inter-continental Hotel stands squarely at the southern extremity where Park Lane meets Piccadilly – a grand hotel with all the anonymity, discretion, internationalism and efficiency that goes with the appellation. You find the regulation carriage attendant, dressed to kill; helpful and knowledgeable hall-porter; news-stand; coffee-shop; marbled lobby in which residents and visitors sit and cement eight figure deals. It is the newest of Park Lane's grand hotels, yet for some ten years it has enjoyed the enviable reputation of running the most efficient banqueting operation in London, which is high praise.

Peter Kromberg, an anglicised German in his early forties, runs the kitchens. If I had to spend the rest of my life on a desert island with a *maître chef des cuisines*, he is the man I would choose. Now there is no good reason why an agreeable character should be a cook of excellence but in Mr Kromberg's case this is so and Le Soufflé Restaurant, while being only a small percentage of the Inter-continental's catering operation, is his flagship, to which he devotes more than fifty per cent of his time. Kromberg is a chef's chef. If you are after a man who stalks the tables in a tall white hat, kissing the clientèle, flashing medallions from his chest, go elsewhere. If the ultimate affectations of nouvelle cuisine, or flaming crêpes suzette by which you can read the "Financial Times" are your idea of high gastronomy, there are other places. Kromberg is a quiet, immensely efficient professional, who cares for gastronomy and practises what he preaches.

Walk into the main entrance and Le Soufflé is to the right: a standard, comfortable hotel restaurant, furbished by the contract designer with a view to offending no-one. Look with attention and you will notice that the china is Villeroy & Boch, which is unusual and expensive and brilliant; the waiters are primarily young, and in the ante-room they serve 1966 vintage claret by the glass, which is good news.

Kromberg did not invent Le Soufflé concept. He arrived, it was there and he made a success of it. Josef Lanser, an Austrian by birth, is the Maître d'Hôtel – listed on the menu as Maître de Hôtel, of which he would approve for he is a man of formality. They are pleased to see you but they don't jump up and down with joy; they like you to sit where you want to sit and, unlike so many restaurants, let you order what you wish to order. Le Soufflé is a restaurant of quality devoid of gimmickry – unless you believe that a soufflé is a gimmick – with which opinion I would not argue a lot.

The chef would be proudest of his fish: from a lime-flavoured seafood soup, via a warm lobster salad with crab fritters and asparagus tips, to the terrine of smoked salmon and langoustine in a tarragon jelly dressed with a hazelnut oil vinaigrette. If you want to confine your fish intake to the main course, there is a spectacular wild mushroom soup amongst the first courses; or you could start with the excellent sautéed rabbit with oyster mushrooms, and follow with the steamed Dover sole filled with lobster mousse riding on a lake of caviar-garnished champagne sauce. There is also a great Park Lane rarity: a main course for under £10: boned breast of farmed chicken in a buttered orange sauce with wild rice and a dandelion salad. For £36.50, there is a Choix de Chef: seven elegant courses, three on either side of a pink champagne sorbet. The sweet trolley rolls smoothly across

the plush carpet, groaning with good-looking confections to compete with the half dozen soufflés that are available from the kitchen: chocolate and candied kumquats, banana and raisins and rum, hazelnut with wild cherries and a Kirsch sabayon ... and probably anything else you have set your heart on. Ask Kromberg which soufflé he would recommend and he would advise you to eat whichever appeals. Ask him what he himself would eat and the answer is a cheese soufflé, which is probably where the whole soufflé trade began.

Of the chefs he employs in the kitchens, two are occupied solely in making soufflés. The wine list is not as long as you would find further up Park Lane but what is there is chosen with care and the prices asked shock less than they do in adjacent establishments.

It is a substantial achievement to impose style and individuality upon a hotel restaurant where the discriminating customer is steadily outnumbered by the transient resident. Peter Kromberg and Josef Lanser have done this with skill and with care, and the fact that they leave gratuities to the discretion of the clientèle is a measure of the confidence they have in the public's appreciation of their work.

Pot-au-feu de saumon aux racines et gros sel

(Salmon with root vegetables, seasoned with Maldon salt)

Serves 6
1 lb (455 g) new Jersey or Belle de
  Fontainey potatoes
6 x 1 in (2.5 cm) thick marrow bones
  (ask your butcher to cut them)
salt
12 bunch carrots, peeled
2-3 young leeks, trimmed and cut into
  3 in (7.5 cm) pieces
½ celeriac, peeled and cut into wedges
2 medium-sized bulbs young fennel,
  quartered
1 tablespoon Maldon salt
6 x 4 oz (110 g) salmon steaks, with
  skin but all bones removed
30 fl oz (850 ml) cold court bouillon
  (be careful with the vinegar)
1 ½ fl oz (40 ml) extra virgin olive oil
juice of 1 – 2 lemons
approx. 24 cherry tomatoes, peeled
1 large bunch fresh chervil, stalks
  removed and leaves coarsely snipped

Steam the new potatoes, then peel them.
Place the marrow bones in a pan with salted
water. Bring to the boil and simmer for 5
minutes, then remove and cool. Precook all
the vegetables individually in lightly salted
water, except for the cherry tomatoes. Drain
and set aside. Lightly oil the bottom of a large,
shallow, flameproof casserole, then sprinkle
with some of the Maldon salt. Arrange the salmon steaks on top, well spaced, then place the
marrow bones and precooked vegetables,
including the potatoes, in between. Add the
cold court bouillon. Bring to the boil, turn off
the heat, cover and leave for 5 minutes.
Remove the salmon, marrow bones and
vegetables and arrange on a large serving
dish. Cover with foil and keep warm.
Reduce the cooking liquid according to
taste. Strain, then gradually whisk in the
olive oil and lemon juice to taste. Pour into a
saucepan, add the cherry tomatoes and
chervil and bring to the boil. Pour over the
salmon *pot-au-feu*, then sprinkle the
remaining Maldon salt over the fish.

Le pigeon en vessie aux ravioles et son tartare

(Pigeon in a parcel with ravioli and its tartare)

Serves 6
For the ravioli :
7 oz (200 g) strong white flour, salt
2 egg yolks, 1 whole egg
1 tablespoon vegetable oil
4 oz (110 g) goose liver pâté, cut into cubes
2 oz (55 g) duck breast, ham or smoked
  goose, sliced very thin
egg wash
For the pigeons :
3 large boned pigeons, bones and
  giblets reserved
freshly-ground pepper
2 oz (55 g) white breadcrumbs
2 oz (55 g) mushroom duxelles
  (mushrooms chopped, cooked in a
  little butter and thickened with
  double cream)
1 tablespoon chopped mixed fresh herbs
2 oz (½ stick/55 g) soft butter
2 oz (55 g) sieved goose liver pâté
3 pigs' bladders, well washed
1 ½ tablespoons port wine
1 ½ tablespoons Madeira
For the sauce :
2 oz (55 g) mirepoix of onions, celery
  and carrots
1 ¾ pints (1 litre) chicken stock or water
¾ oz (scant 2 tablespoons/25 g) butter
½ shallot, chopped
1 tablespoon truffle juice
For the pigeon tartare :
4 pigeon breasts, skinned, boned and
  chopped (reserve legs, bones and
  skins for the sauce)
½ garlic clove, chopped
¼ teaspoon chopped fresh ginger
½ teaspoon chopped leek
½ teaspoon chopped fresh chives
½ teaspoon chopped fresh chervil
½ teaspoon chopped fresh tarragon
¼ teaspoon chopped fresh coriander
  leaves
pinch curry powder
pinch cumin powder
1 teaspoon soy sauce
2 teaspoons hazelnut oil

First make the ravioli dough. Sift the flour
with a pinch of salt into a mound on a work
surface. Make a well in the middle and add
the egg yolks, egg and oil. Work the ingredients together to form a soft ball. Wrap and
leave to rest for about 2 hours.
Season the pigeons inside with salt and pepper. Place the crumbs, duxelles, herbs, butter, chopped pigeons' livers and hearts and
half the goose liver pâté in a bowl and mix
well together to form the stuffing. Season
with salt and pepper. Fill the pigeons with
this mixture, then close using a trussing
needle and thread. Place carefully into the
bladders, add the port wine and Madeira,
then close hermetically with string.
In a large saucepan, bring 7 pints (4 litres)
water to the boil, place the bladders into the
boiling water and reduce the heat immediately. Cover and simmer for approximately 30
minutes.
To make the sauce, brown the reserved
pigeon bones in a little butter, add the mirepoix and sweat until lightly coloured. Add the
chicken stock or water. Bring to the boil and
boil slowly for about 30 minutes or until reduced to one third. Strain and keep aside.
Meanwhile roll out the ravioli dough very
thinly and cut into eighteen 2 ½ in (6 cm)
squares. Wrap the goose liver cubes with the
duck, ham or goose and place in the middle of
the squares. Spread a little egg wash on the
corners and fold together. Poach the ravioli in
salted water with a drop of oil added.
Remove the bladders from the pan and
pierce over a bowl with the tip of a knife, in
order to retain the cooking juices.
Heat the butter in a saucepan, add the shallots, sweat for a few minutes, then add the
cooking juices and the pigeon stock. Bring
to the boil and reduce to the required consistency, then taste. Add the truffle juice
and the remaining goose liver, correct seasoning and keep warm.
To make the pigeon tartare, mix all the
ingredients together with a table fork. Season, then place in the refrigerator.
Remove the pigeons from the bladders, cut in
half and arrange on serving plates. Cover with
the sauce and garnish with the ravioli. Serve
the pigeon tartare separately, accompanied
by toast fingers and a warm lentil salad.

Soufflé glacé aux fruits de la passion, confit aux fraises

(Iced passion fruit soufflé with a strawberry sauce)

Serves 6
For the strawberry confit:
4 oz (110 g) fresh strawberries
3 oz (85 g) caster sugar
1 oz (30 g) redcurrant jelly
juice of ½ lemon
For the soufflé:
2 eggs, separated
3 oz (90 g) icing sugar
2 fl oz (55 ml) passion fruit juice or
  frozen pulp
a little lemon juice
16 fl oz (455 ml) double or whipping
  cream, whipped
3 ½ fl oz (100 ml) melted chocolate
a little Kirsch

Place all the ingredients for the strawberry confit in a bowl and leave overnight to macerate. Transfer to a saucepan, bring to the boil, skim, then leave to cool.
Whisk the egg yolks with half the icing sugar until white and foamy. Add the passion fruit juice or pulp and lemon juice. Whisk the egg whites with the remaining icing sugar until stiff. Fold the passion fruit mixture into the whipped cream, then fold in the egg whites.
Fill 6 individual moulds half full, add a little of the strawberry confit without juice in the middle, then add the remaining mixture to fill the moulds. Freeze overnight.
Remove the ices from the moulds, dip half way in the melted chocolate, then return to the freezer.
To serve, add a little Kirsch to the remaining strawberry confit and arrange on serving plates, with the soufflés in the middle.

Millefeuille de chocolat amer

(Thin chocoate wafers filled with bitter chocolate mousse)

Serves 6
6 oz (170 g) dark chocolate
  (couverture)
2 egg yolks
2 oz (55 g) sugar
pinch of salt
½ leaf gelatine, soaked
4 oz (110 g) bitter chocolate, melted
1 small cup of hot black coffee
10 fl oz (285 ml) double or whipping
  cream, whipped
1 tablespoon cocoa powder
pistachio nuts, halved
wild cherry sauce, to serve

Melt the dark chocolate and bring to a temperature of 29°C/84°F. Cut a sheet of plastic into strips 1 ½ in (4 cm) wide. Brush the chocolate evenly and thinly over the plastic, then mark the strips with a knife every 2 in (5 cm): you will need 24 pieces. Place in the refrigerator until set, then carefully peel off the chocolate wafers.
Whisk together the yolks, sugar and a pinch of salt until foamy, add the soaked and melted gelatine, then the melted bitter chocolate. (If the mixture becomes a bit too sticky, add some of the hot black coffee.) Fold in the whipped cream and leave the mousse to cool a little.
Lay 6 chocolate wafers on a tray and pipe some chocolate mousse on top. Cover with 6 more wafers. Repeat this procedure to add 2 more chocolate wafers to each millefeuille. Dust the top with the cocoa powder. Garnish with a half pistachio nut and serve on a wild cherry sauce.

RULES

35 Maiden Lane, London W C 2. In the middle of Covent Garden. Open Monday to Saturday. (Vegetarian meals; air-conditioned; no dogs.) Private parties: 3 rooms available. To visit nearby: Covent Garden; theatres; Trafalgar Square. Credit cards accepted: Access, AE, Visa. Tel: (01) 836 5314

Rules is part of our national heritage. An establishment that is 190 years old, it began life as an oyster bar, when dandies and rakes as well as superior intelligences comprised its clientèle; went on as an eating-house with an upstairs facility for assignations – Prinny would meet Lily Langtry in a first floor room and persuaded the proprietor to build a side entrance, so that the couple did not have to walk through the restaurant – and is now proud of its history and spectacularly English in its approach to life. Sadly the *chambres particulières*, which featured so prominently in Graham Greene's "The End of the Affair" have gone to make way for banqueting suites but the Edwardian atmosphere pertains. In the words of John Betjeman it is "a unique and irreplaceable part of literary and theatrical London". Dickens ate here, as did Charlie Chaplin, Henry Irving, Buster Keaton, Clark Gable... and my father brought me to Rules before the war and said "remember, always tip the carver tuppence" and I did remember when I came back in the late 1950s and the carver said "you keep it, sir, you look as if you need it more than I."

The present proprietor is John Mayhew. Amazingly he is only the fourth owner since Thomas Rule told his parents that he was turning over a new leaf and opened the doors of 35 Maiden Lane in 1798. (Being an oysterer at that time, was a distinctly ungentlemanly calling.)

The phrase "the customer is always right" is one that has never had much appeal for the English caterer who well knows that the customer is usually wrong, but on balance is probably worth humouring. What is marvellously missing at Rules is any semblance of the fawning, grovelling, scraping reception on offer elsewhere. It is open from noon until midnight. They are medium-pleased to see you and serve you what is on offer, in their style, in their time, with an occasional flourish. A couple of hundred pictures and cartoons and photographs of previous customers stare down at you from the walls; the painted, enamelled and embossed ceilings house great copper-coloured fans though there is air-conditioning; the waiters are in black and white, more Toulouse Lautrec than Yves St Laurent and there is a substantial selection of historically-English food: Morecambe Bay potted shrimps, smoked Finnan haddock Monte Carlo (which means anointed with a poached egg, though Monaco probably has fewer commercial egg producers than any other country but The Vatican), rack of lamb, angels on horseback. There are dishes of the day to reflect the season, wild boar and venison in the winter, fresh salmon in the spring; asparagus in May, grouse in August when Rules probably sells as many of these birds as any establishment in the land... and serves them with good bread sauce spiked with cloves.

Now Rules does not feature in good food guides, perhaps because guides are snobs and Rules would have little time for snobbery; they get on with serving their customers of whom there are sufficient to fill the place around the clock. If you order the right food, then you will eat quite spectacularly well and where else is there that you can sit on a red velvet settee beneath a picture of Charles Laughton and drink Real Ale from a silver tankard. You might notice that the pint tankard is filled to the brim with froth... the beer doesn't begin until about a third of the way down, but they never said it was anything other than "a tankard", and it is cold and excellent and goes brilliantly with the steak and kidney and mushroom pudding. No-one can go wrong with Rules' Steak and Kidney and Mushroom Pudding. It is because of Rules' Steak and Kidney and Mushroom Pudding that I had no hesitation in including this place in my book. Remember the name: Steak and Kidney and Mushroom Pudding. To my mind, Steak and Kidney Pie is a poor dish, but the pudding, suet crust made golden with a judicious spoonful of black treacle, shivering as it is decanted

onto the plate – yet of sufficient crispness to hold it together until you plunge your knife into the bomb-shaped casing causing tender succulent beef and flavoursome offal to ooze across your plate in a moist, mushroomy, meaty mass... and with it come just about the best roast potatoes you will find in London. The whole shooting match costs £8.50. Then there is treacle sponge pudding with custard, to sort of settle you after the main dish; you would be foolish to pass up this confection which may not abound in subtlety but cannot be faulted when it comes to satisfying a man's

desire to go home with an overall feeling of having eaten well.

The wine list is short and to the point. Mumm's champagne is the "House" tipple at 60% of the price they charge for it across the road at the Savoy. There is well-chosen Sancerre, some fairly hit and miss clarets at single figure prices and an excellent late bottled Sandeman's port at a modest £3 a glass.

Go there for the atmosphere, the decency of the establishment; go there because so many good people have been there and do not forget about the s and k and m pudding.

44

Smoked salmon with scrambled egg

Serves 1
4 oz (110 g) "peat smoked" Scottish
  salmon
clarified butter
2 eggs
3 tablespoons single cream
freshly-ground black pepper
grated nutmeg
sprigs of fresh parsley or dill to
  garnish

Arrange the smoked salmon slices on a serving plate. Heat the clarified butter in a
sauté pan. Beat the eggs, cream and seasonings (without salt) together, then pour into
the pan and gently scramble. Place the eggs
on top of the salmon and garnish with sprigs
of parsley or dill.

Oak smoked meats with Cumberland sauce

Serves 4
12 oz (340 g) oak-smoked mutton, ham,
  venison and beef, thinly- sliced
salad leaves to garnish
For the sauce:
1 lb (455 g) fresh redcurrants
20 fl oz (565 ml) water
sugar (see recipe)
1 orange
1 lemon
port
ground cinnamon

The smoked meats are produced in traditional smokehouses in Cumbria from
choice cuts. The mutton and ham take over
a year to cure, smoke and mature. The
meats are smoked over oak to which flavouring woods, such as juniper, beech and
cherry are added.
Pick over the redcurrants and discard any
damaged fruit, then place in a saucepan
with the water, cover and place in a bain
marie filled with boiling water. Poach until
the juice has separated from the fruit. Pour
the fruit and its juice into a jelly bag and
hang over a bowl overnight to strain.
 Measure the juices into a saucepan and for
every 20 fl oz (565 ml) of juice, add 12 oz
(340 g) sugar. Bring to the boil and cook for
30 minutes, skimming frequently. Test the
liquid by putting a little onto a cold plate. If
it sets when cold, the jelly is ready. Transfer
to the refrigerator to set.
Remove the peel from the orange and
lemon and cut into fine julienne. Squeeze
the juice from both fruit.
When ready to serve, place the jelly in a pan
with the other ingredients and bring back to
the boil, then allow to cool. The sauce
should be of pouring consistency when
cold. Arrange the meats on serving plates
and pour round the sauce. Garnish with a
variety of salad leaves.

Roast teal with braised red cabbage

Serves 4
4 teal, hung and cleaned
soft butter for roasting
For the red cabbage:
½ large red cabbage
1 onion
4 oz (110 g) bacon
1 cooking apple
¼ bottle red wine
bacon stock
2 tablespoons cider vinegar
4 oz (110 g) brown sugar
4 oz (110 g) sultanas
pinch ground mixed spice

Preheat the oven to 180°C/350°F/Gas Mark
4. Thinly slice the cabbage and onion and
cut the bacon into small dice. Place in a
heavy flame and ovenproof pan, cover and
cook for a short while. Peel and slice the
apple, then mix into the cabbage and onion
with all the other ingredients. Cover and
bake in the oven for 1-1 ½ hours until the
cabbage is tender.
Increase the oven temperature to
220°C/425°C/Gas Mark 7. Brush the teal
with butter and roast in the preheated oven
for approximately 15 minutes – 5 minutes
on each side and the last 5 on the back.
Remove from the oven and allow to rest in a
warm place.
Serve the teal with a toasted croûte spread
with pâté and garnish with game chips,
watercress and radish. Serve the red cabbage on a side plate.

Pike mousse wrapped in spinach with saffron sauce

Serves 4
17 oz (500 g) skinned and boned pike flesh
salt and freshly-ground pepper
grated nutmeg
2 large eggs
9 fl oz (255 ml) double cream
spinach leaves, washed and stalks removed
sprigs of dill
turned and cooked carrots to garnish
For the saffron sauce:
1 shallot, finely chopped
butter
2 pinches of saffron threads
1 bay leaf
5 fl oz (140 ml) white wine
20 fl oz (565 ml) double cream
salt and freshly-ground pepper
green peppercorns

Pass the pike flesh through a fine mincer twice, then place in a food processor and add the seasonings and eggs. Process until all the ingredients are thoroughly blended. Remove the mixture from the processor and place in a bowl over ice. Add the cream gradually, beating well after each addition. Set aside in the refrigerator.
To make the saffron sauce, sweat the shallots in a little butter, then add the saffron, bay leaf and white wine. Bring to the boil and reduce by about two-thirds. Pour on the cream and reduce again to the recquired consistency. Strain through a fine chinois (conical sieve) and taste and adjust seasoning. Add a few green peppercorns according to taste.
Blanch and refresh the spinach leaves, then arrange in greased dariole moulds with the top side of the leaves facing the sides of the mould. Spoon the mousse into the centre and fold the excess leaves over the top. Cover with foil and steam for approximately 20 minutes.
When cooked, carefully turn out of the moulds and drain off any excess liquid. Place the mousses on serving plates and pour the saffron sauce around. Garnish with sprigs of dill and turned carrots.

Apple hat pudding

Serves 14
3 lb (1.35 kg) cooking apples, peeled and finely diced
8 oz (225 g) raisins
strong stock syrup
ground cinnamon
ground cloves
13 fl oz (370 ml) golden syrup
7 fl oz (200 ml) cream
For the suet pastry:
1 lb (455 g) suet
2 lb (910 g) self-raising flour
8 oz (225 g) sugar
20 fl oz (565 ml) water

To make the pastry, mix all the dry ingredients in a bowl, add the water and knead into a ball. Roll out to a thickness of about ¼ in (0.5 cm) and cut into circles large enough to line buttered dariole moulds without joins.
Combine the apples, raisins and stock syrup with cinnamon and cloves to taste, then fill the lined dariole moulds with this mixture, being sure to fill the centre completely. Roll out the pastry trimmings and cut out lids for the moulds. Place the pastry lids in position, seal with foil and steam for approximately 20 minutes.
Turn out carefully onto serving plates. Warm together the golden syrup and cream and pour round the apple hats.

Apple and blackberry pie

Serves 4
12 oz (340 g) cooking apples, peeled and sliced
6 oz (170 g) blackberries, picked over and washed
cinnamon
sugar
For the sweet pastry:
1 egg
2 oz (55 g) sugar
5 oz (1 stick plus 2 tablespoons/140 g) unsalted butter
8 oz (225 g) flour
egg wash
icing sugar

To make the pastry, cream the egg and sugar together until pale and creamy, then add the butter in pieces and mix for a few seconds. Gradually add the flour and mix lightly until smooth. Rest in the refrigerator for 30 minutes.
Preheat the oven to 220°C/425°F/Gas Mark 7. Fill 1 large or 4 individual pie dishes with the raw fruit mixture, flavouring it with cinnamon and sugar to taste. Roll out the pastry to a thickness of ¼ in (0.5 cm) and cover the apple mixture. Decorate with pastry trimmings and glaze with egg wash. Bake in the preheated oven for 10-15 minutes. Dust with icing sugar and serve with a good egg custard.

Gravetye Manor

In the late 1940s Francis Coulson had taken the road north and opened Sharrow Bay – the first country house hotel in the land (see page 120); Peter Herbert opened Gravetye Manor, the second, in 1957. He had previously been co-owner of the Gore Hotel in Kensington and had come to the attention of the public via his Elizabethan Banquets, conceived to mark the Coronation of the Second Elizabeth with the trappings that pertained during the reign of the First: serving wenches, strolling players, mead, wild boar. The Gore flourished, the banquets were a success and remained on the London scene for five years. Mr and Mrs Herbert moved south, bought the manor at Gravetye. The house had been a sometime smugglers' hide-out, manufacturing base for heavy-weight cannon balls for the Woolwich Arsenal, then home of William Robinson, most famous innovator of the English Garden; he died at Gravetye in his nineties, before the last war. It is a marvellously cultured house, laid out, as were Robinson's gardens, in quietly excellent taste: wood panelling, open fireplaces, oil paintings of real quality... and while there are all manner of young, efficient, important-looking men in dinner jackets, who look as if they hold positions of influence: head of this, master-of-that, manager-of-t'other, Peter Herbert unobtrusively dictates – and I doubt that much goes on about which he does not know.

The Hotel exudes cultured professionalism. The rooms are luxuriously appointed, comfortable, large, with genuine antiques and authentic modern aids to life – like colour TV, phone, bespoke bath-robes, an amazing range of bottles of gel and shampoo in the bathroom. Before meals, drinks are served in the drawing room and there is brought an array of innovative appetisers like anchovy-flavoured cream cheese baked into a pillow of crisp pastry, moist slices of anchoïade, proud twirls of smoked salmon – which they produce at the end of the garden in a smokehouse that was once a potting shed. The menu is presented written in a fine calligrapher's hand containing the welcome news that there is no smoking in the dining room, service is included in the price of the meal, they do not accept credit cards (a sure sign of success) and they will be pleased to take personal cheques or forward the account – which, dammit, is how one gentleman treats another.

Peter Herbert discovered Michael Quinn, one of the most talented of the 1960s chefs, who was transferred after 10 years to the Ritz Hotel, where he never seemed to achieve the same fine flourish that distinguished his reign at the Manor. He is now replaced by the eldest Herbert son, Leigh – who read natural sciences at Cambridge, worked in the vineyards of Burgundy, had a spell with the Brothers Roux, became a successful restaurateur in Australia and is back now in his true vocation. He for whom the fatted calf was slaughtered when he returned from distant parts is in charge of the kitchen. Chef Patron is his official title, his father, never a high profile man, having withdrawn some furlongs down the drive. I doubt his influence will greatly diminish.

It is the ambition of the Gravetye kitchen to purchase only what they cannot grow themselves and to obtain the best local produce, like the pheasants that fall out of the sky to the Sussex shotguns, the fish from the local rivers and nearby sea, some served fresh, some home-smoked. The cooking is skilful and accurate: not for them the startling reductions that end up as a teaspoonful of raspberry vinegar-flavoured glaze. A salad of warm ham hock on a selection of good leaves, with lentils that are spiked with Dijon mustard is a favoured starter – much imitated around the county. They prepare pot-roasted breasts of duck, with lemon and ginger, the slices fanned upon the handsome porcelain plate on a well-executed *jus*. The vegetables are crisp, the julienne of cabbage particularly good, and there is the classic *Pommes dauphinoise* with or without garlic, served in individual cocottes. Wild mushrooms play a part in the repertoire of Leigh Stone-Herbert's kitchen and a salad trolley is wheeled around the restaurant bearing a selection of oils and vinegars, spices and herbs to enable the waitress to create the dressing of your choice.

The wine list is marvellously complete. There are many wines for sensitive pockets, also some great wines which are not; indeed should not be anything but expensive (and there are half bottles for those who have heard about the West

Sussex Constabulary). The wine waiter knows his job : "I don't think you need decant the Shiraz", I said to the young man ; he decanted it, explaining that the wine benefitted from the extra oxidisation, and there was a definite shadow of deposit at the base of the bottle... and he was right, without the least sign of being smug.

What one finds in country houses, though seldom in country house hotels, are savouries. Not so at Gravetye where soft roes and mushrooms on a slice of brioche, or a brie fritter with redcurrant jelly (why not gooseberry?) adorn the pudding menu and where an apple and caramel tart on a puff pastry base served with the smoothest of cinnamon ice creams was outstanding. There is also Château Rieussec, by the glass, at the perfect temperature and coffee and petits fours beyond the call of duty.

In its 32nd year there is not a hint of staleness about this attractive, stylish operation which goes from strength to strength and is distinguished by exhibiting, on the main road, a notice deterring people from taking pot-luck up the drive in search of unreserved meals.

Near East Grinstead, West Sussex, RH19 4LJ. In the Sussex downs, 30 miles from London. Open all year round. (No children under 7; no smoking in restaurant; no dogs.) Private parties: up to 18 in private room. Guest accommodation: 14 rooms all with bath/shower. To visit nearby: Chartwell (Winston Churchill's home); Hever Castle; historic villages e.g. Lindfield, Petworth and Alfriston; famous gardens e.g. Wakehurst, Sheffield Park. No credit cards; cheques accepted with banker's card. Tel: (0342) 810567

Poached lobster in puff pastry

Serves 8
4 x 1 lb (455 g) live lobsters
1 sheet of puff pastry, 12 x 8 in (30 x 20 cm) and ¼ in (0.5 cm) thick, kept chilled
2 egg yolks
milk
For the poaching liquor:
1 carrot, chopped
1 medium onion, chopped
1 stick celery, chopped
1 small bunch mixed fresh herbs
salt to taste
For the lobster stock:
1 tablespoon olive oil
1 carrot, chopped
1 onion, chopped
1 stick celery, chopped
1 small leek, chopped
3 ripe tomatoes, chopped
2 cloves garlic, crushed
11 fl oz (310 ml) dry white wine
1 bunch mixed fresh herbs
10 black peppercorns, crushed
For the sauce:
5 ½ fl oz (155 ml) dry white wine (Chenin Blanc or Sauvignon Blanc)
7 fl oz (200 ml) whipping cream
2 x ½ in (1 cm) cubes very cold unsalted butter
salt and freshly-ground pepper
8 leaves of fresh basil
4 ripe tomatoes, skinned, seeds removed and cut into eighths

Planning ahead
The poaching of the lobsters and the preparation of the stock can be done well in advance.

Place all the poaching ingredients and water in a pot large enough to take the 4 lobsters comfortably. Simmer together for 15 minutes. Kill the lobsters by chopping lengthways through the heads (only) and cook in the simmering, poaching liquor for 9 minutes. Keep at simmering point, do not boil. Lift out the lobsters and plunge them into ice-cold water to prevent them from cooking any further.

Detach the claws and the tail from the heads and carefully remove the flesh from the shells. Reserve the heads. The claws can be easily cracked by tapping them smartly with the back of a heavy kitchen knife. The tail shell can be carefully cut along the underside with kitchen scissors. Using a sharp knife, carefully cut the flesh of each tail into 8 medallions. Set these and the claw flesh aside on a plate, covered with cling film, in a cool place.

To make the stock, remove the shells from the reserved lobster heads to leave the legs, etc. Carefully break off the feathery gills and spiny sac from each head. Discard the shells, gills and sac. Using a heavy knife or small cleaver, chop the remaining trimmed heads coarsely. Fry these pieces in a heavy pot with the olive oil over a medium heat, stirring continually until starting to brown. Throw in the vegetables and garlic and continue stirring until all the liquid has evaporated and the mixture is soft and browning. It should have a rich, aromatic perfume. Add the white wine and reduce by half, stirring all the time, then add just enough water to cover the lobster and vegetables. Bring to the boil, then reduce the heat to a gentle simmer, carefully skimming the surface. Add the bunch of herbs and peppercorns. Simmer gently for about 30 minutes, skimming frequently, until reduced to approximately half its original liquid volume.
Strain off the liquid into a bowl, squeezing as much as possible out of the solids that remain: the best flavour comes from the last drops! There should be 1-1 ¼ pints (0.5-0.75 litre) of stock.

To bake the pastry, ensure that it is very cold and, using a very sharp, cold knife, cut the rectangle into 8 pieces of equal size. Place them, well spread out, onto a dry, cold and very lightly greased baking sheet. Put into the refrigerator to chill. Preheat the oven to 200°C/400°F/Gas Mark 6. Thoroughly mix together the 2 egg yolks with an equal volume of milk and use to paint the pastry pieces, evenly and smoothly. Bake in the preheated oven until cooked to a rich golden colour, remove and set to cool on a wire rack.

To make the sauce, place the wine in a heavy saucepan over a medium heat and reduce to one-third of its volume. Add 11 fl oz (310 ml) of the lobster stock and reduce by half. Add the whipping cream, bring to the boil and reduce the heat to a gentle simmer. Reduce the sauce until it *just* coats the back of a spoon. Whisk in the butter until fully incorporated. Remove the pan to a very low heat, so that the sauce is not even simmering. Season to taste.

Immediately before serving and acting quickly, cut the pastries horizontally very near their bases and put to warm in a gentle oven. Add the basil leaves and lobster pieces to the hot sauce and agitate over a gentle heat to infuse, 1 ½ minutes should be sufficient to warm the lobster through. It must *not* boil. Add the tomato pieces. Place the lower halves of the pastry slices onto 8 hot serving plates. Using a slotted spoon, divide the lobster, tomato and basil equally between the plates. Whisk the sauce vigorously, bring to the boil and strain onto the plates. Place the upper halves of the pastry on top of the lobster and serve.

Prune, armagnac and mascarpone tart

Serves 8
8 large, top quality prunes, steeped in
  tea
armagnac (or brandy if necessary)
shortcrust pastry to line a 10 in (28 cm)
  flan tin
17 oz (510 g) mascarpone cheese
dark brown sugar
For the caramel sauce:
9 oz (255 g) sugar
10 ½ fl oz (300 ml) water
peel of 1 lemon

Drain the prunes from the tea, chop coarsely and macerate for 5 hours in 3 ½ fl oz (100 ml) of armagnac or brandy.
Preheat the oven to 190°C/375°F/Gas Mark 5. Lightly grease a 10 in (28 cm) flan tin. Roll out the pastry as thin as is manageable and carefully line the tin. Bake blind in the preheated oven until golden brown, then allow to cool.
Beat the mascarpone in a bowl with a wire whisk until it begins to thicken and holds its shape. Remove the prunes from the armagnac and fold about 2 ½ fl oz (70 ml) of the armagnac (or to taste) into the mascarpone. Spread the chopped prunes over the bottom of the pastry case. Spoon the mascarpone into the case and spread it evenly using a palette knife, so that it is almost level with the top of the case. Allow to rest in a cool place for at least 1 hour.
To make the caramel sauce, place the sugar and 3 ½ fl oz (100 ml) water in a heavy saucepan and dissolve over a high heat, then cook to a rich dark caramel. Turn off the heat and add the remaining water being very careful for the caramel will spit violently. When the eruption has settled, bring slowly back to the boil, stirring continually. Pour into a bowl, add the lemon peel and allow to cool to room temperature. Remove the lemon peel.
To serve, sprinkle the surface of the mascarpone very lightly with sieved dark brown sugar. Cut the tart into 8 equal pieces and place on serving plates. Pour the caramel sauce around.

Grilled fillets of red mullet with black noodles

Serves 8
8 fresh red mullet, 8 oz (225 g) each
soft butter
sea salt crystals
8 ripe tomatoes
3 cloves garlic, lightly crushed
2 fl oz (55 ml) virgin olive oil
chopped fresh herbs, mainly dill,
  tarragon, parsley, chervil and basil
For the black noodles:
9 oz (255 g) strong white flour, sifted
salt
1 egg
1 teaspoon olive oil
1 ½ fl oz (40 ml) squid ink

Planning ahead
The squid ink can be extracted from fresh squid. The ink sacs contain very thick, oily ink which needs to be passed through a fine sieve – 2 lb (1 kg) of large squid should provide the necessary amount of rich ink. Alternatively, some delicatessens specializing in Japanese foods may stock bottled cuttlefish ink.

To make the noodles, place the flour and a pinch of salt in the bowl of a food processor. Turn to high speed and add first the egg, then the olive oil and finally the squid ink. Allow to form a ball of firm homogeneous dough. (Depending on the strength of the flour, it may be necessary to add a little more flour, if the dough is a little sticky.) Wrap the dough in cling film and allow to rest for a few hours, then, using as little flour as possible, roll out the dough to a thickness of ⅛ in (2 mm), preferably using a pasta roller for convenience. The dough will need to be rolled in 9 or 10 pieces. Allow the sheets of dough to rest for an hour or so, then cut into strips about ½ in (1 cm) wide, again preferably using a pasta roller. Store the noodles in a cool, dry place until needed.
Clean and fillet the red mullet, taking care to remove all scales and bones. Wash and dry the fillets, then brush with softened butter. Lightly oil a grill pan, arrange the 16 fillets on it and sprinkle them with sea salt crystals.

Wash and coarsely chop the tomatoes, then liquidize them. Pass the tomato juice through either a fine sieve or a piece of muslin into a heavy saucepn. Add the garlic and warm through, then leave to infuse while the noodles and mullet are cooking. Preheat the grill. Boil 2 pints (1 litre) of salted water and gently drop in the noodles. They will need about 4 minutes to cook and should be still firm. Strain through a colander, rinse with boiling water and keep warm.
Grill the mullet, skin side up, under a fierce heat for about 4 minutes, without turning. The skin should be browning and crisp, the flesh still moist and slightly pink. Toss the noodles in a spoonful of olive oil, then season with salt and pepper. Divide them equally between 8 hot serving plates. Place 2 grilled fillets on each web of noodles.
Bring the tomato juices to the boil and turn off the heat. Remove the garlic cloves and vigorously whisk in the olive oil in a thin stream, to form a rich emulsion. Check the seasoning, throw in the chopped herbs and stir the sauce. Pour it around the noodles and mullet and serve with a selection of vegetables.

ALEXANDER HOUSE

In the lay subsidy rolls of 1332 it is stated that John Atte Fenn lived at The Mansion, Turners Green and someone (a departing Pilgrim Father perhaps or a later guest with a sense of humour) has carved the date 1620 into the oak panelling in one of the drawing rooms; the date is suitably faded. A tithe record of 1842 shows the owner to be Sir Timothy Shelley – the estate was then known as Fen Place – and earlier this century the Governor of the Bank of England dwelt in the marbled halls. The present proprietors came along in 1984, named the mansion Alexander House after the company's chairman, Earl Alexander, son of the eponymous Field Marshall of Tunis who commanded the 8th Army in the last war. I mention this to allay fears that the place may not be "of the establishment".

Alexander House when you get to it, is breathtakingly unexpected: turn off an unpromising-looking road in the hinterland of Gatwick Airport into a drive which gets more impressive by the yard – and it is long – and there is this imposing façade with a large crested porch set upon four pillars; a morning-coated butler bows into the headlights of your car (I went for dinner) and treats you as if you were the master come back from a journey. Upstairs, there are suites with bed, sitting, withdrawing, dressing and bath rooms; if you want a four-poster bed, you need do no more than mention it. There is, of course, a helicopter landing pad in the gardens, golf courses proliferate in the neighbourhood, riding by arrangement, croquet, hang gliding... probably game fishing and elephant hunting also. It is a country house hotel geared to the whims of the consumer, where they do their very best to provide customers with whatever the customer might conceivably require.

Everyone is helpful, not an ego-trip in sight. Such places are rare.

The dining-room is genuinely beautiful, tall-ceilinged, decor of greys and reds with high-quality glass and silver, Irish linen cloths and napkins, excellent flower arrangements and a staff who are predominantly young and interested in the jobs they are doing. If you were to say it sounds as if they have gone a shade over the top, I would not disagree, but they have gone over the top with considerable style. There is no mention of money, of house-rules, of 'we would like you to do this or that, at such and such a time'. You are the guest. They are there to ensure you have a perfect time while you are under their roof. Pre-dinner drinks and tid-bits are served in the main hall, under the crystal chandelier, near the grand piano... or you can have them in the library where the books are leather-bound, the fireplace Adam, the paintings impressive and the easy chairs covered in heavy silk. One appetiser was soft and creamy, piped into a profiterole; the other a tartlet of crisp pastry filled with a sliver of wild mushroom. The Campari arrived in a Waterford glass, the ice cubes in their own bucket, the fresh orange juice in a jug. There are two menus – an *a la carte* and a six course Menu Exceptionnel (in my book you do not use words like that to describe what you do; you await the customer's judgement). I found here a quite brilliant slice of goose liver dusted in wholemeal flour, fried in clarified butter, served with caramelised segments of citrus fruit, which made me wholly forgive the chef for adding salt to the soup with a shovel. Lobster is a speciality: sliced, on a bed of green tagliatelle with a sauce of coral. The monkfish I ate was the freshest, firmest, most beautifully cooked fish one could desire – poached in a court bouillon, given a thin shine of butter and dressed with a nicety of fresh dill. As you would expect, there is country-house food like saddle of venison with a startling beetroot mousse that was even redder than the Cumberland sauce; game appears in season and best Aberdeen Angus beef cut in pink slices that are charred at the edges. Cheeses are absolutely first class. There are half a dozen rare species of chèvres and a bright and knowledgeable driver of the cheese trolley, who identified and recommended and brought hot rolls as accompaniment.

There is a wine list – which may well have been replaced since my visit for there were wines listed and crossed off, unlisted yet available and no published information as to shippers; but if you search and ask then you will discover. Between a low-priced house wine and the serious clarets pushing three figures, there is an eclectic selection of interesting and good value bottles: a marvellous Alsatian Gewurztraminer, George Duboeuf's excellent Moulin a Vent 1986 in bottles and magnums. When it came to ordering (sorry, asking for) digestifs, they not only had the very best Eau de Vie de Framboise, they had it at the correct temperature, which is rather colder than the end of an eskimo's nose.

Alexander House, it states on the prospectus, "does not resemble a commercial establishment. You are treated as a guest..." They achieve what they set out to do, and if there is a lack of ultimate culinary finesse of the level you might encounter in establishments in which food is the entire raison d'être, being cossetted, humoured, spoilt and generally treated with the most careful consideration is greatly to be welcomed also.

Turners Hill, Sussex, RH10 4QD.
35 miles from London, 6 miles from
M23. Open all year round. Private
parties: up to 120. Guest accommodation: 12 rooms all with bath/sho-
wer. (No facilities for young children; no dogs; tennis; croquet;
putting; snooker.) To visit nearby:
Wakehurst Place Gardens; Ling-
field and Plumpton race courses;
Brighton. Credit cards accepted:
Access, AE, Diners, Visa.
Tel: (0342) 714914 and 716333

Terrine de sole et de homard

(Terrine of sole and lobster)

olive oil
3 large fillets of sole
1 large cooked lobster, approximately 2 ½ lb (1.1 kg)
julienne of carrots, leeks and celery, blanched
chopped fresh chives, dill and parsley
salt and freshly-ground pepper
lobster coulis to serve
<u>For the mousseline:</u>
4 large fillets of sole
1 teaspoon salt
pinch of freshly-ground pepper
pinch of cayenne pepper
1 egg white
16 fl oz (455 ml) double cream

To make the mousseline, place the fish, salt and peppers in a food processor and purée, then add the egg whites and process again. Pass through a fine sieve into a bowl set over a basin of ice. Add the cream a little at a time, beating well after each addition, then pass through the sieve again. Chill in the refrigerator for at least 1 hour.
Line a terrine, 11 x 4 x 2 ½ in (28 x 10 x 6 cm), with a film of olive oil and pipe a layer of mousseline onto the bottom. Flatten out the first sole fillet and lay it in the terrine, skin side up. Break the tail shell of the lobster and remove the meat, keeping it whole. Discard the black intestinal vein. Crack the claws and remove the meat, breaking it as little as possible. Try to straighten the tail and flatten slightly, then cut in half lengthways. Lay half the lobster down the centre of the sole, red side down. Fill the gaps round the ends with some of the claw meat and any small pieces. Lay the vegetable julienne down the centre and cover with the second half of lobster, red side up. Fill up the spaces round the ends again, then add a second flattened sole fillet, skin side up, to make an envelope with the first and allowing a small gap between the fish and the sides of the terrine. Pipe in mousseline tightly to fill the gap all round, then continue to fill the terrine to the top with the mousseline.

Bang the terrine on the working surface to compact the contents, then lay in the last flattened sole fillet. Sprinkle with the herbs and season lightly.
Preheat the oven to 160°C/325°F/Gas Mark 3. Cover with foil and a lid, then poach slowly in a bain marie in the bottom of the preheated oven for about 40 minutes. Leave to cool for about 10 minutes, then place a 2 lb (1 kg) weight on top until cold.

Foie gras sauté aux fruits caramélisés

(Pan-fried foie gras with caramelized orange and grapefruit)

Serves 4
selection of French salad leaves
walnut oil-based vinaigrette
8 segments pink grapefruit
8 segments white grapefruit
8 segments orange
4 slices fresh foie gras
salt and freshly-ground pepper
wholemeal flour
peel of 1 orange, cut into strips and blanched
<u>For the caramel sauce:</u>
2 oz (55 g) sugar
juice of 1 orange
Madeira to taste

To make the caramel sauce, place the sugar in a copper pan and add just enough water to dissolve the sugar. When dissolved, cook until a dark golden brown, being careful to keep the sides of the pan clear of splashes of sugar which will burn. Remove from the heat and carefully add the orange juice and Madeira to taste. Sieve and leave to cool.
Rinse and pat dry the salad leaves, place in a bowl and toss in the vinaigrette. Arrange on plates with the fruit.
Season the foie gras well with salt and pepper, dust with wholemeal flour and sauté in a very hot pan, without fat. Dry on kitchen paper, then arrange in the centre of the plates. Place the blanched peel on top of the fruit and spoon the caramel sauce over.

Mignon de veau au habayon de citron vert

(Fillet of veal with lime sabayon)

Serves 4
4 medium size medallions of fillet of veal
salt and freshly-ground pepper
oil and butter
juice of 3 large limes
10 fl oz (285 ml) white wine
12 fl oz (340 ml) strong chicken stock
6 fl oz (170 ml) whipping cream
½ each red, yellow and green pepper
1 large courgette
1 small head fennel
8 large mange tout
3 shallots
finely-chopped garlic, bay leaf and thyme
4 tablespoons tomato coulis
6 egg yolks, beaten
4 teaspoons tomato concassé
12 segments of lime
sprig of fresh parsley

Season and flour the veal. Sauté lightly in oil and butter, then remove from the pan, pour over the juices and keep warm. Add the lime juice to the same hot pan, thereby reducing it to almost nothing, pour in the wine and reduce again to a syrupy consistency. Add the stock and reduce by two-thirds. Stir in the cream and set aside.
Prepare the vegetables and cut into ¼ in (0.5 cm) pieces. Sauté the courgette, fennel, mange tout and mixed peppers separately in olive oil, drain and keep crisp. Sauté the shallots with the chopped garlic and herbs, then mix all the sautéed vegetables together with the tomato coulis.
Put the egg yolks in a bowl and strain the cream sauce into it. Whisk over a double boiler until a trail from the whisk remains firm momentarily. Correct the seasoning with salt, pepper and lime juice if required. Ensure the veal is hot, then cut the medallions in half horizontally. Arrange on serving plates with the rest of the ingredients.

Selle de chevreuil à la mousse de betterave

(Saddle of venison with beetroot mousse)

Serves 4
1 lb (455 g) trimmed saddle of venison
white wine
olive oil
salt and freshly-ground pepper
butter
1 heaped tablespoon redcurrant jelly
1 shallot, finely diced
small amount crushed garlic
2 fl oz (55 ml) raspberry vinegar
4 fl oz (110 ml) port
6 fl oz (170 ml) red wine
5 fl oz (140 ml) veal stock
5 fl oz (140 ml) game or venison stock
20 olive-shaped pieces of cooked
  beetroot
1 oz (30 g) hard unsalted butter
sliced truffle and fresh parsley to
  garnish
For the beetroot timbales:
olive oil
3 shallots, chopped
sprig of thyme
¼ clove garlic, crushed
1 lb (455 g) cooked small beetroot,
  diced
3 fl oz (85 ml) red wine vinegar
2 fl oz (55 ml) red wine
4 large tomatoes, skinned, seeds
  removed and diced
2 heaped tablespoons redcurrant jelly
1 ½ whole eggs
2 ½ egg yolks

Marinade the venison in white wine and oil
for 24 hours.
To make the beetroot timbales, heat the oil
in a large frying pan, add the shallots,
thyme and garlic and fry for 2-3 minutes.
Add the diced beetroot, season with salt and
pepper and heat through, then add the
vinegar and wine and bring to the boil. Add
the tomatoes, transfer to an ovenproof dish
and cover. Cook in a preheated oven at
190°C/375°F/Gas Mark 5 for 1 ½ – 2 hours
until the beetroot is very soft. Remove from

the oven, add the redcurrant jelly and cook
on top of the stove for about 15 minutes
until dry. Transfer the mixture to a food processor, mix in all the eggs, then taste and
adjust the seasoning.
Lightly oil some egg cups or similar moulds
and fill them with the mousse. Place the
moulds in a bain marie and cook in a preheated oven at 150°C/300°F/Gas Mark 2
until set. It is advisable to take a single sample egg cupful from the mixer and carry out
the final step to ensure it will set. If not, further whole egg(s) can be mixed in.
Remove the venison from the marinade and
pat dry. Season with salt and pepper and
pan-fry in a little butter and oil until pink.
Remove from the pan, pour juices over the
meat and keep warm. To the same pan add
the redcurrant jelly, shallot and garlic, cook
over a high heat until slightly caramelized,
then deglaze by adding first the vinegar,
then the port. Reduce until syrupy, add the
red wine and reduce again by half. Add both
the stocks and reduce once more until the
liquid will coat the back of a spoon.
Warm up the mousses if necessary. Sieve the
sauce into a pan and warm up the beetroot
olivettes in it. Turn out the mousses onto
serving plates near the centre and arrange
the beetroot around. Return the sauce to
the heat and shake in the butter, a knob at a
time – do not allow to boil. Adjust the seasoning and consistency if required. Spoon the
sauce around the plate. Slice the venison
thinly and arrange above the mousses. Garnish with the truffle and parsley sprigs.

Assiette de sorbets "Alexander"

*(Mixed sorbets in "tulip" biscuits
with raspberry sauce)*

Serves 8
For each variety of sorbet:
5 ½ fl oz (155 ml) water
6 ½ oz (185 g) sugar
1 oz (30 g) glucose
6 fl oz (170 ml) fruit pulp
raspberry coulis to serve
For the biscuits:
3 ½ oz (100 g) ground almonds
5 oz (140 g) icing sugar
1 ½ oz (40 g) plain flour
2 egg whites, stiffly beaten
2 fl oz (55 ml) milk

Planning ahead. The sorbets should be
made well in advance. Three different flavours are made to give an interesting blend
of colour, with 2 seasonal fruit flavours and
1 of Champagne.

To make each sorbet, boil the water, sugar
and glucose together into a syrup, then
allow to cool. Add the fruit pulp and turn in
a sorbet machine. Alternatively, place the
mixture of syrup and fruit pulp in a freezer
container and freeze for 2 hours. Remove
from freezer and beat well, then freeze
again. Beat again after a further 2 hours,
then freeze until firm.
To make the 'tulip' biscuits, sieve the
almonds, icing sugar and flour together,
then slowly incorporate with the egg whites
and adjust to a spreading consistency with
the milk as necessary. Preheat the oven to
200°C/400°F/Gas Mark 6. Spread a batch of
the mixture on a baking sheet in thin discs
approximately 3 in (7.5 cm) in diameter.
Bake in the preheated oven for 3-5 minutes
until golden brown. Remove from the oven
and place each disc in a tea cup, press down
with the bottom of another cup and allow to
cool until hard. Repeat as required.
To serve, place scoops of assorted sorbets in
each tulip basket and decorate with raspberry coulis. For a more elaborate presentation a "cage" of caramel can be added.

MANLEYS

Manleys Hill, Storrington, Sussex RH20 4BT. 50 miles from London. Open Tuesday to Saturday; closed 2 weeks January, 1 week August, 1 week September. (Vegetarian meals; children's helpings; no smoking in dining room; air-conditioned; no dogs.) Private parties: 10 in main room, 24 in private room. Guest accommodation: 1 apartment with bath. To visit nearby: Parham House; Arundel Castle; Goodwood House and race course. Credit cards accepted: Access, AE, Diners, Visa. Tel: (090 66) 2331

Storrington sounds like a village one should know: "Oh yes, Storrington" and they said, "south of Horsham, on the Worthing Road", and I said, "Oh, *that* Storrington". I did not know it, indeed, but for Manleys restaurant it seems an ordinary run-of-the-mill West Sussex village, inhabited by people who could not quite make it to the coast yet wanted to live in the fashionable South, as opposed to the not-yet-yuppie East or the hardly-smart-at-all North. (West is best: any estate agent will tell you so.)

The directions I got were to drive down the A24 and turn right at Washington. South of Horsham I found the village of Ashington, thought I must have misheard – or the "W" had come off the village sign – and turned right. I was wrong. Uniquely among the civilised nations of the world, we have adjacent villages separated by a single consonant. Manleys is in the main street just beyond the Marley turn-off.

The house stands back from the road, a substantial old building with an ample car-park in front. Inside you find unvarnished old oak beams across the ceiling, half-timbered walls, alcoves with large vases of chrysanthemums and overall a motif of silver and white. There are two communicating dining rooms, the further housing a bar. It is a very formal, proper, stylish restaurant with starched white linen; a large pristine candle on each table; silver vases with fresh flowers (some with orchids) and well-trained young waiters and waitresses calling guests "Sir" and "Madam" and doing all the right things, like serving from the correct side. They explained that the canapés with the drinks – very cold, chived, garlicked cream cheese on baguette – and the appetiser before the meal – minced

ham in filo pastry – came with the compliments of the chef. There is a choice of other free appetisers.

Karl and Margaret Löderer, who own the establishment, are the ideal couple for their profession: he cooks, she runs the front of house. He is an anglicised Austrian, quiet, disciplined, admirably exact in all he prepares. She is Scottish, exuding Glaswegian hospitality, care, warmth and efficiency. Prior to starting their own place, Karl worked as chef at Gravetye Manor (see page 46), where they speak of him with pride and affection... and where he found the calligrapher who also writes his menus.

Seven first courses (impressive in a restaurant seating not many more than forty) include smoked quail on a bed of red cabbage tinged with cloves, and marinated shellfish in a coriander and vinegar dressing – dishes of such impeccable pedigree that the note on the menu informing the clientèle that the chef will cook for you any dish of your choice, within reason, actually makes appeal. He produces food of such consistent excellence that if you were to order your dream menu, he might be your man; he would certainly do it as you wanted it, for he is not the temperamental egomaniac so often found in upmarket kitchens.

There are a dozen main courses amongst which I found the best single dish encountered in the entire research for this book: a local sea bass of brilliant freshness, in a sauce of fish stock and fennel, lemon and cream that complemented it to perfection. Fish and sauce tasted as if they were made for each other – which, of course, they were; it is a rare achievement to attain such perfection. Mr Löderer also produces the best Rösti (perhaps it takes an umlaut in your name to prepare this), steaming

the julienne of potatoes before roasting them to a crackling crispness; you would be foolish to pass these by. The serious young staff, under the watchful gaze of la patronne, bring food beneath silver domes, display handsome synchronisation as they lift them simultaneously from all plates at a table and eschew such idiotic habits as asking whether you would like pepper on a dish before you have tasted it. Local scallops, made into a soufflé or mousse is another speciality – with attendant sauce, of which the chef is a master.

His puddings are another strong suit: passionfruit soufflé that would win a prize, anywhere; spun sugar baskets filled with home-made sorbets and, as he is Austrian, not only can you get *Salzburger nockerln* but also *Kaiser schmarrn mit himbeersaft*, which are pieces of fried pancake batter with a coulis of best raspberries. He makes his own friandises: a candied grapefruit peel was outstanding, his white chocolate with slivers of mint excellent.

The wine list shows, the way recognised restaurants seem to feel they have to show, first growth clarets of exclusive vintages at three figure prices but tends to leave Burgundies to Paul Jaboulet, which must disappoint those who want to experiment a bit. On the credit side there are well chosen Rhines and Moselles, including one that sparkles and is affordable and will see you through all those free first courses, and show you to be a person of discrimination.

You would not put Manleys into the category of "a jolly place" but then they do not try to be a jolly place. It is a serious eating-house with a deep commitment to serving the best food in a stylish atmosphere, brought to your table by staff who are proud of their calling. It would be a very good restaurant in which to convince French gourmets that the pursuit of gastronomy is not confined to any one country.

There is a double bedroom on the first floor. This might be just the thing for a couple who wish to sample the range of Eaux de Vie and know about the West Sussex police force's rigid attention to detail when it comes to enforcing the drink drive law.

Suprême de pigeonneau rôti aux lentilles et salade de mâche

(Roast pigeon breast with lentil and lambs lettuce)

Serves 4
4 pairs pigeon breasts (from corn-fed pigeons), boneless and skinned
6 tablespoons double cream
4 tablespoons game stock
4 medium sized fresh sage leaves, shredded
1 tablespoon chopped chives
salt and freshly-ground pepper
For the lentil salad:
8 tablespoons brown lentils
4 medium shallots, finely chopped
6 rashers smoked bacon, cut into thin strips
4 tablespoons olive oil-based vinaigrette
To serve:
mâche (lambs lettuce)
olive oil-based vinaigrette

Preheat the oven to 190°C/375°F/Gas Mark 5. Brush the pigeon breasts with olive oil and roast in the preheated oven for 10 minutes. Keep warm.
To make the lentil salad, cook the lentils in water at a simmer for 45 minutes, until tender, then drain. Meanwhile sweat the shallots and sauté the smoked bacon. Mix the cooked ingredients together with vinaigrette and leave to cool.
Place the cream, game stock and sage in a saucepan, bring to the boil and cook until reduced by half. Pass through a fine sieve, then add the chopped chives and season to taste with salt and pepper.
To serve, place the lentils in dariole moulds. Pour the sauce on the warmed serving plates and unmould the lentils in the centre. Slice the pigeon breasts and place beneath the lentils. Toss the mâche in vinaigrette and arrange at the top of the plate.

Caille rôtie et fumée et sa galette de pommes de terre

(Roast smoked quail with a potato galette)

Serves 4
4 super large quail
For the red cabbage:
6 rashers smoked bacon, sliced
1 tablespoon finely-chopped onion
1 large red cabbage, sliced
2 apples, peeled and sliced
10 fl oz (285 ml) red wine
5 fl oz (140 ml) game stock
2 tablespoons redcurrant jelly
For the potato galette:
8 medium sized potatoes
1 tablespoon mixed fresh herbs, chopped
2 tablespoons olive oil
For the sauce:
9 fl oz (255 ml) demi glace
2 tablespoons truffle juice
slices of truffle to garnish
skinned grapes to garnish

To cook the red cabbage, sauté the smoked bacon and onion, then place in a flame and ovenproof pan with the red cabbage, apples, red wine, game stock and redcurrant jelly. Cover and bring to the boil. Preheat the oven to 180°C/350°F/Gas Mark 4, then transfer the red cabbage mixture to the oven and braise for 1-1½ hours until tender. Increase the oven temperature to 190°C/375°F/Gas Mark 5. Brush the quail with olive oil and roast in the oven for 12 minutes or until slightly pink, then cool smoke the birds for 12 minutes.
To make the potato galettes, finely shred the potatoes and flavour with the mixed herbs. Form into round cakes about ¼ in (0.5 cm) thick and fry in olive oil until golden brown on both sides.
Place the demi glace in a pan and reduce by half. Pass through a fine sieve, then add the truffle juice.

Escalope de turbot et tian de coquilles St Jacques

(Turbot escalope with a scallop and ginger tian)

Serves 1
1 boned centre of turbot, about 8 oz (225 g)
For the prawn sauce:
8 oz (225 g) uncooked whole Dublin Bay prawns
clarified butter
4 oz (110 g) finely diced carrot, parsnip, celeriac and shallot mixed fresh herbs
16 fl oz (455 ml) fish stock
8 fl oz (225 ml) double cream
salt and freshly-ground pepper
dash of brandy
1 tablespoon butter
For the tian:
1 courgette
2 scallops, diced
1 tomato, skinned, seeds removed and diced
grated fresh root ginger to taste
For the garnish:
tomato concassé
truffles, sliced
girolles, steamed
Seychelles prawn tails, lightly sautéed in olive oil

To make the prawn sauce, cook the diced vegetables in clarified butter until soft, then add the prawns and herbs and cook for a few minutes. Pour on the fish stock and cook over a medium heat until reduced by two-thirds. Pour over the cream plus a dash of brandy. Season with salt and pepper and reduce again by half. Strain through muslin, then finish with the butter. Keep warm.
To make the tian, cut the courgette in thin strips and use to line a dariole mould, leaving the ends overhanging. Mix together the scallops, tomatoes and ginger, then fill the mould with this mixture and fold over the courgette strips. Cover with foil and steam for about 5 minutes, until tender.
Lightly season the escalope of turbot and steam for 3 minutes on each side.

Magret de canard mariné et grillé avec choux vert au gingembre

(Marinated grilled duck breast with green cabbage and ginger)

Serves 4
4 large duck breasts (either Aylesbury or Barbary), boned and skinned
1 carrot
1 stick of celery
1 leek
9 fl oz (255 ml) demi glace
½ medium sized green cabbage, finely sliced
1 tablespoon sesame oil
1 small clove garlic, finely chopped
1 in (2.5 cm) piece of fresh root ginger, peeled and grated
For the marinade:
4 tablespoons honey
4 tablespoons chopped shallots
4 tablespoons grated fresh root ginger
4 tablespoons olive oil
4 tablespoons dry sherry
4 tablespoons soy sauce

Mix all the marinade ingredients together, add the duck breasts and leave to marinate for 12 hours.
Cut the carrot, celery and leek into julienne, then blanch and refresh. Sauté the ginger and garlic in the sesame oil until beginning to colour, then add the shredded cabbage, cover and cook until tender.
Remove the duck from the marinade and pour the marinade into a pan with the demi glace. Bring to the boil and reduce until syrupy.
Grill the duck under a very hot grill until still slightly pink. Warm up the julienne of vegetables in butter and place a little in the middle of each serving plate. Slice the duck and arrange on top. Add a mound of cabbage to each plate and pour round some of the sauce. Serve with potatoes.

Salzburger nockerln

Serves 4
6 egg whites
6 oz (170 g) caster sugar
3 egg yolks
pinch of flour
grated peel of 1 orange
grated peel of 1 lemon
1 heaped tablespoon honey
1 oz (2 tablespoons/30 g) clarified butter
1 generous tablespoon double cream
vanilla-flavoured icing sugar
4 fl oz (110 ml) rum (optional)

Preheat the oven to 190°C/375°F/Gas Mark 5. Whip the egg whites until creamy, then whisk in the sugar. Mix together the egg yolks, flour and grated peels, then fold into the egg whites. Combine the honey, butter and cream and pour into a warm ovenproof dish, 6 x 4 x 2 in (15 x 10 x 5 cm).
Shape the meringue mixture on top into a mountain and bake in the preheated oven for 12 minutes. Dust with vanilla sugar and serve. For a dramatic presentation, the dish can be flambéed in rum at the table.

PROVENCE

Provence at the Gordleton Mill, Silver Street, Hordle, Lymington, Hampshire SO41 6DJ. In the New Forest on Avon Water, 90 miles from London. Open Tuesday to Sunday, except Sunday dinner; closed 4 weeks January/February. (No children under 8; no dogs.) Private parties: 30 in main room; 14 in private rooms. Guest accommodation: 5 rooms all with bath/shower. To visit nearby: New Forest; Beaulieu Motor Museum; Winchester and Salisbury Cathedrals; Portsmouth Naval Museum. Credit cards accepted: Access, Diners, Visa.
Tel: (0590) 682219

Gordleton Mill – a bespoke five-roomed hotel of which Provence is the 30-seater restaurant – lies in the southern perambulation of the New Forest between Lymington and Sway, on Avon water: this is not quite the river Avon from which are taken the best fish in Hampshire nor anything to do with the Bard's Avon, some hundred miles due north.

The Provence hit the guides only in 1988, getting praise from one and a fifteen-out-of-twenty rating from another, which is good going for a newcomer. The reason behind this elevation is Jean-Pierre Novi, the chef/proprietor. The Novi family own the "Riboto de Taven", a rated, starred restaurant in Les Baux, France, and, like the adjacent "Oustau", which has an embassy in London, SW1 (see page 28), Provence restaurant, Silver Street, Hordle (its official address) is an outstation run by the son of the mother-house and his wife Claire, to bring joy to the gastronomically-disadvantaged people of Hampshire.

Gordleton is a mill house – but the obduracy of the local planners prevents the construction of a restaurant overlooking the water – everyone's favourite view. As a consequence, the dining room faces the lawn and you must concentrate on the beauty within rather than the aspect beyond the window. It is "a pretty restaurant"; warm reddish carpet, "House and Garden" curtains and pelmets, Edwardian "boudoir" chairs, handsome glasses, okay silver, large scalloped plates that are white for main courses and sometimes a startling black for puddings, which look sensational when you order a *Crème de praline* and a bit ominous with chocolate mousse. There are bowls of fresh flowers on the tables, a beautiful bow-fronted corner cupboard and, as a conversation piece, a huge pickling jar containing strange floating objects, which, on closer inspection, reveal themselves to be cèpes preserved in liquor, dead-ringers for kidneys in formaldehyde.

The service is in the old tradition: slow, deliberate, attentive; they know that you have come to spend the evening and it is more important to get it right than to have you out before a certain hour. With the apéritif arrives a dish of *amuse-gueules:* prettily-fried quails' eggs on slices of baguette; feuilleté of prawns; shining almonds and there is a set no-choice three course menu as well as a slightly more expensive one where you may choose from seven starters, seven main courses, six puddings and a French cheese board that attracts a supplement. Customers are requested not to smoke, soft Muzak plays (but can be turned off by request), prices are inclusive – which really ought to qualify for an extra award – and when you sit in the dining room, ever and anon the door to the kitchen opens and there wafts towards the diners the deeply nostalgic smell of Provence ... butter sizzling around garlic with an overtone of rosemary and basil; only the Pernod and (mercifully) the Gauloises are missing.

Chef Jean-Pierre remains behind the scenes by his cooker; his wife is the intermediary, explaining, recommending, ensuring that people are happy and the staff do their job efficiently and engagingly, running the front of house. The atmosphere is genuinely friendly, no-one whispers, which means you overhear interesting conversations – and while you await the first course, there comes a dish of beautiful, small mussels in a saffron cream sauce garnised with a fennel-like fern: it is not fennel (fennel has no part to play in a saf-

fron sauce), it is the top sprig of a baby carrot, tasting of nothing, looking attractive.

The food continues to be impressive, well-presented and strong in taste; the preparation of vegetables is entirely admirable: a plate with beautifully undercooked French beans, carrots, courgettes, mange touts and small rissolées potatoes.

The fish dishes are probably those of which the Novis are most proud: sea bass and local mullet, steamed and sauced with a fish stock laced with star anis, served beside a mousse of Jerusalem artichokes – a vegetable that has come out of the wilderness; there is salt cod, both steamed and served in a light veal stock and flaked, garlicked and baked in puff pastry set on a white wine glaze. Madame Novi glides past, to bring more guests to fill her tables, mentions the rabbit with candied lemon, the partridge roast with mandarin orange and brings the wine list, which is chosen with such care that the five typed pages actually make good reading. You cheer up no end when they bring you a further list showing wines from the Midi. At the London "Auberge", Coteaux d'Aix-en-Provence – les Baux wines are priced to cause a thin patina of perspiration to form on your brow. In the New Forest a Mas du Gourgonnier '84, both the grapy white and the soft, full red, cost well under £10 a bottle including service. This comes from the vineyards south of Les Alpilles, near the village of Mouries, where they have irrigated the land with complicated ducts to produce large quantities of desirable grapes and, no, I do not know why they should be able to make wine that is so much less expensive than the produce of nearby vineyards; I suspect it is to do with the absence of greed by the vintners of Gourgonnier.

The cheese tray arrives with some ceremony and a good strong odour. Pride of place goes to a perfectly ripe Brie à la Fougère, there is also a selection of chèvres, no English cheese at all but slices of very prettily baked walnut bread to show that they care. The waiter hovers helpfully: a glass of port, a marc de Champagne?, it is all there, though no-one leans on anyone to order more than they want; they bid you "au revoir" knowing that they will.

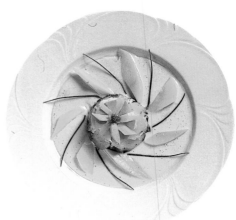

Escalope de saumon sauvage au coulis de tomate verte

(Escalope of wild salmon with a green tomato coulis)

Serves 4
4 oz (110 g) blanched spinach
4 oz (1 stick/110 g) unsalted butter, softened
2 fl oz (55 ml) olive oil
1 lb (455 g) green tomatoes, skinned and diced
1 red pepper, skinned and diced
salt and freshly-ground pepper
½ teaspoon sugar
1 ¼ lb (570 g) wild salmon fillet, cut into 4 escalopes
melted butter, to glaze

Make some spinach butter by placing the blanched spinach and butter in a food processor and processing until well mixed. Leave to chill in the refrigerator.
Warm the olive oil in a saucepan and add the tomatoes. Season with salt, pepper and the sugar, then cook over a gentle heat for 5 minutes. Little by little add the spinach butter, stirring continuously and at the last minute, add the red pepper.
Place the salmon escalopes under a very hot grill and cook for 2 minutes, it should be still rosy pink. Pour some of the coulis on each plate and place the salmon on top. Glaze the salmon with melted butter and serve immediately.

Mousse de volaille à la mangue et au gingembre

(Chicken mousse with mango and ginger)

Serves 4
For the mousse:
1 chicken breast
salt and freshly-ground white pepper
2 egg whites
3 ½ fl oz (100 ml) whipping cream, very cold
3 ½ fl oz (100 ml) milk, boiled and cooled
¾ oz (25 g) peeled, grated and blanched ginger root
2 mangoes, peeled and sliced
For the sauce:
2 egg yolks
3 tablespoons water
7 oz (1 ¾ sticks/200 g) butter, melted and clarified
juice of ½ lemon
3 ½ fl oz (100 ml) whipping cream

Mince the chicken breast in a food processor. Season with salt and pepper, then mix in the egg whites. Pass the mixture through a sieve. Return to the food processor and quickly mix in the cold cream, the milk and the ginger. Leave to chill in the refrigerator. Preheat the oven to 180°C/350°F/Gas Mark 4. Line 4 ramekins with the mango slices and pour in the mousse. Place in a bain marie and cook in the preheated oven for about 40 minutes, until firm.
To make the sauce, whip the egg yolks and water in a saucepan over a gentle heat until thickened, then remove from the heat and, little by little, add the warm melted butter, salt, pepper and the lemon juice to finish. Whip the cream until it forms soft peaks, then add it slowly to the sauce. Whip the sauce until smooth.
To serve, unmould the mousses onto serving plates and pour a ribbon of sauce around.
For a more elaborate presentation, fresh mango slices with chive strands can be arranged around the mousses.

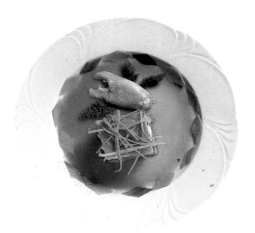

Feuillantine de brandade de morue au coulis de homard

(Salt cod in puff pastry with a lobster coulis)

Serves 4
11 oz (310 g) salt cod
20 fl oz (565 ml) court bouillon
1 x 17 oz (500 g) live lobster
salt and freshly-ground pepper
few drops of red wine vinegar
11 oz (310 g) puff pastry
1 oz (30 g) finely-chopped garlic
4 oz (110 g) boiled and peeled potatoes
3 ½ fl oz (100 ml) olive oil, warmed
   slightly
3 ½ fl oz (100 ml) whipping cream,
   warmed slightly
For the coulis:
1 onion, chopped
1 leek, white part only, sliced
2 measures cognac
9 fl oz (255 ml) dry white wine
bayleaves
a sprig of fresh thyme
a few sprigs of fresh parsley
2 ripe tomatoes
4 ½ oz (1 stick plus 1 tablespoon/125 g)
   butter

Soak the salt cod for 6 hours in cold running water or in several changes of cold water. Drain, then poach in the court bouillon for 5 minutes.
Bring a pan of water large enough to take the lobster to the boil, add some salt and a few drops of red wine vinegar. Cook the lobster in the boiling water for 2 minutes. Remove the head and leave the tail and claws to cool down a little in the liquid. While still warm, crush the shells and extract the meat from the tail and the claws. To make the coulis, fry the onion and leek in a little olive oil, then add the crushed lobster shell and lightly brown. Next add the cognac and flambé to reduce the alcohol, then add the white wine, bayleaves, thyme, parsley, tomatoes and salt and pepper. Bring to the boil, then cook for 10 minutes to

reduce. Pass the sauce through a sieve, then, over a gentle heat, whisk in the butter, little by little. Set aside and keep warm. (Do not warm over heat as this would cause the sauce to separate.)
Preheat the oven to 220°C/425°F/Gas Mark 7. Roll out the pastry and cut it into 12 rectangles, 2 x 3 ½ in (5 x 9 cm). Place on a baking sheet and leave to rest in the refrigerator for 30 minutes. Bake in the preheated oven for about 15 minutes until well risen. Clean the poached salt cod of any skin and bones and mix it in a food processor with the garlic and boiled potato. Slowly add the warm olive oil, then gradually add the warm cream.
To serve, place 1 puff pastry rectangle on each plate, spread over some of the salt cod mousse, lay another piece of pastry over this and spread on some more mousse. Cover with another pastry piece and top with a slice of lobster meat. Pour the sauce over the top and serve warm. The dish can be further decorated with a julienne of vegetables, such as carrot and leek.

Millefeuille de chocolat amer à la mousse de chocolat blanc

(Dark and white chocolate millefeuille)

Serves 4
9 oz (255 g) bitter chocolate
4 oranges
3 ½ fl oz (100 ml) grenadine
mint leaves, to decorate
For the mousse:
8 egg whites
2 oz (55 g) sugar
4 oz (110 g) white chocolate

Melt the bitter chocolate in a bain marie, then spread thinly and evenly on a baking sheet covered with baking parchment. When the chocolate starts to set, mark it into 12 even rectangles 1 ½ x 3 in (4 x 7.5 cm), using a knife. Place in the refrigerator until set.
Peel the oranges without including any pith. Cut the peel into fine julienne and blanch 3 times. Cook the julienne in the grenadine until candied. Cut away the pith from the oranges and segment the flesh.
To make the white chocolate mousse, whisk the egg whites until they form soft peaks. Slowly add the sugar and carry on whisking until firm. Melt the white chocolate over a gentle heat, then cool before folding into the egg whites with a plastic spatula. Leave to chill in the refrigerator.
To serve, place a rectangle of dark chocolate on each plate, spread with a layer of white chocolate mousse about ¾ in (2 cm) thick , repeat, then top with a third rectangle of chocolate. Decorate with the orange julienne, the fresh segments and some mint leaves. This can also be served with a fresh fruit coulis, chocolate leaves and flowers.

THE CARVED ANGEL

2 South Embankment, Dartmouth, South Devon, TQ6 9BH. On the south coast of Devon, 200 miles from London. Open Tuesday to Sunday, except Sunday dinner; closed all January. (Vegetarian meals; children's helpings; no dogs.) Private parties: 30 in main room. To visit nearby: Devon coast; National Trust Gardens; Slapton Sands; Exeter Marine Museum. No credit cards; cheques accepted.
Tel: (08043) 2465

The town of Dartmouth is exactly what it says: a town at the mouth of the Dart. The river is wide and Dartmouth lies on the southern bank, approachable by ferry from Kingswear if you are coming down the coast. The ferry takes about five minutes; the queue in the summer can increase this to half an hour – not much more because one is able to drive around the estuary in that time; the ferry charge roughly reflects the cost of petrol required for that journey. Dartmouth is the archetypal seaside town: gift shops, cafés, boarding houses, tearooms, a bookmaker called Blewitt, a grocer whose window cannot have changed a lot since good Queen Victoria sat upon the throne... and in the sweeping parade, facing such navigation as meanders up-river to the harbour quay, between a papershop and a building society is the solid, well-built, four storey Carved Angel – contemporary ground floor overhung by elaborate mock-Tudor upstairs – a restaurant of charm and innovative ideas and brilliant, predominantly local food, cooked in the French manner by the most distinguished disciple of Elizabeth David. For eleven months, Joyce Molyneux and her staff work away in the kitchen – at the back behind a few plants that screen her from the ground floor restaurant commanded by the ebullient Meriel Boydon. Comes the annual January closure, builders and decorators and painters move in and when this is out of the way the show is once more on the road – in a new set: two chieftains and six Indians and in the very best Liberal traditions everyone takes turns at every job. Tuesday's dishwasher becomes Wednesday's waitress (they are closed on Mondays), Thursday's pastry cook might dispense wine on Friday... and on occasion you find

Meriel at the stove and Joyce running the front of house. This is team work of a very high order, in which the customer is involved as an enthusiastic, supportive spectator.

There is a downstairs restaurant, larger than the two upstairs rooms, which can be booked for private parties; it seats about 30 customers under the smug gaze of the oak-carved angel who gave his name to this eating-house. The tables are round – which I always welcome, even though cost controllers insist that they use available space uneconomically – comfortable steel and wickerwork chairs, chunky blue and white patterned china, serviceable modern cutlery and wine racks left around the place as if light-handed customers were outside their experience. "No," they say reflectively, "we don't think anyone has ever stolen anything from us". This could be the reward for pursuing the catering equivalent of open government in which there is no feeling of them and us, everyone is on the same side (service is included, credit cards excluded, consideration when smoking requested, drinking of champagne by the glass, £3, encouraged). I have a friend who came in to book a table and caught Joyce Molyneux buying one of a pair of salmon brought by a fisherman. She persuaded him to buy the other one, extolling its virtues. It is that sort of place.

There may be, as you come in, the soft smell of a provençale fish soup hovering over the restaurant – which will be served in a tureen so that you may ladle the broth into your own bowl and add spoonfuls of a powerful rouille and garlic croûtons as and when you feel like it. *Crab soufflé suissesse*, a brilliant dish using local ingredients; parcels of puff pastry, filled with scallops and mussels

enveloped in a purée of leeks and baked under a topping of sesame seeds is another favourite – as are goujons of sole fried in the crispest of batters.

The cooking is classical with a creative approach – as in roast rabbit with bread sauce and a sloe and apple jelly. Under the heading "offal" you will get the most beautiful selection of liver and kidney, sweetbreads and brains in black butter. Puddings are traditionally rich – sticky toffee, chocolate chestnut cake with Devonshire clotted cream, but choose your time of year and you may find an autumn fruit salad of pears, clementines, prunes and pecans in honey and red wine served with a quince parfait. A summer speciality is salmon from the River Dart; local mutton pie is highly rated in the winter.

George Perry-Smith, who owns a piece of The Carved Angel and was Joyce Molyneux's partner at Helford, after making his name at "The Hole in the Wall" in Bath, is responsible for the length and quality of the wine list. There are over 200 labels, with a wide selection of clarets and burgundies, lots of half bottles and representatives from North America, Australia and New Zealand as well as England. The policy in respect of house wines is admirable: there are five of them, all carefully chosen, all available by the bottle, half, or glass, at prices that would not stretch the most modest pocket and all open if you want a taste. With the pudding there is a dessert wine from the Midi, which, glory be, is not Beaumes de Venise and costs £1.50 a glass. There is also a delicious Sauternes – Château Bastor de Rivesaltes 1981 at £2 a glass. Porbeagle is a word that one comes across now and then in a crossword puzzle; it is a small shark with a pointed nose and a crescent-shaped tail and at The Carved Angel you can eat it cooked in butter with lemon and parsley, which is exactly as you should eat fish that you have not previously encountered. It is served as a main course – or as a first course – and if you wanted it on toast, as a savoury instead of the good selection of cheeses (excellent goats' cheese comes with a carefully dressed salad), they would do that with a smile. It is an establishment which, should you have been in doubt, will restore your faith in the overt decency of the British restaurant industry.

Avocado, melon and strawberry salad with elderflower dressing

Serves 4
2 ripe avocados
1 small Galia or Ogen melon
8 oz (225 g) strawberries
watercress, or chervil and parsley, to garnish
<u>For the dressing:</u>
3 tablespoons elderflower or tarragon vinegar (see note)
1 teaspoon caster sugar
5 fl oz (140 ml) groundnut oil
salt and freshly-ground pepper
5 fl oz (140 ml) single cream

To make the dressing put the vinegar, sugar, oil, salt and pepper into a blender and process. Add the cream and process again to mix.
Peel the avocados, halve and slice. Cut the melon into quarters, remove the seeds, peel and slice. Hull the strawberries and cut in quarters, then mix with a little dressing.
Arrange the melon, avocado and strawberries on plates. Brush the melon and avocado slices with some of the dressing. Garnish with watercress or chervil and parsley. Serve the rest of the dressing separately.
Note: To make elderflower vinegar, fill a preserving jar lightly with sprigs of elderflower. Pour over white wine vinegar to fill the jar, cover and leave for 4 weeks. Strain through a muslin.

Goat's cheese and hazelnut soufflé

Serves 4
1 tablespoon dried breadcrumbs
1 tablespoon grated Parmesan cheese
5 fl oz (140 ml) single cream
5 fl oz (140 ml) milk
pinch chopped fresh thyme
1 oz (2 tablespoons/30 g) butter
1 oz (30 g) flour
4 oz (110 g) soft, fresh goat's cheese
2 egg yolks, beaten
salt and freshly-ground pepper
freshly-grated nutmeg
3 egg whites
1 oz (30 g) roasted hazelnuts, finely chopped

Preheat the oven to 220°C/425°F/Gas Mark 7. Butter four ½ pint (¼ litre) soufflé dishes and coat with a mixture of the breadcrumbs and Parmesan.
Heat the cream and milk together with the thyme. Make a roux with the butter and flour. Add the hot milk mixture gradually, stirring until smooth, then cook out thoroughly. Allow to cool.
When cooled, crumble the cheese into the sauce and stir in the beaten egg yolks. Season with salt, pepper and nutmeg. The amount of seasoning will depend on the saltiness or otherwise of the goat's cheese but should be pronounced enough to counteract the softening effect of the egg whites. Whip the egg whites until stiff and fold in. Divide the mixture between the soufflé dishes, sprinkle with hazelnuts and cook in the preheated oven for 10-15 minutes. The soufflés should be well risen but still moist inside.
Serve with a little salad tossed with a hazelnut oil dressing.

Saddle of rabbit stuffed with grapes

Serves 2
1 saddle of tame rabbit, boned (bones reserved)
piece of caul
1 oz (2 tablespoons/30 g) butter to finish
watercress and parsley sprigs to garnish
For the stuffing:
1 oz (30 g) chopped onion
1 oz (2 tablespoons/30 g) butter
about 24 large grapes (Muscatel, if possible), blanched, peeled and seeds removed
1 tablespoon brandy
½ oz (15 g) soft breadcrumbs
1 teaspoon chopped fresh parsley
1 teaspoon chopped fresh tarragon
salt and freshly-ground pepper

Ask the butcher to bone the saddle of rabbit. Use the bones to make 10 fl oz (285 ml) stock. Preheat the oven to 180°C/350°F/ Gas Mark 4.
To make the stuffing, sweat the onion in the butter without colouring. Divide the grapes between 2 bowls. Stir the brandy into one half and into the other mix in the onion, the breadcrumbs, herbs and seasoning.
Lay the boned saddle of rabbit on a board, skin side down and season. Spread the grape and onion stuffing over the meat, fold the belly flaps over and wrap in the piece of caul to make a neat parcel. Roast in a pre-heated oven for 10-15 minutes, then put to rest for another 5 minutes.
Pour the roast juices into a pan, add the stock and boil up well. Strain, then add the brandied grapes and stir in the butter piece by piece. Taste and adjust seasoning.
Carve the saddle neatly and arrange on 2 plates. Pour the sauce around. Garnish with watercress and parsley.

Lobster Newburg

Serves 4
2 x 1 ½ lb (680 g) lobsters, boiled
4 tomatoes, skinned, seeds removed and diced
4 tablespoons dry sherry
salt and freshly-ground pepper
4 egg yolks
6 fl oz (170 ml) double cream
sprigs of dill and parsley to garnish
For the stock:
heads and shells of lobster
1 onion
1 carrot
1 stick celery
1 oz (2 tablespoons/30 g) butter
1 bay leaf
sprig of fresh thyme
a few sprigs parsley
1 tablespoon brandy
20 fl oz (565 ml) fish stock
5 fl oz (140 ml) white wine
2 tomatoes, halved

Split the lobsters, remove the tail meat (discarding any intestine) and set aside on a plate with the green meat from the heads. Crack the claws and add the meat to the rest.
To make the stock, chop the onion, carrot and celery and sweat in the butter in a saucepan for 5 minutes without colouring. Add the lobster heads and shells, smashing down well to release the flavour. Add the herbs, brandy, fish stock, white wine and tomatoes. Cover closely and cook for 30 minutes. Strain, pressing well through the sieve, then return to saucepan and boil until reduced to about 10 fl oz (285 ml).
Put the lobster meat and diced tomatoes in a flat pan with the sherry and lobster stock. Season. Reheat gently. Mix the egg yolks and cream together to make a liaison. Stir the liaison into the lobster mixture. Cook gently to thicken. Taste and adjust seasoning.
Arrange the lobster on a plate, coat with the sauce and garnish with dill and parsley. Serve with boiled rice or a saffron pilaff.

Fresh cream cheese with rose petal jelly and wild strawberries

Serves 6
20 fl oz (565 ml) milk
20 fl oz (565 ml) single cream
1 teaspoon rennet
wild strawberries, to decorate
For the jelly:
2 lb (900 g) cooking apples
1 ¼ pints (710 ml) water
4 fragrant dark red roses
sugar (see method)

Planning ahead
The jelly should be made a few days in advance and the cream cheese the day before serving.

To make the rose petal jelly, wipe and slice the apples. Put into a pan with the water, bring to the boil, cover and simmer gently for about 1 hour, adding the rose petals after 30 minutes. The apples should be really soft. Place in a muslin-lined sieve, tie and hang up over a bowl overnight. The next day, measure the juice into a saucepan and to every 20 fl oz (565 ml) add 1 lb (455 g) sugar. Place over a medium heat, stirring until the sugar is dissolved, then bring to the boil and boil until setting point is reached, about 5-10 minutes. Check after 5 minutes by putting a little jelly on a saucer in a cold place. The jelly should wrinkle after about 15 minutes cooling. Pot the jelly into heated sterilized jars. Cover and seal.
Mix the milk and cream together in a saucepan. Warm to blood heat, then add the rennet, stirring in well. Leave in a warm place to set, about 30 minutes.
Line 6 heart-shaped porcelain moulds with muslin. Spoon in the curds, fold the muslin over and stand the moulds on a rack to drain for about 3 hours or overnight. Unfold the muslin and turn out onto serving plates.
Spoon a little rose petal jelly on the side and arrange a cluster of wild strawberries beside.
Variation
This can be served with any other soft fruit or fruit sauce or conserve. The beauty is the fresh, light, milky taste of the cheese contrasted with the fruit.

GIDLEIGH PARK

Somewhere beyond Buckfastleigh one turns off the main road, makes for Bovey Tracey, then Moretonhampstead, looks for a sign to Chagford, passes the board which announces that the Devon village has been twinned with Bretteville sur Laize (where they probably also puzzle about Chagford when they see the notice on the perimeter of their parish) and then, in the square, turn right at Lloyds bank, and take the next fork to the right where it says "unsuitable for heavy traffic". A mile along this thin drive, beyond the "CAUTION Nervous Horses" marker (if I were a horse, I would be nervous, living out there in the wilderness) is a sign telling you to "KEEP HEART you are en route for Gidleigh Park" and the large 1930s Tudor mansion eventually comes into sight.

Gidleigh Park was the English retreat of an Australian sheep farmer – who lived here for a while before the war – where after it became a 20-room hostelry (with three bathrooms); the Hendersons, who are American, bought it in 1977 and made it into a fourteen-suite country house hotel. In God's good time they were recognised by the cognoscenti and have been collecting awards for some years now: a césar from one, an oak leaf from another and most recently The Times (London) designated it "Hotel of the Year 1989". They do a thriving trade, are fully booked more often than not, accept reservations for dinner from non-residents... but you may well miss out if you cannot be a proper player of the whole country house scene.

In the entrance hall there are a dozen pairs of Wellington boots and a stand filled with Hotel umbrellas beneath a notice asking you not to steal them, for they are available for sale for £15 + VAT – rather than £17.25. It is "different" from other places.

There is a bar where you can choose from a brilliant selection of malt whiskies – which they serve in brandy balloons; one wall is covered in maps of the locality, perhaps to stimulate conversation about how hard it is to find... and there are Siamese cats which roam the corridors. Outside the bar is a terrace, leading to two croquet lawns. Fellow guests are there to eat and to walk; also to read back numbers of "New Yorker" and "Private Eye" magazines in the drawing room, which is luxuriously comfortable, with well-mannered ferns handsomely arranged in vases. Staff are quietly available to take orders.

Despite its distance from the fleshpots of civilisation, things run smoothly at Gidleigh Park. There are two dining rooms each seating around 20 people; starched white cloths, small vases of fresh flowers, home-baked rolls and butter-milk bread, good slabs of butter and, in a corner of the room, a cheese trolley with 20 cheeses – soft, medium, hard; cow, goat, sheep – among which a Parmesan-like Spenwood is outstanding.

There is a four course menu with half a dozen choices of starters and main dishes and a seven course speciality menu changes daily – has sorbet after cheese, before lemon soufflé with lime sauce – and by request they will prepare vegetarian, or Vegan dishes. Be a good guest and they will reciprocate as hosts, in the manner of these establishments – but this is not some "tell us how you would like it" place. They make it quite clear that they will do it their way: if one member of a party wants the speciality menu, all must have it ("how can we serve a four course meal and a seven course meal at one table?" they ask with some reason). They put 35p on each bill which goes towards a charity for blossoming poets and authors unless you request that this be *not* done; if smoking cigarettes, please do so with consideration for other guests, is the instruction to diners.

The atmosphere is country house hotel: muted conversation, waitresses dressed in Laura Ashley, orphan-Annie dresses, quietly moving around the two dining rooms, asking after each dish whether it was alright? A knowledgeable, well-organised wine waiter performs his duty faultlessly, decants wines with skill, at a sideboard, over a candle. The proprietor is a wine buff: he prefaces the 400 bin pan-American list with "policies and prejudices". To select a few phrases that may give the reader a glimpse into his opinions: "to the best of our knowledge Gidleigh Park offers the best choice of American wines out-

side the USA"; "the list is really designed for people who like fine wine and know a bit about it"; "we buy wines that *we* like"; "some restaurants offer more brandies, malt whiskies, etc, but I don't know any which has as many *good* ones". There are also dessert wines by the glass and some brilliant and rare wines from the Cruover machine, for which it is worth travelling all the byways of the west country, but it is the range and variety of the American wines that command most respect. To put it another way, the proprietor is right.

The food is cosmopolitan, with excellent ingredients. Good appetisers are served with your pre-dinner drinks and quite exceptional petits fours come with the coffee – splendidly cold and crisp, and fresh. No room here for "After Eight" mints.

If you want to get lost in a luxurious, idiosynchratic, *different* scenario, surrounded by excellent food, amazingly fine wines and thoroughly nice staff, there can be few places that make more appeal.

Chagford, Devon, TQ13 8HH. Near
Exeter in the middle of Dartmoor,
220 miles from London. Open all
year round. Private parties: 18 in
main room. Guest accommodation:
14 rooms all with bath/shower.
(2 croquet lawns; all-weather tennis
court; pets welcome.) To visit
nearby: Dartmoor National Park
with its prehistoric settlements;
ancient Devon villages. Credit cards
accepted: Access, AE, Diners, Visa
(cash/cheque preferred).
Tel: (06473) 2367/8/9 and 2225

Fresh pasta with rabbit and pesto sauce

Serves 4
1 farmed rabbit
4 oz (110 g) mixed wild mushrooms (to include chanterelle and black trumpets)
salt and freshly-ground pepper
olive oil for cooking
For the pasta:
3 oz (85 g) strong plain flour
1 oz (30 g) semolina
1 egg
1 teaspoon olive oil
½ teaspoon salt
For the pesto:
1 oz (30 g) pine kernels
1 clove garlic
1 oz (30 g) grated pecorino cheese
2 fl oz (55 ml) olive oil
2 oz (55 g) fresh basil leaves
For the sauce:
1 onion
1 carrot
1 leek
1 fl oz (30 ml) tomato purée
2 fl oz (55 ml) red wine
40 fl oz (1.1 litres) cold water
1 teaspoon arrowroot

First joint the rabbit into 2 front legs, the 2 fillets which run along the back and the 2 hind legs. Cut out and reserve the liver and kidneys. Chop the front legs and carcase for the stock. Lift all the membrane from the fillet and hind legs. Remove the bones from the thighs and cut the remaining meat into two lengthways. Clean the wild mushrooms with a small sharp knife. Cut out and reserve the stalks. Wash and pat dry.
To make the pasta, combine all the ingredients and knead the dough until homogeneous and smooth. Cover with a damp cloth and refrigerate for at least 4 hours.
Cut the ball of dough into 4 pieces and roll out into long rectangles. If you have a pasta machine, roll it first through the finest setting, then through the spaghetti cutters. If not, roll out the dough as thinly as possible, allow to rest and contract for 20 minutes (I hang the pasta across clean broom handles), then cut into thin strips.

Drop the pasta into boiling, salted and slightly oiled water for 1 minute. Drain thoroughly, taking care to shake out as much water as possible. Toss in a little olive oil and keep until required. (Do not keep the cooked pasta in cold water. It will become dry and brittle.)
To make the pesto, blend the pine kernels, garlic and cheese with the oil in a liquidizer or food processor. Add the basil leaves one by one until completely puréed. Transfer to a small bowl until needed, covering the pesto with a thin layer of olive oil or cling film, otherwise it will discolour quite quickly.
To make the rabbit sauce, peel and chop the vegetables and place in a roasting tray with the front legs and rabbit carcase. Roast in a preheated oven at 200°C/400°F/Gas mark 6 until golden brown. Spread the tomato purée over the bones and return to the oven for a further 10 minutes. Transfer the bones and vegetables to a medium-sized saucepan, skim off any grease from the tray, then deglaze with the red wine and 10 fl oz (285 ml) of the water. Add the remaining water to the saucepan with the vegetables and bones and bring to the boil. Simmer for at least 2 hours. If the stock reduces too quickly, top up with more cold water. Skim the stock as it reduces and always after you have added more water.
Strain into a clean, smaller saucepan, add the deglazed stock from the roasting tray, bring to the boil and cook until reduced to 5 fl oz (140 ml). Thicken with the arrowroot dissolved in a little water. Reboil, then strain through muslin into a container and set aside.
To complete the dish, season the rabbit (including the liver and kidneys) and mushrooms with salt and pepper, then sauté quickly on both sides with a little oil. Remove the kidneys and livers, which require no more cooking. Place the rabbit and mushrooms on foil and complete the cooking in a hot oven – 200°C/400°F/Gas Mark 6, about 3-4 minutes. The rabbit cooks quickly and will become dry if overcooked.
To serve, reboil the sauce. Mix the pasta with the pesto and twirl the pasta round a carving fork into 4 servings. Place each onto a warmed plate. Carve the rabbit, kidney and liver into long slices and arrange with the wild mushrooms around the pasta. Pour the sauce around the meat.

Monkfish with mustard and cucumber sauce

Serves 4
1 monkfish tail, filleted
salt and freshly-ground pepper
½ lemon
For the stock:
1 medium-sized leek
1 medium-sized shallot
1 small bunch parsley
1 teaspoon olive oil
1 cucumber, peeled and peel reserved
20 fl oz (565 ml) water
For the sauce:
1 tablespoon Dijon mustard
1 fl oz (30 ml) dry sherry
2 fl oz (55 ml) double cream
1 oz (2 tablespoons/30 g) unsalted butter

To prepare the fish stock, cut the bone and all the fish trimmings into roughly 1 in (2.5 cm) pieces. Clean and cut the leek, shallot and parsley similarly. Grind a little black pepper over the pieces. Warm the olive oil in a medium saucepan, then sweat the fish and vegetables until you can smell cooked fish rather than raw. Add all the peelings from the cucumber and the water. Bring to the boil, then turn down the heat and simmer for 20 minutes. Strain into a smaller saucepan and reduce by simmering until 5 fl oz (140 ml) remain.
To make the sauce, cut the cucumber into thin slices or strips. Lightly salt and pepper them. Keep to one side in a warm spot. Whisk the mustard into the fish stock and sherry and bring to the boil. Add the cream. Reboil, then simmer for 5 minutes. Whisk in the butter. Take off the heat.
To complete the dish, slice the monkfish into medallions no more than ¼ in (0.5 cm) thick. Heat a dry pan until you sense it is about to start smoking. Place the fish slices onto the hot surface of the pan and let them seal on each side. Dust with a fine spray of salt. They will cook in 2-3 minutes. Lift out the slices onto a piece of kitchen paper and squeeze lemon juice over them.
Test the sauce to see whether it may need a little salt, then spoon onto warm plates. Lift the cucumber. Squeeze it lightly and place onto the sauce. Lay the monkfish on top and serve.

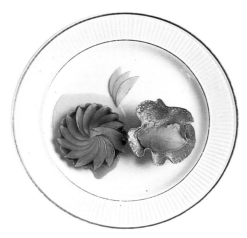

Ragout of wild mushrooms and baby vegetables

Serves 4
1 bunch baby carrots
8 baby artichokes
juice of ½ lemon
2 tomatoes
4 oz (110 g) slender French beans
1 bunch baby leeks
4 oz (110 g) mange-tout peas
8 oz (225 g) broad beans
8 oz (225 g) mixed wild mushrooms
  e.g. chanterelles, morilles, black
  trumpets, amethyst deceivers
salt
5 fl oz (140 ml) double cream

This dish has no formal set of ingredients and should be an entirely seasonal combination of what is best at the market.
Cut the greenery away from the carrots and peel them. Cut the outer leaves away from the artichokes, then carefully trim down to the choke. Boil for 5 minutes in water with the lemon juice. Rinse in cold water, then use a teaspoon to remove the hairy, fibrous part in the middle.
Skin the tomatoes, cut into quarters and scrape away the seeds. Top and tail the French beans, leeks and mange-tout peas. Pod the broad beans, then drop them into boiling water for a few seconds. Refresh them with cold water, then peel away the skins.
Scrape as much grit away from the wild mushrooms as you can. At the last moment, wash them in plenty of cold water and dry them with kitchen paper. Bring about 10 fl oz (285 ml) water to the boil in a good-sized saucepan. Salt the vegetables rather than the water. Put the vegetables into the boiling water in the order they need to be cooked – carrots first, then leeks, beans and peas. Cook off the wild mushrooms with a little butter in a frying pan. Lift out the vegetables and mushrooms and place on plates or in soup dishes, along with the tomato and artichokes. Boil the water in which the vegetables were cooked with the cream and the pan juices from the mushrooms. Spoon this over the vegetables.

Home-cured beef (bresaola) with salad

Serves 12
1 x 4 lb (1.8 kg) topside of beef
For the brine:
½ bottle red wine
1 lb (455 g) salt
¼ oz (7 g) saltpetre
4 oz (110 g) brown sugar
1 tablespoon peppercorns
1 tablespoon crushed juniper berries
1 sprig thyme
8 oz (225 g) sliced carrots
6 chillis
1 cinnamon stick
For the dressing:
5 fl oz (140 ml) extra virgin olive oil
2 tablespoons sherry vinegar
1 tablespoon mustard
1 egg yolk
salt and pepper
assorted salad leaves

Bring all the brine ingredients to the boil, then allow to cool. Marinate the beef in this brine for 4 days. Remove and hang the beef in a warm, dry place for 2-3 weeks, or until hard.
Carefully cut away the dried outside, then slice thinly onto serving plates. Mix the mustard and olive oil dressing and gently toss the salad leaves in it.

Nectarine and caramel tart

Serves 4
For the caramel ice cream:
8 oz (225 g) sugar
10 fl oz (285 ml) double cream
10 fl oz (285 ml) milk
8 egg yolks
For the sweet pastry:
8 oz (225 g) plain flour
3 oz (85 g) ground almonds
4 oz (110 g) caster sugar
6 oz (170 g) butter, soft but not melted
2 egg yolks
½ teaspoon vanilla essence

For the filling:
4 ripe nectarines
6 oz (1 stick plus 4 tablespoons/170 g)
  unsalted butter
9 oz (255 g) sugar
1 fl oz (30 ml) armagnac

To make the ice cream, dissolve the sugar in a little water. Boil hard until it caramelizes. It will turn a light brown colour, just past golden yellow. Take the pan off the heat at this point and let it develop into a rich brown colour as it cools slightly. Otherwise when you add the cream and milk it will splatter violently. Pour on the cream and milk carefully.
Whisk onto the egg yolks and stir over a low heat until slightly thickened and the consistency of thin custard. Cool, then process through an ice cream machine. Alternatively, freeze in the usual way and break up the frozen mousse in a food processor.
To make the pastry, sieve all the dry ingredients together. Rub in the butter, egg yolks and vanilla essence with your fingertips. Form into a ball, then rest the pastry for at least 1 hour in the refrigerator. This pastry is quite difficult to handle and will be worse if not well cooled and rested.
Roll out onto floured cling film to ⅛ in (3 mm) thickness. Turn the pastry onto the tart cases 4 in (10 cm) in diameter and remove the cling film. Patch up any untidy parts with pastry trimmings (although the pastry is very short, it does not tend to shrink).
Rest the tart cases for another hour, then preheat the oven to 180°C/350°F/Gas Mark 4 and bake blind for 10 minutes. Check the pastry during the baking and if the cases are bubbling or rising, gently pat them down with a cloth or kitchen paper.
Cut the nectarines in half and discard the stones. Purée 4 halves and spoon into the pastry cases. Put the butter, sugar and armagnac into a small saucepan (ideally copper) and cook until the mixture caramelizes.
Slice the remaining nectarine halves and fan them on top of the purée. Coat with the caramel sauce while still warm. Serve with the caramel ice cream. The ice cream can be served in coupelles for a more elaborate presentation.

BALLYMALOE HOUSE

There is something wondrously unlikely about Ballymaloe on the outskirts of the village of Shanagarry: you drive down the uncharted roads of County Cork, passing in the way of hostelries an extravagant number of pubs that sell Murphy's stout (in this corner of Ireland, Guinness is something drunk by "foreigners") and salt-and-vinegar-flavoured crisps, then the Allen estate appears like a mirage and turns out to be a genuine oasis. A Georgian house with a Norman keep, it was the family home and grew – started as a market garden, became a restaurant, sprouted a cookery school, blossomed into a hotel, begat a farm shop and a gift shop and a golf course.

Myrtle married Ivan Allen forty years ago and they bought the estate where she began as a farmer's wife. Today it is a beautiful, professionally-run, first class hotel and restaurant, which exudes confidence in its own ability and is preoccupied with caring for the well-being of its customers. There are Allen sons and daughters, nieces, nephews and grandchildren; Allens farm and grow, cook and serve, organise and supervise with the gentle hand of Myrtle at the tiller. She moves from kitchen to dining room, shop to school and you can tell by the arrangement of the flowers, the straightness of the silver on the Irish linen tablecloths, the wholesomeness of the home-baked bread and the farm-churned butter that she is heeded – and admired – by those who work with her.

Ballymaloe (the final syllable is pronounced "oo") is no showman's cuisine. They serve real food, reared or grown on the farm, tinged with herbs from the garden, and if you recall that there are chefs who boast of the quality of their *pâté maison*, Myrtle Allens' can outperform them for the terrine comes from her own pigs, as do the bacon, the sausages and the black pudding, served with her own black treacle bread, as often as not by her grandchildren.

The restaurant seats around sixty. There is a set menu with an occasional choice of courses – like two soups of such appeal that there is not a couple in the dining room who do not have one of each kind and share each other's. Fish at Ballymaloe is the only thing that is 'brought in'. It comes from the fishing port of Ballycotton, ten minutes down the road, where the boats are met by the buyers and Myrtle's man gets pride of place in the queue. It is here that son-in-law Jim will pick his lobsters, destined to be served that night either hot in a soft lemon sauce or cold with mayonnaise of quality. Monkfish and scallops and salmon in a cucumber hollandaise make their appearance, as does plaice. If "plaice" has about it a pejorative ring, it is time you tried that which comes from the kitchen of Ballymaloe, where it has spent only an hour or two since leaving the sea. Mrs Allen cooks each fish in its own liquor – no all-purpose *court bouillon* for her – and there is a *Fritto misto di mare*, served with both a garlicky *maître d'hôtel* butter and a tartare sauce.

There is nothing trendy, no cult that impresses Mrs Allen: if cooks have to have a fashion, she says, mine is to recapture some forgotten flavours and preserve those that may soon die. Her treacle bread now has less treacle than it did, her Irish stew is such a perfect balance of mutton neck chops, carrots, onions, potatoes, parsley, chives and stock, that there is no need for thickening. It is a cuisine that is totally without pomp: soups that are hot and flavoursome, real chickens, cheeses of strength and merit, a pudding trolley that is so calorific that you decide to start slimming on the morrow, for today there is a blackcurrant and redcurrant fool, a chocolate cake of startling intensity, praline ice cream, orange meringue, apple vol-au-vents and an all-enveloping cream to cling to the fresh raspberries. If there is a weakness, it may be in the wines: decent house wine, a good showing of 1970 clarets but, as yet, a dearth of produce from California, Australia and New Zealand and very little in the way of Hock and Moselle. It will not ever be thus for a grandson is being dispatched to the vineyards in search of knowledge.

What is remarkable about Ballymaloe is the atmosphere: the sheer niceness of the staff, the total absence of whisperers among the customers and the camaraderie that builds up between diners sitting at adjoining tables enthusing about the meal.

Shanagarry, Midleton, Co. Cork, Ireland. On the south coast of Ireland. Open all year round except 3 days at Christmas. (Vegetarian meals ; children's helpings ; dogs by arrangement.) Private parties : 35 in main room, 18 and 30 in private rooms. Guest accommodation : 30 rooms all with bath/shower. (Rooms for disabled ; heated outdoor swimming pool ; tennis courts ; small golf course.) To visit nearby : fishing harbours ; rocky inlets ; long beaches. Credit cards accepted : Access, AE, Diners, Visa.   Tel : (021) 652 531

Cod with cream and bay

Serves 4
4 x 8 oz (225 g) chunks of cod, 1 in
  (2.5 cm) thick, without skin or bone
2 teaspoons butter
2 tablespoons chopped onion
seasoned flour
1 bay leaf
salt and freshly-ground pepper
8 fl oz (225 ml) double cream

This is a traditional, regional Irish dish
from the south coast, which must often have
been made without much reference to a
recipe. The cream, fish, butter, onion and
bay leaf are things that would have been
close to hand.
Preheat the oven to 190°C/375°F/Gas Mark
5. Take a flameproof and ovenproof sauté
pan that holds the fish exactly. Melt the butter in this pan and fry the onions in it for 2
minutes. Push them to one side of the pan.
Dip the fish into the seasoned flour and
place in the pan to cook for 1 – 2 minutes on
each side. Add the bay leaf, a little more seasoning and the cream.
Cover with a tightly-fitting lid and cook in
the preheated oven for about 10 minutes or
until the fish is cooked through. Remove
the bay leaf and serve the fish surrounded
by the cream.

Sauté of calves liver with whiskey and tarragon

Serves 4
1 oz (2 tablespoons/30 g) butter
4 x 4 – 6 oz (110-170 g) slices calves'
  liver
seasoned flour
4 tablespoons whiskey
10-12 fl oz (285 – 340 ml) concentrated
  stock (ordinary strength stock boiled
  until reduced by half)
chopped garlic, to taste
4 teaspoons chopped fresh tarragon
  leaves
4 tablespoons cream

Heat the butter in a heavy frying pan until it
foams. Dip the livers in seasoned flour and
fry on both sides in the butter until cooked
to required degree, then push to one side of
the pan. Pour in the whiskey and ignite
carefully. When the flames have died down,
add the stock, garlic and tarragon. Bring to
the boil and reduce over a high heat until
the sauce is syrupy. Stir in the cream and
serve.

Chicken gruyère

Serves 4
1 x 3 ½ – 4 lb (1.5 – 2 kg) chicken
bouquet of thyme, ¼ bay leaf and
  marjoram
5 fl oz (140 ml) cream
For the stock :
½ onion, sliced
½ carrot
parsley sprigs
thyme sprigs
½ bay leaf
For the stuffing :
4 oz (110 g) sliced onions
½ oz (1 tablespoon/15 g) butter
salt and freshly-ground pepper
French mustard
2 teaspoons finely-chopped fresh
  marjoram
pinch of chopped fresh rosemary
approx. 4 oz (110 g) Gruyère cheese
1 teaspoon oil

Preheat the oven to 190°C/375°F/Gas Mark
5. Cut the legs and breasts with wings attached from the chicken carcase. Remove the
leg and wing bones and reserve.
To make the stock, put the reserved bones
and the chicken carcase in a saucepan just
big enough to hold them. Add a few slices of
the onion, the carrot and herbs, cover with
cold water and simmer while you prepare
the rest of the dish.
To make the stuffing, fry the onion in half
the butter until soft and golden. Remove
from the heat, season and leave to cool a
little. Cut a pocket into the breast meat.
Spread the French mustard inside the legs
and into the pocket in the breasts. Put in the
cooked onion, a sprinkling of marjoram
and rosemary and a slice of cheese. Roll up
the joints and tie with string. Melt the
remaining butter with the oil in a flameproof and ovenproof casserole. Put in the
chicken joints and brown all over. If the pot
is burned, remove the chicken, wipe it out,
put in fresh butter and return the chicken
joints. Add any remaining onions and the
bouquet of herbs. Cover with a tight-fitting
lid and cook in the preheated oven for
40-45 minutes until the chicken is cooked
through.
Place the joints on a serving dish, removing
the string. Spoon around the onions and
keep warm.
Strain the stock and add 8 fl oz (225 ml) of
this to the casserole, skimming off any sur-
plus fat. Boil up well, then stir in the cream.
Reduce again to thicken slightly. Taste and
add seasoning if necessary. Pour this over
the chicken and sprinkle with more herbs.

Ballymaloe brown bread

For four 5 x 8 in (13 x 20 cm) loaves :
3 ½ lb (1.5 kg) wholemeal flour
1 oz (30 g) salt
1 – 2 well-rounded teaspoons black
  treacle
45 fl oz (1 ¼ litres) water at blood heat
2 – 4 oz (55 – 110 g) fresh yeast
For one 5 x 8 in (13 x 20 cm) loaf :
1 lb (455 g) wholemeal flour
2 teaspoons salt
1 teaspoon black treacle
12 fl oz (340 ml) water at blood heat
1 oz (30 g) fresh yeast

When making this bread, remember that yeast is a living fungus. In order to grow, it requires warmth, moisture and nourishment. The growing process produces carbon dioxide, which makes the bread rise. Hot water will kill yeast. Have the ingredients and equipment at blood heat. The yeast will rise on sugar or treacle : we use treacle. The dough rises more rapidly with 4 oz (110 g) yeast than with only 2 oz (55 g). The flour we use is wholemeal, stone ground. Different flours produce breads of different textures. The amount of natural moisture in flour varies according to the atmospheric conditions. The quantity of water should be altered accordingly. The dough should be just too wet to knead : in fact, it does not require kneading. The main ingredients – wholemeal flour, treacle and yeast – are highly nutritious.

Mix the flour with the salt and warm it in a very cool oven. Mix the treacle with some of the water in a small bowl and crumble in the yeast. Put the bowl in a warm position such as the back of the cooker. Grease the bread tins and put them to warm along with a clean teatowel.

Look to see if the yeast is rising : it will take about 5 minutes and will be frothy. Stir it well and pour it with the remaining water into the flour to make a wettish dough. Put the mixture into the tins and put the tins back in the same position as used to raise the yeast. Put the teatowel over the tins. Preheat the oven to 230°C/470°F/Gas Mark 8. In approximately 20 minutes the dough will have risen to twice its original size.

Bake in the preheated oven for 45-50 minutes or until nicely browned and the loaves sound hollow when tapped.

Note : dried yeast may be used instead of fresh. Use only half the weight as given for fresh. Follow the same method but allow longer to rise.

Praline ice cream

Serves 6 – 8
2 tablespoons sugar
4 fl oz (110 ml) water
2 egg yolks
½ teaspoon vanilla essence
10 fl oz (285 ml) double cream,
  whipped
2 tablespoons crushed praline

Boil the sugar and water together in a saucepan to the thread stage, 107°C/225°F. (It will look thick and syrupy and when a metal spoon is dipped in, the last drops of syrup will form thin threads.)

Beat this a little at a time into the egg yolks. Add the vanilla essence and beat to a thick creamy white mousse. Fold in the cream, transfer to a freezer container and freeze. When semi-frozen, stir in the praline and return to the freezer until completely frozen.

Vol-au-vents filled with apples in Irish Mist

Serves 12 – 14
1 ¼ lb (570 g) puff pastry
5 fl oz (140 ml) double cream, whipped
1 ½ teaspoons Irish Mist
icing sugar

For the pastry cream :
10 fl oz (285 ml) milk
vanilla pod or vanilla essence
3 small eggs
4 oz (110 g) sugar
1 oz (30 g) flour, sifted
For the apples in Irish Mist :
4 eating apples
3 oz (85 g) caster sugar
juice of ½ lemon
1 ½ tablespoons Irish Mist

Preheat the oven to 240°C/475°F/Gas Mark 9. Roll out the puff pastry to a thickness of ¼ in (½ cm). Stamp out into 3 in (7.5 cm) rounds. You should have 12-14 rounds. Mark the centre by half cutting with a 1 ½ in (4 cm) cutter. Bake in the preheated oven for 15-20 minutes, until risen and browned. Cool, remove the lids and scrape out the soft pastry inside. Set aside.

To make the pastry cream, bring the milk to the boil with a small piece of vanilla pod or add a few drops of vanilla essence once it has boiled. Separate the yolks and whites of 2 eggs. Beat the yolks and the whole egg together and pour the boiling milk onto them. Beat in the sugar and flour. Transfer to a heavy saucepan and stir over a very low heat until the custard is thick and cooked, being careful to prevent sticking or lumps forming. Strain into a clean bowl. Beat the egg whites stiffly and fold them in. Cool before using. (If the mixture seems too runny, you can set it with 1 teaspoon powdered gelatine soaked in a little water.)

To make the apples in Irish Mist, peel, quarter and cut the apples into ⅛ in (3 mm) slices. Put them into a stainless steel or enamel saucepan, add the sugar and lemon juice, cover the pan tightly and cook over a gentle heat until the apples are soft but not broken. Cool, then stir in the liqueur.

Stir the cream, the liqueur and some of the juices from the apple into the pastry cream. Fill the vol-au-vent cases one-half to two-thirds full with this mixture. Fill to the top with the apple mixture. Replace the pastry lids and dredge heavily with icing sugar.

DUNDERRY LODGE RESTAURANT

Being a caterer in Ireland must be a bit like making ice cream in hell: the climate is against you. Until a few years ago there was a prohibitive 33% value added tax on restaurant meals, which discouraged anyone who owned a gas-ring and a saucepan from going out. When the tax was abated people remembered and stayed away and only the very plushest restaurants made a go of it. Then there is Irish licensing legislation, where the publicans have a strong lobby and the voice of the restaurateur is a lone cry in an emerald wilderness, with very few exceptions. Licences have to be purchased at great expense and involve a profusion of niggling regulations: non-residential eating-houses are restricted to serving wine; no apéritifs like Campari or Dubonnet; no gin to go with a pre-meal tonic; no port or brandy when the feast is done.

There is another major problem that you will encounter prior to eating excellently at Dunderry Lodge, which is finding the place. It is on the plains of County Meath and is only "not far away from Navan", if you were expecting to go to the other end of the country. Asking people is not always helpful; locals are so keen to be of assistance that "drive a few yards down this road and you will see it on your left" could mean absolutely anything — like it is eight miles down another road on the right, or I am a stranger to these parts but could direct you to Mullingar.

Let us suppose you find it.

Dunderry Lodge before the Healys bought it in 1977 was a series of ramshackle farm buildings — what is today's restaurant was not much more than a shed — but they restored it with skill and good taste. It is now admirably furnished, nicely lit and fresh flowers abound. There is an area to the right of the entrance where you drink pre-dinner wine and look at the menu; the dining area overlooks the gardens on the far side. In the catering trade the road to success entails one person doing the work of several — and the Healys do that alright, as they will tell you over a glass of white wine (because you can't get Guinness). Catherine runs the kitchen and Nicholas runs the dining room... or to put it another way, Catherine does all the cooking, delegates virtually nothing and has for help only a couple of women who come in to do the vegetables and plate up the first courses. Nicholas does all the front of house stuff, takes orders, serves, supervises the wine cellar and organises the bills. Catherine, a keen cook but an untrained chef, who has spent working holidays in starred restaurants of Europe, now excels in her trade. She was with Roger Vergé at the "Moulin de Mougins" on the Côte d'Azur and worked for some weeks with Albert Roux at Le Gavroche (see page 22). The Vergé influence seems more dominant for strong flavours burst from the elegant dishes that emerge from her kitchen. The salads and herbs come from her garden and over the years her fame has spread, so that suppliers now bring their produce to her, when previously it was she who searched for fish and meat, fruit and vegetables of quality. Her mousse of Jerusalem artichokes is renowned; she makes ravioli filled with truffled sweetbreads or a forcemeat of mussels; has a way with game, of which there is much locally, and her desserts are superb: light and unexpected and unstodgy, there are plums in port and ginger ice cream; œufs à la neige; honey and lavender sorbet.

Nicholas was a professional caterer, knows just how it should all be done and frightens the living daylights out of many of his customers, who come back regardless. Like many of us who are or were in the trade, he realises that if a punter is left on edge, he will be less likely to make a fuss, that much easier to serve. He corrects the pronunciation of a French wine to one party, taps his pen against his pad as another table is deciding what to order for pudding, raises his eyebrow as someone orders red wine with lobster, generally keeps the clientèle up to the mark... but win him over and you will not find a pleasanter man in the county.

If it is the lightness and sureness of Catherine's touch that charms you and the handsomely-balanced wine list that Nicholas has produced which takes you back to try another bottle, another year, another shipper, there is also a whole host of gastronomes who rave about the cheese tray at Dunderry. The Irish cheese industry is relatively new but when they get it right, it is admirably right. I would like to put in a special word for Carryckbyrne and for the strongly-flavoured Derrynaflan, another that may well catch the public taste and is available on the menu, which gives excellent value for money.

If, in the assessment of this restaurant I have dwelt a bit on the personalities, it is because the Healys are Dunderry just as Dunderry is the Healys. There does not seem much point writing of staff or atmosphere in a place when everything depends on how two people perform — and how you react to their performance. This is no orchestra; it is a duet. Nicholas and Catherine Healy have put their energy, their skill (and their money) into this venture; it is a rewarding experience to spend some of yours on seeing how they do it — their way.

Dunderry, Robinstown, Navan, Co. Meath, Ireland. Towards the north-east of Ireland, in the middle of Co. Meath, 26 miles from Dublin. Open Tuesday to Saturday (except Saturday lunch) ; closed Christmas to mid February, Bank Holidays and Easter week. (Al fresco dining ; no dogs.) Private parties : up to 25. To visit nearby : Tara ; Bective ; Boyne valley. Credit cards accepted : Access, AE, Diners, Visa.
Tel : (046) 31671

Baby squid with tagliatelle and pesto

Serves 6
1 lb 5 oz (600 g) baby squid
salt
11 oz (310 g) fresh tagliatelle
purple basil leaves
For the pesto :
2 oz (55 g) fresh basil leaves
1 clove garlic, chopped
2 oz (55 g) pine nuts
freshly-ground black pepper
2 oz (55 g) grated Parmesan cheese
4 fl oz (110 ml) extra virgin olive oil

To make the pesto, pound the basil leaves, garlic and pine nuts with a little salt and pepper in a mortar. Add the cheese and continue pounding. When a good purée is formed, add the oil, a little at a time, beating well after each addition. The finished pesto should be of the consistency of creamed butter.
Poach the squid in salted water until tender – if they are very small, this will only take a few minutes.
Cook the tagliatelle in boiling water until al dente, drain and mix together with the squid and purple basil leaves. Divide the pasta between 6 plates, pour over the pesto and serve immediately.

Fillet of gurnard with a nettle sauce

Serves 6
1 cup nettle leaves from young nettles, without stalks
7 fl oz (200 ml) fish stock
7 fl oz (200 ml) double cream
salt and freshly-ground pepper
6 fillets red gurnard, each 6 oz (170 g)
red chard, cut into julienne strips

To make the nettle purée, plunge the nettle leaves into boiling water and continue boiling until the leaves are quite soft, this will only take 3-5 minutes. Drain, then push the leaves through a sieve to form a good purée. Place the fish stock and cream in a saucepan, bring to the boil and reduce until the mixture coats the back of a spoon. Season lightly with salt and pepper, then stir in the nettle purée.
Place the gurnard fillets in a steamer, skin side uppermost, and steam for 5 minutes. Spoon the nettle sauce onto the serving plates, arrange the gurnard fillets on top and garnish with the julienne of red chard.

Roast grouse on a bed of cabbage

1 good green cabbage
6 whole grouse, drawn
butter
$^1/_2$ bottle red wine
salt and freshly-ground pepper

Separate the leaves from the cabbage and blanch, then keep in iced water until needed.
Preheat the oven to 220°C/425°F/Gas Mark 7. Roast the grouse until it is cooked either rare or pink, according to preference, 15-25 minutes.
Warm up the cabbage in a little butter and place on serving plates. Remove the legs and breast meat from the grouse and arrange on top of the bed of cabbage leaves. Keep warm while preparing the sauce.
Crush the carcases and place in a saucepan with the red wine. Bring to the boil and cook over a high heat until the sauce has reduced to a good consistency. Strain through a fine sieve, return to a low heat and whisk in a little butter. Season with salt and pepper as necessary and pour the sauce over the grouse.

Breast of pigeon with red chard, sauce Beaujolais

Serves 6
6 plump pigeons
6 red chard leaves (use green if red
   unavailable)
$^1/_2$ bottle beaujolais
1 teaspoon balsamic vinegar
butter

Planning ahead
The stock can be made 1 day in advance.

Draw and clean the pigeons. Remove the breasts and reserve. Use the carcases to make a good stock.
Blanch the chard leaves and keep in iced water until needed. Strain the pigeon stock into a saucepan and add the red wine. Bring to the boil, then simmer until the sauce is a good consistency. Add the balsamic vinegar and cook for a further few minutes. Whisk in a little butter and keep warm until ready to serve.
Lightly pan-fry the pigeon breasts in a little butter. Warm up the chard leaves in a little butter, then arrange on the serving plates. Place the pigeon breasts on top, pour over the sauce and serve immediately.

Scallops with courgette flowers filled with a mousseline of scallop

Serves 6
18 whole scallops
3 oz (85 g) scallop meat
1 small egg white
3 $^1/_2$ fl oz (100 ml) double cream
salt and freshly-ground pepper
6 baby courgettes with flower attached
For the sauce :
3 tablespoons white wine
squeeze of lemon juice
4 oz (1 stick/110 g) butter, softened

Clean and trim the whole scallops, then cut in half horizontally, retaining the coral. Set aside in a bowl of cold water.
Place the scallop meat and egg white in a food processor and process to a purée. Slowly add the cream, then season with salt and pepper. Push the mousseline mixture through a tamis (drum sieve) and chill in the refrigerator for at least 1 hour.
Take the baby courgettes and, using a teaspoon, stuff the flowers with the mousseline. Chill until ready to cook.
To make the butter sauce, place the wine and lemon juice in a pan and reduce by two-thirds, then whisk in the butter, a knob at a time and season lightly. Place the scallops and the courgettes in a steamer and steam for 4 minutes, remove the scallops and continue steaming the courgettes for a further 2-3 minutes. Serve with the butter sauce.

Warm salad of snipe with mâche and pine kernels

Serves 6
9 whole snipe
2 pints (1 litre) mâche (lambs lettuce)
1 tablespoon pine nuts
1 tablespoon vinaigrette (made with
   extra virgin olive oil)
butter
1 teaspoon balsamic vinegar

Remove the legs and breasts from the snipe – this will allow 3 breasts and 3 legs per portion.
Toss the mâche, pine nuts and vinaigrette together, then arrange on serving plates.
Melt a little butter in a hot pan and quickly cook the pieces of snipe in it, until either rare or pink, depending on preference, 3 – 6 minutes. Arrange the snipe on top of the mâche, deglaze the pan with the balsamic vinegar and pour over the meat. Serve immediately.

ALTNAHARRIE INN

Ullapool, Wester Ross, Scotland. On the north-west coast of Scotland, across Loch Broom from Ullapool, 60 miles from Inverness. Open all week, dinner only; closed late October to Easter. (no children under 10; no smoking; dogs by arrangement.) Private parties: 14 by arrangement. Guest accommodation: 6 rooms all with bath/shower. (Fishing; hill walking.) To visit nearby: Torridan hills; Isle of Lewis; Inverewe Gardens; Summer Isles. No credit cards.   Tel: (085 483) 230

There is a general belief that good food guides aim off for distance: if the restaurant is in the metropolis – with huge competition all around – it is considerably harder to gain recognition than if yours is the only eating-house in, say, Dyfed (Wales). I am not convinced of the correctness of that assumption but what is beyond argument is that when you travel a very long way for a meal, your critical faculties sharpen over the miles. By the time I had gone to the north east corner of Scotland and waited at the harbour for a boat to take me across a loch to a jetty below the Hotel in which I was to dine, I said to myself "this had better be good". It turned out to be better than that.

In a Brothers Grimm fairy tale, the wicked witch locks up Rapunzel in a tall tower, to which access is restricted to those grappling upwards on the tresses of the girl's hair. Gunn Eriksen Brown does not live up a tower ... but if you want to meet her, the procedure is not dissimilar. You go to Ullapool, find a telephone box, dial 83230 and shout "let down your hair" or, more accurately, "send out your motor launch". Then, when the tide is sufficiently high, along comes the boatman and fifteen minutes later he lands you at an establishment from which there is no escape, but from which no-one in their right mind would want to get away.

Gunn, who comes from Norway is, above all, a perfectionist. She wove, the sculpted and now she cooks – privately in a kitchen to which only she has access – on a "Rayburn" range and four gas rings. There is a set menu for the fourteen nightly diners. Amazing, fresh, innovative food, like the dish that caused Drew Smith in the "Good Food Guide" to call her "one of the most accomplished modern British chefs": breast of wood pigeon with a sauce of its own juices, leeks, grapes and juniper, served with a cake of its liver and brown mushrooms.

Gunn is a worker and a planner and a botanist and as skilled a fishmonger as ever used knife on marble slab. There is soup made of an immaculate stock with slivers of sole, salmon, turbot and monkfish, dressed with herbs and garnished with cream. I ate a mousse of delicate wild asparagus clothed in a pastry crust no thicker than a bank note. With my main meal there was a ravioli of forcemeat flavoured with juniper berries. The cheeses were rich and fresh and chosen with loving care. The dinner broadens after that to give diners a choice of three puddings.

I was 650 miles from home, the seas were running high and I said I would like to try some of the cloudberry ice cream in a pastry shell garnished with spun sugar, as well as a little of the dark chocolate mousse. Fred Brown, the husband of this culinary genius and the most admirable, careful, caring host, was disappointed that I had eschewed the pear tart, and as I did not want to offend, I asked for a little of that, also. Each pudding came in a generous portion, on a goodly-sized plate; each time I said "too much but I'll try a bite" and each time I cleared the lot and decided that of three delicious offerings, the pear tart deserved pride of place: there was a buttery brittleness in the pastry and a sweet-scented lusciousness about the fruit that would make good practitioners bow their heads in envy.

The staff consists of Gunn and Fred, plus an invisible lady, who does the washing up and an Oxford graduate of tender years, who lends distinction to the profession of waitress. She will be gone, perhaps running some corporate empire, when you eat at Altnaharrie but a sister or a cousin or a friend will take her place. There is a whole army of talented folk out there wanting some Eriksen-Brown expertise to rub off on them.

If I have gone on a bit about Gunn, let me write also of Fred. A Glaswegian

veterinarian, he runs the show. He describes the menu when guests are assembled in the sitting room for pre-dinner drinks – with which he offers such preparations as his wife sends from the kitchen to amuse diners before the serious business of eating begins – he serves and takes orders for wine. There is an exceptional selection of reasonably-priced clarets and Burgundies in a "cellar" which has just been completed and in which they intend to sit and gaze at bottles in the long winter evenings when the Hotel returns to being the family home. Then will Gunn go up into

the hills above her house and pick nettles and sorrel, rowan which she uses in a caper sauce, hawthorn, chervil and cress and plan the wooing of her next summer's guests.

Here is a cuisine based on the produce of the hedgerows of the north used to enhance the freshest ingredients under the command of a painstakingly accurate, imaginative cook. There is likely to be one problem : the Inn is open for six or seven months, catering for a full complement of fourteen diners. In the world of high gastronomy there are some 500 guides, magazines and publications that like to inform their readers of the current state of the restaurant scene ... and it cannot be long before each will want to update the entry under Ullapool. Now if each of these gastro-scribes comes with a guest once a year, then almost every other person at Altnaharrie will be there for a motive

other than eating the good food and enjoying the special atmosphere. Some great houses in the land display notices barring "hawkers" and "canvassers" from gaining admission. Perhaps there might have to come a time when "no foodwriters" will be written on the door of Altnaharrie.

Wild mushrooms with an asparagus and wild sorrel sauce in a cave of strudel pastry

Serves 4
**4 large handfuls of a wide variety of
   wild mushrooms, e.g. chanterelles,
   hedgehog fungi, oyster, girolles
butter
8 thin asparagus spears
wild sorrel to garnish**
For the pastry:
**4 ½ oz (125 g) plain flour
2 fl oz (50 ml) cold water
a few drops sunflower oil
½ egg
approx. 2 ¾ oz (5 – 6 tablespoons/75 g)
   butter, melted**
For the sauce:
**3 shallots, finely chopped
2 oz (½ stick/50 g) butter
5 ½ fl oz (150 ml) cream
1 teaspoon coarse grain mustard
a little redcurrant jelly
stalks of asparagus, cut into thin slices
a large handful of wild sorrel, finely
   chopped
salt and coarsely-ground pepper**

To prepare the pastry, mix together the flour, water, oil and egg until well blended. Brush the pastry with a little oil, cover and leave to rest for 30 minutes, then roll the dough onto a floured cloth until it is paper thin. Preheat the oven to 220°C/425°F/Gas Mark 7. Brush half the dough with some of the melted butter, then fold the other half of the dough over the top. Cut the dough into pieces 3 x 5 in (7.5 x 12.5 cm). Drape the pieces of dough halfway round buttered, upturned dariole moulds, making a cave-like shape. Where the dough is gathered at the top, use a string of dough to bind it together. Brush with more of the melted butter and cook in the preheated oven for approximately 10 minutes, until golden and crisp. Remove the moulds.
To make the sauce, sauté the shallots gently in the butter, add the cream, mustard and jelly, then add the asparagus slices and sor-

rel. Taste and adjust the seasoning.
Clean and prepare the wild mushrooms. Sauté them in a frying pan in butter and in another pan gently turn the asparagus tips in butter.
Spoon the sauce onto serving plates, add the pastry "caves" and arrange the mushrooms and asparagus inside. Garnish with a cluster of wild sorrel leaves.

Witch with crab and ginger and a champagne butter sauce

Serves 4
**4 medium witch, heads and little side
   bones removed
sea salt and coarsely-ground pepper**
For the filling:
**5 ½ fl oz (150 ml) soured cream
1 tablespoon mayonnaise
½ tablespoon chopped fresh dill
a few drops of garlic juice
lemon juice to taste
approx. 5 ½ oz (150 g) white crab meat**
For the sauce:
**3 ½ fl oz (100 ml) reduced fish stock
   (made from the bones and heads of
   the fish)
Champagne
approx. 5 ½ oz (1 stick plus
   3 tablespoons/150 g) butter, cut into
   cubes
2 tablespoons cream**
For the garnish:
**1 tablespoon each of leeks and ginger,
   cut into very thin matchsticks 1 in
   (3 cm) long
4 sprigs of fresh dill**

For the filling, mix together the cream, mayonnaise, dill and garlic juice with salt, pepper and lemon juice to taste, then gently fold in the crab meat. Set aside.
Toss the strips of ginger in butter until crisp and golden. Toss the leeks for a second.
To make the sauce, place the fish stock and 1

glass of Champagne into a saucepan and cook until reduced by half. Whisk in pieces of butter, little by little, add seasoning, a touch of cream and more Champagne if needed. Set aside and keep warm.
Preheat the oven to 180 – 200°C/350 – 400°F/Gas Mark 4 – 6. Put the fish into a buttered, ovenproof dish, sprinkle with sea salt and coarse pepper and cook until ready – this varies from oven to oven but be careful not to overcook, the bone should remain pink.
Remove the fish from the oven, gently place the crab mixture on top of the fish and garnish with the leeks and golden ginger. Return to the oven for a minute. Take out and arrange the fish on serving plates, adding a little sauce and a sprig of dill.

Medallions of roe deer with a sauce of its own juices, grapes, juniper and dill and flambéed in armagnac

**knob of butter
4 – 5 medallions of roedeer per person,
   each ¾ in (2 cm) thick
a little armagnac**
For the sauce:
**bones from the roedeer
1 leek
2 oz (½ stick/50 g) butter
3 ½ oz (100 g) grapes
10 juniper berries
a few sprigs of fresh dill
red wine
freshly-ground pepper**
For the garnish:
**a few sprigs of fresh dill
a few cherries
mushrooms
rowan jelly**

To make the sauce, roast the bones with the leek and butter until brown, then transfer to a large saucepan, add the grapes, juniper berries and dill and cover with water. Bring to the boil and cook for a few hours, then strain into a smaller saucepan. Add red wine to taste and reduce to a syrupy consistency. Strain again. You should be left with 2 tablespoons per person. Taste frequently and add pepper as necessary.

Heat a heavy-bottomed frying pan and add a knob of butter. Fry the medallions for a few seconds on both sides, then flambé with a little armagnac. Remove the meat from the pan and add the remaining juices to the sauce. Taste and adjust the seasoning.

To serve, spoon a little sauce onto the serving plates and arrange the medallions on top. Garnish with dill, quartered cherries, mushrooms and a spoonful of rowan jelly.

Norwegian cream cake with a cloudberry filling and a marzipan topping

Serves 8 – 10
For the sponge :
4 eggs
4 ³⁄₄ oz (130 g) sugar
4 ¹⁄₂ oz (125 g) plain flour
¹⁄₂ teaspoon baking powder
For the filling :
2 ¹⁄₄ pints (1.2 litres) whipping cream
3 ¹⁄₂ oz (100 g) cloudberries
orange juice
2 tablespoon ground hazelnuts
2 tablespoons brown sugar
For the marzipan :
2 oz (50 g) ground almonds
2 oz (50 g) icing sugar
white of 1 small egg

To make the sponge, whisk the eggs and sugar together until white and fluffy, being sure to introduce lots of air into the mixture for best results. Sieve the flour and baking powder together, then carefully blend into the eggs and sugar. Pour the mixture into a greased and floured, loose-bottomed 10 in (28 cm) cake tin. Place in a cold oven and set oven to 150°C/300°F/Gas Mark 3. Bake for about 1 hour. Test with a skewer to make sure the middle has cooked. Remove from oven, free from tin and place on a rack until cool, then cut horizontally into 3 layers.

Whip the cream until fairly stiff but not dry. Mix half the cream with the cloudberries. Place the bottom layer of sponge on a dish, moisten with a little orange juice, then cover with a thick layer of cloudberry cream and top with half the hazelnuts and sugar. Repeat with the next layer, then add the third sponge layer. Cut the cake into small heart-shaped portions and cover the sides and tops of each heart with a thick layer of the remaining cream.

To make the marzipan, mix together the almonds, sugar and egg white, then roll out to a thin layer, ¹⁄₁₂ in (1.5 mm) thick. Cut into heart shapes to match the sponge and carefully place on top of each sponge heart. Decorate with small dots of cream and flowers or marzipan roses.

Krumkaker filled with a pistachio ice cream and spun sugar

Serves 10 – 12
For the biscuit :
2 eggs
4 ¹⁄₂ oz (125 g) sugar
4 ¹⁄₂ oz (1 stick plus 1 tablespoon/125 g) margarine, melted and cooled
5 ¹⁄₂ oz (150 g) plain white flour, sieved
a pinch of freshly-ground cardamom

For the ice cream :
2 egg yolks
4 ¹⁄₂ oz (125 g) icing sugar
2 tablespoons cloudberry liqueur
1 tablespoon lemon juice
2 oz (50 g) pistachio nuts, ground to a paste
10 ¹⁄₂ fl oz (300 ml) whipping cream
2 egg whites
For the spun sugar :
3 ¹⁄₂ oz (100 g) caster sugar

To make the biscuit, mix the eggs and sugar together until light and fluffy. Gently fold in the melted margarine, then add the flour and cardamom – the mixture should have a thick spooning consistency. The krumkaker are made in an old-fashioned Norwegian double cast-iron mould (called a *krumkake jern*), which is heated over an open fire or on top of the cooker. There is also a modern Teflon-coated electrical appliance that does the same job. Place a spoonful of the mixture onto the hot iron and cook until golden brown. Quickly remove from the iron and shape in the inside of a cup.

To make the ice cream, mix the egg yolks and icing sugar together until pale and light. Add the liqueur and lemon juice, then the pistachio paste. Whip the cream and gently mix into the eggs and sugar. Whip the egg whites until firm, then gently fold into the mixture. Freeze until the mixture is the consistency of a slightly soft ice cream.

For the spun sugar, melt the sugar with a little water until thick and golden. Remove from the heat. Wear rubber gloves to protect your hands and use a fork to draw fine threads of the sugar around your hands in all directions to give a spun effect.

To serve, fill the krumkaker with a scoop of ice cream, decorate with spun sugar and serve immediately.

INVERLOCHY CASTLE

Torlundy, Fort William, Scotland, PH33 6SN. On the west coast of Scotland, 3 miles north of Fort William. Open all week; closed mid November to mid March. (No smoking in dining room; no dogs.) Private parties: 8. Guest accommodation: 16 rooms all with bath/shower. (Golf; fishing; horse riding; tennis; snooker; sailing by arrangement.) To visit nearby: Ben Nevis; Fort William; the Isle of Mull; the Isle of Skye; Glenfinnan. Credit cards accepted: Access, Visa. Tel: (0397) 2177/8

It began with Miss Shaw – I am not sure anyone knew her by any other name. Miss Shaw came to Inverlochy Castle as housekeeper to the Hobbs family, who had bought the fine baronial pile in 1944, which with hindsight, was a terrific year for buying property. Built in the 1860's, the imposing grey mansion is embellished with turrets and towers and battlements, the hall has immensely high, painted ceilings, the drawing room is huge – with elaborate plasterwork, there are 500 acres of land.

Mr Hobbs senior was a Canadian; his son, on inheriting the castle, decided that it was a shade too large for him so he and his wife, Grete, turned it into a hotel. Miss Shaw, who had cooked, became The Chef. She was a self-taught cook, acquiring knowledge by looking over other cooks' shoulders and deciding that she could do as well. Bring her a grouse and she roasted it. Ask her for a soup and she made it with care, using decent ingredients and adding cream. She baked many breads, as the Scots do, and she made pies and fashioned pastry crusts around fillets of Aberdeen Angus beef and her orange soufflé was known throughout the county as being the most reliable high flyer north of Hadrian's Wall.

Slowly – because in those days gastronews travelled at hardly any speed at all, the cuisine of Miss Shaw became recognised. Good Food Guides, international gastronomes, American gourmets, even Michelin and Gault Millau, accepted that in an unlikely castle in a remote part of Scotland, which mobile telephones are still unable to penetrate, was a considerable new talent. Mrs Hobbs, daughter-in-law of the wartime purchaser, made the Hotel beautiful, Miss Shaw made it famous and it flourished as places deserve to flourish with the bestowal of such love and expertise.

Michael Leonard became the manager – is now the managing director – a young veteran with 13 years of Inverlochy service and when Miss Shaw retired in 1981 (and joined the great celestial brigade above a year later), the impetus carried them along. Michelin took a close look and, exceptionally, retained the castle's star status. Graham Newbould is the chef and when you learn that this young man spent six and a half years among the pots and pipkins of the kitchens of HRH The Prince of Wales, your faith in the perspicacity of our future king will take an upward lurch. Mr Newbould cooks with exceptional skill, has a substantially larger repertoire than did his famous predecessor, whose orange soufflé (please give one hour's notice) he faithfully emulates.

Inverlochy is run with stunning panache: a restrained notice on the A82 discreetly discloses its name. At the end of the smoothly-tarmacadamed drive you will find cars none of which would qualify for "special offers" by insurance companies, for this is the carriage trade at its least inhibited. You are welcomed into the grand drawing room with open fires and a chandelier for which Dukes and Marquesses would kill. They call you by name, they treat you as if you owned the place. They suggest, never recommend. Drinks are brought, canapés make their appearance – goose liver on circles of wholemeal bread, fried in clarified butter; twirls of smoked salmon in a bouchée; miniscule tartlets of crabmeat – and one of the superior staff (the head waiter or the managing director) brings menu and wine list: the former shows a four course set meal with a choice at each stage; the latter is a work of admirable length, wide range, many good bottles from the New World, a splendid selection of half bottles and responsibly – not extravagantly – priced fine clarets of the great vintages. The staff are of the country house school of waiting: nicely starched, impersonal, efficient, speak when they are spoken to.

There is a consommé of chanterelles
which I found absolutely brilliant, as
good a clear soup as I have ever eaten
(pace Paul Bocuse), scallops, fresh
prawns in herb butter represented cooking at its best and if you choose the
time of year, there are mallards and
pheasant, grouse and woodcock, prepared with a fine flourish of which Miss
Shaw would have approved. Vegetables
are of the school of nouvelle cuisine and
impeccable. There is a cheese board of
half a dozen carefully-chosen varieties
– with a marvellously aromatic Irish

camembert kept in the larder in case
you show anything but total approval of
those on display. And then, when the
petits fours arrive with the coffee and
there are chocolate truffles straight
from the refrigerator, comes the only
disappointment of the evening. You get
a bill. You feel hurt... I mean you have
been a guest, a good guest, eaten up,
thanked them and surely nice people
do not mention money... but it arrives
and not only is it less than you expect,
but the service is included, the final
sum being written on the bottom line of
your credit card receipt – which always
makes me leave an extra gratuity.
Michael Leonard runs the ship with a
firm hand; Graham Newbould is a chef of
whom we shall hear much more and if
that is the training you receive at High-
clere House, where the Prince and Princess of Wales reside, there will be an
unholy scramble to employ his successor.

Glazed Loch Linnhe prawns

Serves 4
6 live prawns per person, washed
8 oz (2 sticks/225 g) unsalted butter
2 egg yolks
small bunches of tarragon, parsley,
  chervil and chives, chopped and
  mixed together
salt and freshly-ground pepper
juice of ½ lemon

Blanch the prawns in boiled water for
1 minute and refresh in iced water – blan-
ching them makes peeling the shell off
much easier. Separate the tails from the
head, peel the tails and run a knife down the
middle to remove the black intestinal vein.
Place the butter, egg yolks and herbs together with a little seasoning and the lemon
juice in a food processor and process until
the mixture becomes light in texture and
white in colour.
Reheat the prawn tails in hot water or in a
steamer. When hot, fold them into the
whipped butter and place into a deep,
flameproof soup plate. Place under a
preheated salamander (grill) until golden
brown. Serve straightaway, garnished with
a hot prawn head.

Mousseline of queen scallops

Serves 4
2 oz (55 g) samphire, blanched
16 queen scallops
puff pastry fleurons to garnish
For the mousseline:
4 large spinach leaves, blanched
6 oz (170 g) queen scallops
2 oz (55 g) Dover sole fillets
1 egg white
8 fl oz (225 ml) double cream
salt, cayenne pepper
½ oz (15 g) chopped fresh chives

For the sauce:
bones of 3 Dover sole
2 oz (55 g) sliced shallots
2 oz (55 g) mushroom trimmings
5 fl oz (140 ml) dry white wine
5 fl oz (140 ml) Noilly Prat
pinch sugar
pinch saffron threads
10 fl oz (285 ml) double cream
1 oz (2 tablespoons/30 g) butter

To prepare the mousseline, line 4 buttered
ramekins with the blanched spinach leaves.
Place the scallops and fish fillets in a food
processor with the egg white and purée,
then pass through a fine sieve. Transfer the
mixture to a bowl on ice and allow to cool.
When cool, slowly beat in the cream, season
with salt and cayenne pepper and add the
chives. Place the mousseline into the lined
ramekins, wrap over the spinach leaves and
cover with buttered foil.
Preheat the oven to 180°C/350°F/Gas Mark
4. Place the ramekins in a bain marie and
cook in the preheated oven for 10 minutes.
To make the fish sauce, place the bones,
shallots, mushroom trimmings, wine,
Noilly Prat, sugar and saffron in a saucepan
and bring to the boil. Cook until reduced to
approximately 1 tablespoon. Add the
cream, bring back to the boil and whisk in
the butter. Correct seasoning.
To serve, turn out the ramekins onto
warmed serving plates. Pour a little sauce
around and sprinkle the warmed samphire
on top. Arrange 4 lightly steamed queen
scallops per serving on the sauce and garnish with a puff pastry fleuron.

Grilled breast of wood-pigeon

Serves 4
1 lb (455 g) potatoes
16 baby turnips
8 oz (225 g) red cabbage, shredded
grated apple, red wine
8 woodpigeon breasts, skinned
salt and freshly-ground pepper
clarified butter
1 orange, segmented

For the sauce:
¼ bottle red wine
2 fl oz (55 ml) cider vinegar
2 shallots, finely chopped
juice and peel of 2 oranges
juice of 1 lemon
2 tablespoons redcurrant jelly
¾ oz (25 g) English mustard powder
3 ½ fl oz (100 ml) port

Planning ahead: Make the sauce 1 day
before needed.

To make the sauce, place the wine, cider
vinegar and shallots in a pan, bring to the
boil and reduce by half. Peel the oranges
and reserve the peel. Add the orange and
lemon juice together with the redcurrant
jelly to the sauce, bring back to the boil,
skim, then remove from the heat and allow
to cool. Finely shred the orange peel and
blanch. When the sauce is cool, stir in the
mustard, orange peel and port, then allow
to rest for 24 hours.
Peel the potatoes, shred them finely and
place in a small frying pan, which has been
heated with a little oil and butter. Fry the
potatoes on each side until golden brown.
Peel and boil the baby turnips. Cook the red
cabbage with a little grated apple in red
wine. Warm up the sauce. Season the
breasts of woodpigeon and brush with clarified butter, then place on a hot charcoal
grill and grill for approximately 2 minutes
on each side.
To serve, place the potatoes on a warmed
serving plate, then add the red cabbage.
Place the grilled breasts of woodpigeon on
top and coat with the Cumberland sauce.
Garnish with the orange segments, blanched zest and baby turnips rolled in butter.

Roast saddle of roedeer with apple purée and rosemary sauce

Serves 4
10 – 12 oz (285 – 340 g) roedeer saddle
  on the bone per person
salt and freshly-ground pepper
onion, carrot, leek and celery

¼ bottle red wine
a good bunch of fresh rosemary plus
   an extra sprig
5 fl oz (140 ml) game or veal stock
1 oz (2 tablespoons/30 g) butter
2 cooking apples
1 oz (30 g) brown sugar
2 cloves
juice of ¼ lemon
For the marinade:
½ bottle red wine
1 carrot, chopped
1 leek, chopped
1 onion, chopped
1 stick celery, choppped
18 juniper berries, crushed
peel of 1 lemon
2 cloves
1 tablespoon redcurrant jelly

Planning ahead: Begin marinading the meat a day in advance.

Bring all the marinade ingredients to the boil, then allow to cool. Remove the eye of meat from the bone. Trim off any sinew from the meat and reserve the bones. Marinade the meat for 24 hours.
To make the sauce, roast the bones until brown, tip off any excess fat, add a little chopped onion, carrot, leek and celery and allow them to brown (be careful not to burn the vegetables as this will give the sauce a bitter taste). Add the wine and bunch of rosemary, bring to the boil and reduce to 1 tablespoon. Add a little of the marinade and reduce again. Add the game or veal stock and reduce by half. Strain the sauce, correct the seasoning and beat in the butter to finish.
Peel, core and quarter 1 of the cooking apples. Sweat the apple in a little butter with the sugar, a sprig of rosemary, the cloves and lemon juce. When cooked, pass the apple through a fine sieve to make the purée. For the garnish, peel the remaining apple and cut into shapes. Cook in a little water, butter and sugar until tender.
To cook the meat, preheat the oven to 230°C/450°F/Gas Mark 8. Take the meat from the marinade, season and place in a hot roasting tray with a little oil and butter. Roast in the preheated oven for about 5 minutes. Remove the meat from the pan

and allow to rest for 5 minutes, then slice thinly. Arrange the meat on a warmed serving plate, coat with a little sauce and serve with a quenelle of apple purée ·and the turned, cooked apples, accompanied by a selection of vegetables.

Tears of dark chocolate filled mousse

Serves 4
4 oz (110 g dark bitter chocolate
For the whisky mousse:
6 oz (170 g) dark bitter chocolate
1 egg
1 egg yolk
2 fl oz (55 ml) whisky
5 fl oz (140 ml) double cream, lightly
   whipped
For the white chocolate sauce:
7 fl oz (200 ml) milk
4 oz (110 g) white chocolate, finely
   chopped
For the garnish:
fresh raspberries
mint leaves
set chocolate shapes

Melt the chocolate in a double boiler until smooth, 46-48°C/115-118°F. Cool to 36°C/97°F, then paint the chocolate on flexible plastic strips. When on the point of setting, nip the 2 ends together to make a tear shape. Leave until set, then peel of the plastic.
To make the mousse, melt the chocolate in a double boiler. Whisk the egg and egg yolk together in a pan over a bain marie until light and fluffy, then whisk the chocolate at the same temperature) into the sabayon. Add the whisky to the cream, then fold into the egg and chocolate mixture. Allow the mousse to set, then pipe into the tearshaped chocolate cases.
To make the sauce, bring the milk to the boil, remove from the heat and stir in the white chocolate until smooth. Allow to cool.
To serve, pour the white chocolate sauce onto the serving plate and place 2 chocolate tears on top. Garnish with raspberries, mint leaves and set chocolate shapes.

Roasted strawberries and pink grapefruit sorbet

Serves 4
6 strawberries per person
small mint leaves to decorate
For the grapefruit sorbet:
9 fl oz (255 ml) freshly-squeezed pink
   grapefruit juice
3 fl oz (85 ml) stock syrup
1 fl oz (30 ml) white wine
1 egg white, stiffly beaten
For the honey tuiles:
2 oz (½ stick/55 g) butter
2 oz (55 g) honey
2 ½ oz (70 g) demerara sugar
2 ½ oz (70 g) flour, sieved
2 egg whites
nibbed almonds
For the sauce:
14 fl oz (400 ml) fresh orange juice
3 ½ fl oz (100 ml) Grand Marnier
1 oz (30 g) honey
4 oz (110 g) demerara sugar
¾ oz (25 g) pink peppercorns

Mix together the ingredients for the sorbet and freeze in an ice cream machine. Alternatively, mix together the juice, syrup and wine, place in a freezer container and freeze until semi-solid, then remove from the freezer and beat in the egg white. Return to the freezer and freeze until firm.
To make the tuiles, preheat the oven to 180°C/350°F/Gas Mark 4. Bring the butter, honey and sugar to the boil. As the sugar dissolves, add the flour, stirring continually. Finally add the egg whites and mix until smooth. Allow the mixture to cool. Using a club-shaped stencil, spread the mixture over. Coat thinly with nibbed almonds and bake in the preheated oven for 8 minutes, until golden brown. When cooked, place over a small cup or bowl to make a nest shape.
Bring all the ingredients for the sauce to the boil and reduce to a light syrup. Place the strawberries in this syrup and gently mix to coat. Place in a hot oven for 2 minutes. Place 1 tuile in the middle of each serving plate, fill with a scoop of sorbet and decorate with a small mint leaf. Remove the strawberries from the oven, arrange them around the sorbet and serve immediately.

THE PEAT INN

David Wilson was in industry in 1970, "y'know, everyone had a job and mine was with Rio Tinto Zinc", and he did not care for it and got a job in catering, then another – and in 1972 he and his wife bought a pub at a forsaken crossroads some two hour's walk from St Andrews – provided you turn right and left at the correct places.

Seldom has anyone stood longer and more securely at a crossroads and his address is now The Peat Inn, Peat Inn, Fife... for his neighbours, tired of gastronomes calling at their houses asking for directions on how to get to the Inn, have changed the name of the hamlet to reflect its most notable citizen. It was, when the Wilsons arrived, "a pub – with a room for a hop" in which the locals celebrated weddings, funerals, hangings, whatever came up. Not a lot came up, so David Wilson divided the function room into dining rooms and a

kitchen; he cooked and his wife, Patricia, wrote the menus with a bold hand and arranged the flowers and did the accounts; they also trapped – the way the Scots have to trap – the local food before it could make its way south to the prosperous markets and kept it for their customers. Aberdeen Angus beef, lobsters, loganberries, grouse, scallops, are all Celtic exports of which the local population sees little as they make their way to Smithfield, Billingsgate, Covent Garden in London or Rungis in Paris.

Among the successful Scottish eating houses there is a tendency to country-house gentility; much play-acting involves booking a table, then being greeted and treated as if you were an honoured guest who has just happened along. In the recognised restaurants of Scotland, you encounter a lot of "set dinners" served to you as if that was what you really desired, by maîtres d'hôtel who behave like Edwardian butlers, while waiters and waitresses are encouraged to pretend they are footmen and tweenies. In these places you get no fish-knives because in the 1950s Miss Mitford decreed that they were non-U, and was believed by people who wanted to prove their social desirability via the cutlery. "We're a real restaurant – not a gastronomic tombstone," says David Wilson, whose menu measures 20 by 20 inches and on any one day has nine starters including a truffled duck baked in a brioche; a fish soup redolent of saffron; lobster salad, soups spiked with herbs from his garden and in the way of main courses, grouse and mallards, venison, salmon, crayfish and *The Fish Market*, which is a selection of the day's best catch in a light, creamy chive sauce.

David Wilson lends a startling, individual talent to the preparation and pre-

sentation of the very best local ingredients, is marvellously unpompous, and runs the restaurant with a rare sense of humour. He has style; he looks like a huntsman who has fallen on good times and is a doer in a world of talkers. Lunch trade was slow, inevitably on the winter weekday when I first went there. For my pudding I was served two circles of millefeuille dusted with icing sugar – which had been caramelized; between those lids, set in a perfect, liqueur-flavoured, whipped cream, were the very plumpest blackberries, finest loganberries, most succulent strawberries – the whole confection surrounded by slices of moist white peach riding on a sea of a blend of sabayon and crème pâtissière with four perfect ferns of sweet sicily at the points of a compass. The table-cloths are red, covered with lace doylies, the napkins and the flowers clash a bit but both are in prime condition; the carpet is there to reflect some future – or perhaps previous – colour scheme and the chairs are serious, high-backed things which make you sit up straight. All this becomes totally irrelevant when you start to eat your meal – perhaps a fillet of poached brill garnished with tufts of thyme and chervil and lemon thyme, sitting on a fresh tomato sauce – and you become hooked, as was the fish a very few hours before.

The "house style" entails innovative, light sauces, handsomely sculpted, original vegetables, like samphire (which one has difficulties finding far from the Wash), baby turnips, marvellous beetspinach; his potatoes are cut into slices, arranged to make golden medallions to accompany the roast meats. There is no whispering at The Peat Inn, for great food loosens the tongue and the lack of social pretension, the plethora of fish-

knives, the liqueur glasses filled with toothpicks are all signals to gastronomes that the food is for serious eating; décor is only essential where the food is suspect.

Do I hear you ask about the wines at this excellent, unpretentious crossroads inn? Well, there are 354 bins on the list... none out of stock, priced with sanity rather than greed, a handsome array of half bottles and a quite brilliant selection of Burgundies via the very best shippers... and there is a recently-built annex where you can stay the night in comfort, in view of which there really is no good reason for missing out on a digestif glass of one of his comprehensive selection of single malt whiskies.

As you leave Peat Inn (the village) there are a dozen houses in which they eat stovies and one where they braise a breast of duck in juniper and sherry vinegar, glaze it beneath a grill and serve it with thin slivers of beetroot, courgettes and a mousse of celeriac; all seem to live together in harmony.

Peat Inn, Cupar, Fife, KY15 5 LH, Scotland. 6 miles south-west of St Andrews, close to the Firth of Forth. Open : Residence all week, restaurant Tuesday ro Saturday ; both closed 2 weeks January, 2 weeks November. Privates parties : up to 24 in main room, 12 in private room. Guest accommodation : 8 suites all with bath/shower. (Fishing ; golf.) To visit nearby : St Andrews ; fishing villages of East Fife ; Hill to Tarvit, house and gardens ; Kellie Castle ; Falkland Palace. Credit cards accepted : Access, AE, Diners, Visa. Tel. : (033484) 206.

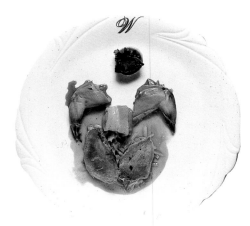

Ragout of wood pigeon and wild Scottish mushrooms

Serves 6
3 pigeon breasts, with skin
vegetable oil
12 oz (340 g) assorted wild mushrooms,
   e.g. chanterelle, boletus
4 oz (1 stick/110 g) unsalted butter
5 fl oz (140 ml) vegetable stock
salt and freshly-ground black pepper
2 teaspoons chopped fresh chervil

Preheat the oven to 230°C/450°F/Gas Mark 8. Sauté the pigeon breasts in a little vegetable oil, turning to cook both sides, then place on a roasting tray, skin side up and cook in the preheated oven for about 6 minutes. Remove and keep warm.

Rinse, pick over and clean the mushrooms. Cut or slice them until the different mushrooms are approximately the same size. Put in a sauté pan with a little of the butter and cook over a medium heat until the juices start to run. Add the vegetable stock and simmer for 2 minutes. Using a slotted spoon, transfer the mushrooms to a tray and keep warm. Bring the cooking liquid back to the boil and simmer to reduce until syrupy. Finish the sauce by whisking in the remaining butter a knob at a time. Reduce again until the sauce coats the back of a spoon. Check the seasoning.

To serve, cover warmed serving plates with the sauce. Divide the mushrooms equally among the plates, placing them in the centre. Remove the skin from the pigeon breasts, cut the breasts lengthways into julienne strips, season with salt and pepper, then scatter over the mushrooms. Sprinkle the chervil on top and serve immediately.

Whole lobster in a lightly spiced sauce with Barsac

Serves 6
6 live lobsters
For the sauce :
5 fl oz (140 ml) fish stock
5 fl oz (140 ml) double cream
pinch curry powder
sprig of fresh coriander
thin sliver of fresh root ginger
salt and freshly-ground pepper
2 fl oz (55 ml) Barsac (sweet white
   wine from Sauternes region)
2 oz (½ stick/55 g) butter

Fill a large pan with water and bring to the boil. Place the lobsters in the boiling water, bring back to the boil, then cook for just 2 minutes. Remove and allow to cool slightly. To make the sauce, put all the ingredients, except the Barsac and butter, in a saucepan and bring to the boil, simmer for 10 minutes. Add the Barsac and simmer for a further 5 minutes, then pass the sauce through a fine sieve. Return the sauce to the heat and whisk in the butter, a knob at a time. Adjust the consistency of the sauce by reduction if it is still thin or by adding a little fish stock if it is too thick. Season to taste.

To serve, remove the whole tail from the lobster, then with fingers or heavy scissors, break off the shell, keeping the tail meat intact. Remove the black intestine running up the centre of the tail and discard. Keep the meat warm. Crack the claws and remove the meat in one piece. Keep warm. Repeat with the other lobsters.

Warm the sauce, then spoon on to warmed serving plates. Place the lobsters on top of the sauce and serve immediately with a selection of vegetables.

Roast young partridge on a bed of cabbage with its juices

Serves 6
6 young partridge, plucked, drawn and
   livers reserved
salt and freshly-ground pepper
bacon rashers to cover partridge
   breasts
10 fl oz (285 ml) game stock
3 – 4 oz (¾ – 1 stick/85 – 110 g) butter
1 small Savoy cabbage
vegetable oil

Preheat the oven to 230°C/450°F/Gas Mark 8. Season inside the partridge with salt and pepper, then place in a roasting tin well spaced. (Use 2 tins if necessary.) Cover the breasts with bacon and pour in just enough game stock to cover the bottom of the tin. Place in the centre of the preheated oven and roast for about 10 minutes. Remove and leave to rest in a warm place.

To make the sauce, pour all the juices from the roasting tin into a saucepan and add the remainder of the stock. Bring to the boil, whisk in the butter a knob at a time and reduce to the required consistency. Check the seasoning.

Discard the outer leaves of the cabbage and shred the remainder finely. Place in a pan, stir in a little butter and cook lightly. Season. Gently fry the reserved livers in a little oil, then season.

To serve, remove the breasts and legs from the partridge. Spoon a little cabbage into the centre of warmed serving plates, place the bacon on top, then the breasts with the legs placed above to left and right. Spoon the sauce around and arrange the liver on top.

For a more elaborate presentation, the liver can be served in a little pastry case filled with some lightly cooked onion.

Steamed scallops with baby leeks in a citrus vinaigrette

Serves 6
18 large scallops
1 lb (455 g) baby leeks
1 small carrot, cut into julienne
For the vinaigrette:
2 medium oranges, peeled and
    segmented
1 lemon, peeled and segmented
4 fl oz (110 ml) extra virgin olive oil

Remove the scallops from their shells, trim and separate the corals. Rinse thoroughly in cold water and reserve the scallops and corals in separate bowls. Chop part of 1 leek into julienne strips and reserve. Chop the white parts of the remaining leeks finely and wash in cold water.

To make the vinaigrette, place the orange and lemon segments in a food processor or liquidizer and process to a thick purée, then gradually add the olive oil, mixing as you pour. Pass through a fine sieve into a saucepan and set aside.

Slice the scallops in half horizontally, then place in a steamer with the corals. Steam for 1-2 minutes, depending on the thickness of the scallops. Steam the leeks separately for 2 minutes (or plunge into boiling water for a similar time).

To serve, warm the vinaigrette and pour onto warmed serving plates. Using a slotted spoon, spoon the leeks on top and arrange the scallops around. Cut the corals into small pieces and place between the scallops. Garnish with the julienne of carrot and leek.

Feuilleté of fruits with vanilla cream sauce

Serves 6
1 lb (455 g) strawberries
3 Granny Smith apples
8 oz (225 g) puff pastry
egg and milk wash
icing sugar
For the caramel:
1 lb (455 g) sugar
5 fl oz (140 ml) boiling water
½ vanilla pod, split
For the crème pâtissière:
9 fl oz (255 ml) milk
1 vanilla pod, split
4 egg yolks
2 ½ oz (70 g) sugar
1 oz (30 g) flour, sifted
For the vanilla cream sauce:
7 fl oz (200 ml) milk
1 vanilla pod, split
2 egg yolks
2 tablespoons caster sugar

Hull and wash the strawberries, then cut in half. Peel and core the apples, then dice into pieces about ¾ in (2 cm) square.

To make the caramel syrup, put the sugar in a pan and cook over a gentle heat until melted and caramelized, 5-6 minutes. Gently stir in the boiling water, then add the vanilla pod and mix well. Add the diced apple and cook until golden but still firm, 2-3 minutes.

To make the crème pâtissière, bring the milk to the boil with the vanilla pod. Cream the yolks and sugar together until creamy, then gently fold in the flour, mixing to a smooth paste. Pour on the boiled milk, whisking rapidly, return to the saucepan, remove the vanilla pod and cook over a low heat without boiling, whisking all the time until the sauce is smooth and creamy. Leave to cool, stirring occasionally.

To make the vanilla cream sauce, bring the milk and vanilla pod to the boil. Beat the yolks and sugar together, then gradually pour the boiled milk onto them, whisking continually. Pour back into the pan and remove the vanilla pod. Cook over a low heat in a double boiler until the sauce is

thick enough to coat the back of a spoon. Leave to cool.

Roll out the puff pastry on a cold surface to a thickness of about ¼ in (0.5 cm), then cut out 6 strawberry shapes about 3 ½ in (9 cm) deep and 3 ½ in (9 cm) across. (You may find it easier to use a cardboard template to cut these.) About ¼ in (0.5 cm) in from the edge of each shape, cut a line half-way through the pastry all the way round to form the lid. Score lightly to decorate. Place the shapes on a baking sheet and refrigerate for 30 minutes.

Gather the pastry trimmings into a ball and roll out to form a flat sheet no more than ⅛ in (3 mm) thick. Trim this to the size of a 12 x 10 in (30 x 25 cm) baking sheet, then gently transfer to the sheet and refrigerate for 30 minutes.

Preheat the oven to 230°C/450°F/Gas Mark 8. Brush the strawberry shapes with the egg wash and place in the centre of the preheated oven. Bake for 12-15 minutes until golden. Remove from the oven and immediately cut away the lid and remove all the soft dough from inside. Keep the pastry shapes warm until required.

To bake the flat pastry, reduce the oven temperature to 180°C/350°F/Gas Mark 4. Remove the pastry from the refrigerator and place a second baking sheet on top, then place 2 weights of 1-2 lb (½ to 1 kg) each on top to prevent the pastry from rising. Place in the oven and bake until golden, about 10 minutes. Remove from the oven, take off weights and top baking sheet and leave to cool a little, then cut carefully into 12 squares of about 2 in (5 cm). Keep shapes warm until required.

To serve, spoon a little crème pâtissière into the bottom of each strawberry shape, then fill with the prepared strawberries. Dust the lid with icing sugar and place on top. Run the vanilla cream around the serving plates and place the strawberry pastries on top. Arrange a square of flat pastry on each plate and, using a slotted spoon, heap some caramelized apple on top. Dust the remaining squares with icing sugar and decorate with a diamond pattern formed with a hot skewer. Place the lids on top of the apples and serve immediately.

CROMLIX HOUSE

Kinbuck, Dunblane, Perthshire, FK15 9JT, Scotland. In Central Scotland, 4 miles north of Dunblane, 1 hour's drive from Glasgow and Edinburgh, about 430 miles from London. Open all week; closed for 10 days at beginning of February. (Dogs by arrangement.) Private parties: up to 24. Guest accommodation: 14 rooms all with bath/shower. (Tennis; croquet; horse riding; clay pigeon shooting; coarse and game fishing; golf.) To visit nearby: Dunblane Cathedral; Stirling Castle; Wallace Monument; Doune Castle; Scone Palace. Credit cards accepted: Access, AE, Diners, Visa. Tel: (0786) 822125

A massive stone entrance porch leads to a large panelled hall in which an open fireplace burns great chunks of pine. Mounted stags' heads look down haughtily from the walls and a lady, dressed as if she had just stepped off the

104

Bonny Prince's boat, places a glass of malt whisky in your hand. Other staff appear to take luggage from your car to the suite allocated for your stay – a suite that would shame most hotels that use the word to denote something bigger than a double room. Here you get a self-contained mansion, space to swing a red deer in if you had a mind to, a hall, with steps up to drawing room, bedroom with four poster and along the corridor and down some more steps a pantry, dressing room, bathroom. The books on the shelves deal with country pursuits – shooting, conservation, fishing, forestry – and you may just learn more about grouse than you wanted to know. "Stuffed with seasoned butter, wrapped in streaky bacon and roasted in a hot oven for 24 minutes" is my knee-jerk reaction to "grouse". The Hon. Ronald Eden, reclusive owner of Cromlix and its surrounding 5000 acres is an international authority and writer on the species, can tell one breed from another at 40 paces and has monitored their lifestyle and their deathstyle in textbooks on the subject.

It was in 1980 that the Eden family home on the outskirts of the village of Kinbuck was converted into a country house hotel. Cromlix House is not easy to find for the proprietors are wary about publicising the location. The house was built in 1880 and is in excellent order with a particularly fine upstairs library – which can be hired for conferences – drawing rooms and dining rooms, which are unostentatiously grand, if some way from being chummy. People tend to whisper. The dining room deserves to have 30 people seated at a huge mahogany table and you feel a bit lost sitting there in twos and fours but the staff is reassuring and the silver and glass, porcelain and linen

and the excellent pre-dinner wild mushroom canapés are good omens of the joys to come. There is a six course dinner menu with options at each stage except for the sorbet, which is universally-acceptable orange.

The cooking is stylish country house, with a new chef, Mark Salter, following the excellent example of his predecessor, while stamping his own authority on the dishes that emerge from his kitchens. The ingredients are of high quality, the service is smooth and if you loved someone a lot and wanted an intimate place in which to luxuriate in good food and rich wines, I cannot think of a better location. Over pre-dinner drinks the restaurant manager appears, asks if he might propose the menu... and gives the rundown on the evening's fare. Terrines of game – like quail and roe deer (with fresh melon and figs in cassis, served with a ginger and port wine sauce) reminded me of the story of the man who had pigeon and pork pie, asked what were the proportions of the two meats and was told one to one: it transpired that it was one pigeon to one pig. Here the ratio turned out to be altogether more honest. The speciality is seafood and there are scallops and braised lobster in a Meaux mustard dressing to rival the wild salmon and sorrel, which is prepared with a galette of morilles and a Riesling sauce. Scottish Lamb is a delicacy and it comes in a rich rosemary sauce with a timbale of leek and apricot – a thinking man's vegetable.

Puddings were interesting: I have eaten brown bread ice cream but oatmeal ice, unlike frozen porridge, was new to me. Glazed apple pancakes were produced with skill and the cheese tray featured some good chèvres, excellent local farmhouse cheddar and Scottish cream cheese wrapped in toasted oatmeal.

The idea of printing a menu is new to this country house hotel where they prided themselves on the distance they kept from other, commercial establishments. Mark Salter feels that if a menu is to be "proposed" to each guest, there should also be the opportunity for the guest to suggest an alternative. In order not to spend too much time discussing the food, they "propose" the recommended six courses and leave you with the printed sheet of other dishes on offer.

The wine list is far ranging, not a lot for

people on a low budget but then this is patently not a low-budget place to go. The clarets are very fine, the years of the vintages impressive, and the range good as befits an establishment that has regular tutored wine tastings. It is over-all a very stylish place and to remind customers of their sojourn among the lochs and trout streams, the grouse moors and the pheasant drives, they have a newly-formed Cromlix Winter Digest. From November to March subscribers are sent monthly parcels of local foods – like smoked Jacob lamb, salmon, pheasant, game pies and terri-nes, which can be munched while recalling the splendours of Perthshire. "Our aim", it states on the prospectus, "is to provide, in a mood of peace and relaxation, old-fashioned comforts, quiet hospitality and personal service." They have succeeded.

Salad of smoked duck with glazed apples

Serves 4
2 breasts of smoked duck
1 oz (30 g) skinned and sliced hazelnuts
2 Granny Smith apples
2 oz (55 g) sugar
2 oz (½ stick/55 g) clarified butter
9 fl oz (255 ml) hazelnut oil
6 tablespoons raspberry vinegar
salt and freshly-ground pepper
12 fresh raspberries
4 sprigs fresh chervil
4 nasturtium flowers

Detach the skin from the breast meat and cut into fine julienne. Pan-fry until crisp, then strain in a sieve.
Toast the hazelnuts under a grill. Peel the apples, cut in half and remove the core. Cut each half into slices and sprinkle with sugar, then sauté in the clarified butter, browning on both sides. Arrange the slices around the outside of the serving plates.
Preheat the oven to 200°C/400°F/Gas Mark 6. Place the duck breasts on a lightly buttered tray and cover with foil. Warm them in the preheated oven for 2-3 minutes, then slice and arrange inside the apple slices.
Make a vinaigrette with the hazelnut oil and raspberry vinegar and season. Spoon a little vinaigrette over the apple and sliced duck breast, then warm both under a hot salamander (grill). Pour on a little more vinaigrette and garnish with the hazelnuts, raspberries, duck fat, chervil and nasturtium petals.
Variation
Guinea fowl could replace the duck in this dish.

Medallion of monkfish wrapped in a herb crust

Serves 4
4 oz (110 g) dried white breadcrumbs
½ teaspoon chopped fresh rosemary and thyme
2 tablespoons chopped fresh parsley
1 clove garlic, finely chopped and pressed
salt and freshly-ground pepper
14 oz (3 ½ sticks/400 g) unsalted butter
4 medallions of monkfish, each 3 oz (85 g)
7 oz (200 g) crépinettes or caul fat
9 fl oz (255 ml) Beaujolais
1 shallot, sliced
9 fl oz (255 ml) fish stock, reduced to a glaze
cayenne pepper
2 aubergines
4 oz (110 g) each of trumpet and oyster mushrooms
12 sprigs of fresh chervil

Mix the breadcrumbs with the rosemary, thyme and parsley, add the garlic and season. Melt 7 oz (1 ¾ sticks/200 g) of the butter and stir into the breadcrumbs. Take the monkfish medallions and coat them in the herb crust, then wrap in the crépinette.
Place the Beaujolais with the shallot and the fish stock in a saucepan. Bring to the boil and cook until only 1 tablespoon remains. Add a spoonful of cold water, then whisk the remaining butter in knobs, seasoning with salt and cayenne pepper. Set aside and keep warm.
Slice the aubergines and cut into equal-sized rounds using a cutter. Quickly clean and wash the trumpet and oyster mushrooms. Pan-fry both the aubergines and the mushrooms in a little unsalted butter and season with salt and pepper.
Pass the underside of the monkfish through seasoned flour and sauté in some clarified butter to seal. Place in a preheated oven at 200°C/400°F/Gas Mark 6 for 5 minutes, then finish under a salamander (grill). Arrange the mushrooms, monkfish and aubergines on serving plates and pour the sauce round. Garnish with the chervil and serve immediately.

Sautéed west coast scallops with freshwater crayfish tails

Serves 4
12 freshwater crayfish
pinch of caraway seeds
salt and freshly-ground pepper
2 medium-sized leeks
2 oz (½ stick/55 g) unsalted butter
pinch of sugar
¼ clove garlic, finely-diced
2 tablespoons medium-dry white wine
1 teaspoon finely-diced fresh root ginger, blanched
12 West Coast scallops
lemon juice
a little clarified butter
For the choux pastry :
10 fl oz (285 ml) water
4 oz (1 stick/110 g) margarine
5 oz (140 g) plain flour
2 eggs
For the white wine sauce :
1 shallot, finely chopped
1 glass dry white wine e.g. Chardonnay, Riesling
1 tablespoon fish stock
4 oz (1 stick/110 g) unsalted butter
cayenne pepper
For the red wine sauce :
1 shallot, finely chopped
1 glass of red Burgundy
1 tablespoon fish stock
4 oz (1 stick/110 g) unsalted butter
For the watercress sauce :
1 shallot, finely chopped
1 glass dry white wine e.g. Chardonnay, Riesling
1 tablespoon fish stock
4 oz (110 g) watercress, picked over
1 tablespoon beef consommé
1 tablespoon unsalted butter

Cook the whole crayfish in boiling salted water with a pinch of caraway seeds for 1-2 minutes. Transfer to a bowl using a slotted spoon, then strain the cooking liquid on top. Set aside.

Cut the leeks into fine strips and wash well. Place the butter, a pinch of sugar and the garlic in a small sauté pan, mix in the leeks and season with salt and pepper. Cook slowly until the leeks are just soft, then add a splash of white wine to keep the compote moist and finally mix in the ginger. Set aside.

To make the choux pastry, preheat the oven to 180°C/350°F/Gas Mark 4. Pour the water, margarine and a pinch of salt into a saucepan and bring to the boil. Remove from the heat and stir in the flour. Return to the heat, stirring continually until the mixture forms a glossy ball, then cool slightly before adding the eggs, one by one, beating well after each addition. Place the paste in a piping bag fitted with a fine nozzle and pipe the choux onto lightly oiled dariole moulds. Bake in the preheated oven for 5 minutes until light golden.

To make the white wine sauce, place the shallot in a saucepan, pour on the white wine and the fish stock and reduce until only 1 tablespoon remains. Add a tablespoon of warm water, then slowly whisk in the unsalted butter. Season with salt and cayenne and keep warm. Make the red wine sauce the same way.

To make the watercress sauce, place the shallot in a saucepan, pour on the white wine and the fish stock and reduce until only 1 tablespoon remains. Liquidize the watercress with the beef consommé, then add 1 tablespoon of the puréed watercress to the sauce. Slowly whisk in the unsalted butter. Season with salt and cayenne pepper and keep warm.

Season the scallops with salt, pepper and lemon juice. Sauté in a little clarified butter. Peel the freshwater crayfish tails. Reheat the leek compote and place on serving plates. Arrange the crayfish on top and add 1 tablespoon of each of the 3 sauces around the outside. Sit 1 scallop on each of these sauces and garnish with the choux pastry cage.

Charlotte of white coffee mousse with an orange and Grand Marnier sauce

Serves 4
For the sponge:
4 oz (1 stick/110 g) margarine
4 oz (110 g) sugar
2 eggs, beaten
4 oz (110 g) self-raising flour, sifted
redcurrant jelly
For the mousse:
2 eggs
8 egg yolks
5 oz (140 g) sugar
1 ¾ pints (1 litre) double cream
3 oz (85 g) coffee beans
3 oz (85 g) white chocolate
6 leaves gelatine
For the sauce:
5 oranges
4 oz (110 g) sugar
⅓ oz (10 g) cornflour
Grand Marnier to taste

Planning ahead
The sponge for the charlotte should be made at least 1 day before required.

To make the sponge, cream the margarine and sugar together, add the beaten eggs slowly, beating well after each additon, then fold in the flour. Preheat the oven to 180°C/350°F/Gas Mark 4. Line a well-buttered rectangular tin 8 x 4 in (20 x 10 cm) with greaseproof paper and sprinkle with flour. Shake out any excess. Fill with the sponge mixture and bake in the preheated oven for 20-25 minutes. Leave the sponge for at least a day before using. Cut into 4 equal layers and spread each layer with redcurrant jelly. Reform the sponge, then slice lengthways into 4 strips. Slice these strips crossways thinly and use to line 4 timbale moulds neatly.

To make the mousse, beat the whole eggs, yolks and sugar over a pan of boiling water until creamy. Boil half the cream with the coffee beans and leave to infuse. Strain, then cool before adding to the remaining cold cream. Melt the chocolate in a double boiler and soak the gelatine in a bowl of cold water. Add the gelatine to the melted chocolate and dissolve, then add this mixture to the lightly-beaten eggs and sugar. Whisk together well, then fold in the coffee cream. Fill the timbales with the mousse and place in the refrigerator to chill.

To make the sauce, zest the oranges, cut in half and squeeze the juice into a jug. Blanch the zest and refresh. Caramelize the sugar, add the zest, then quickly stir in the orange juice. Bring to the boil and cook until all the sugar has dissolved. Thicken with the cornflour and add Grand Marnier to taste. Unmould the timbales onto serving plates and pour the sauce around. Decorate with fresh orange segments as an extra touch.

LINDEN HALL HOTEL

Longhorsley, Morpeth, Northumberland. In north-east of England, about 290 miles from London. Open all year round. Private parties: up to 300. Guest accommodation: 45 rooms all with bath/shower. To visit nearby: Hadrian's Wall; Crag Side National Park; Durham Cathedral. Credit cards accepted: Access, AE, Diners, Visa.
Tel: (0670) 516611

Take the A1 north from Newcastle and at Morpeth bear left onto the A697; not much further on through a village called Longhorsley, the hotel is clearly marked on the right side of the road. (It is a monstrously rotten supposition that everyone travels from the South; if you are approaching Linden Hall from the North, I apologise; please read these instructions upside down.) The driveway is long and so maddens drivers with its profusion of sleeping policemen – which are plumper than most – that the first six might persuade you to call it a day... were it not that backing over sleeping policemen is even worse; after that things look up.

Linden Hall was built by the Bigge family in the first years of the last century. The Bigges were bankers, ergo local politicians. Charles led the Northumbrian Whig party from 1794 until his retirement from politics in 1841, was offered a baronetcy for his good works and declined it "with typical modesty". The following year, Bigge, aged 70, bad farewell to his wife and ten surviving children and set off on an extensive tour

of the world; when he got back two years later three more of his children had perished and it all got worse. He died aged 76 and his son, Matthew, succeeded the old boy both as landlord of the estate and senior director of what had become The District Bank. The bank had what Mr Nigel Lawson would call "a blip" in 1857 and was forced to stop trading. The Hall, having been guaranteed to depositors, was sold, not just lock and stock but among the 1000 items listed in the catalogue were "The Servants Pillows". It was as serious as that. One is tempted to write "here endeth the Bigges" but one of Matthew's sons became vicar of Stamfordham, begat a son called Arthur, who came to the attention of Queen Victoria during the Zulu war, was subsequently knighted, became Lord Stamfordham.

But the Hall was gone to the Ames family, then to the Adamsons who lived there for much of this century and it came to pass that in 1978 the house was again on the market. The purchasers were a company called Callers/Pegasus, furniture people who had gone successfully into the travel business and with brothers Mr Roy and Mr Ian Callers at the helm, the place was transformed into the fine establishment it is today: not just a country house that takes guests but a real hotel.

The restaurant has rightly gained a reputation as an oasis of good living in something of a culinary backwater; it comprises two rooms and if you sit in the first there is much through-traffic to keep up the onlooker's interest; in the further room you need not fear of encountering loneliness – for the staff are fit and young and patrol their territory with admirable frequency. Being an ex-furniture-become-travel businessman is the perfect background for a

hotelier: there are the most luxurious carpets and curtains... and the guests come from around the globe. The restaurant buzzes with French and Italian and American people (not a smattering of the local accent to be heard) and the indigenous clientèle are the sort of people you meet in trendy London eating-houses.

But then the staff are similarly upmarket and young, and international and of both sexes, equally divided. The maître d'hôtel wears a dinner jacket; the rest are dressed in smart blue jackets with gold buttons and starched white shirts or blouses. The cooking is honest and careful and the menu tells you like it is: a symphony of seasonal lettuce leaves accompanied by smoked goose, duck and ham with satsumas in an almond vinaigrette. The chef uses imagination, has a flair for presentation and among his tours de force are the freshest of fish – like brill and salmon served on a marvellously-light, buttery lemon and rosemary sauce. The vegetables are good and fresh and undercooked and the "special pudding, created this day" was a well-crafted pastry swan, its body made of fresh peach ice cream decorated with a profusion of twirls of spun sugar and a sprig of mint to cheer you up. There is a small selection of English cheeses, among which there was the most perfect Stilton; also an English Gouda and a Durham cheese, which had more to do with jingoism than high gastronomy.

The wine list is 16 pages long, contains sound advice at the head of each region and is nicely opinionated: there are seven Beaujolais on the list, all of them shipped by Georges Duboeuf, six of them 1986. The house champagne is excellent and under £17 a bottle, which is good news; the house wines are

£6.95 and there are bottles from California, Australia and New Zealand, which are well chosen and priced with consideration rather than avarice.

This is a really well-run, comfortable, good-looking restaurant, where the food reflects not just the quality of the local produce, but the proximity of the sea and the moors. It is entirely proper that a house that has had such a solid history of private opulence should in the third century of its existence be sharing its grandeur.

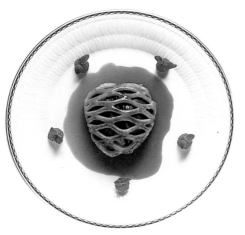

Stuffed breast of wood-pigeon in a trellis of puff pastry with a marsala sauce

Serves 1
1 plump woodpigeon
1 egg, separated
1 oz (30 g) grapes
1 oz (30 g) shelled pistachio nuts
2 fl oz (55 ml) double cream
salt and freshly-ground pepper
3 oz (85 g) puff pastry
1 oz (30 g) finely-chopped shallots
1 oz (2 tablespoons/30 g) butter
2 fl oz (55 ml) marsala
5 fl oz (140 ml) rich game stock
5 fresh raspberries
oregano leaves

Remove the breasts and the leg meat from the pigeon. Place the leg meat and the egg white in a food processor and purée, then pass through a fine sieve into a bowl. Peel the grapes, quarter and remove the seeds, then mix into the purée together with the pistachio nuts. Place in the refrigerator to chill. When chilled, place the bowl over ice and slowly fold in the cream. Season with salt and pepper. Return to the refrigerator to chill.
Preheat the oven to 200°C/400°F/Gas Mark 6. Make a lengthways cut down the centre of the pigeon breasts and fill with the farce. Place both breasts together. Roll out the puff pastry and cut into strips. Wrap the strips in a trellis pattern round both breasts. Glaze the pastry with the egg yolk. Bake in the preheated oven for 15-20 minutes.
Meanwhile, sweat the shallots in $^1/_2$ oz (1 tablespoon/15 g) of the butter until golden. Add the marsala and reduce to a syrup, then add the game stock and reduce by two-thirds. Whisk in the remainder of the butter and pass through a fine sieve.
Place the pigeon in the centre of a serving plate, surround with the marsala sauce and garnish with the raspberries and oregano leaves.

A medley of lettuce leaves with scallops in a pink peppercorn dressing

Serves 1
3 large scallops
5 fl oz (140 ml) fish stock
2 fl oz (55 ml) olive oil
1 teaspoon white wine vinegar
1 teaspoon pink peppercorns
mixed lettuce leaves, e.g. frisé, escarole, radicchio, lollo rosso, rocket, mâche (lamb's lettuce), pourpier, watercress
salt and freshly-ground pepper
For the garnish:
mixed fresh herbs, e.g. chervil, fennel, coriander, chive
tomato petals

Lightly poach the scallops in the fish stock for 1-2 minutes, then remove from the cooking liquor and allow to cool. Place the olive oil, white wine vinegar and pink peppercorns in a bowl and mix well together. Gently toss all the lettuce leaves with 1 tablespoon of the dressing and season lightly with salt and pepper. Arrange the leaves on a serving plate in a neat nest. Thinly slice the scallops and place around the salad. Arrange the herbs and tomato petals on top. Finally moisten the scallops with the remainder of the dressing.

Grilled fillet of salmon on a nest of cucumber noodles in a saffron sauce

Serves 1
8 oz (225 g) fillet of salmon
flour for dusting
about 2 oz ($^1/_2$ stick/55 g) butter
1 oz (30 g) finely-chopped shallots
1 small clove garlic, finely chopped
pinch of saffron threads
2 fl oz (55 ml) dry white wine or vermouth
4 fl oz (110 ml) fish stock
5 fl oz (140 ml) double cream
$^1/_2$ cucumber, peeled
salt and freshly-ground pepper
tomato rose
fennel leaves

Lightly dust the salmon with flour, then sear with a red hot branding iron, marking the fillet in a criss-cross fashion. Dot with butter, then place under a hot salamander (grill) for 3-4 minutes each side.
Meanwhile, sauté the shallots in about 1 oz (2 tablespoons/30 g) butter until golden brown. Add the garlic and saffron, then the white wine or vermouth, bring to the boil and reduce to a syrup. Stir in the fish stock and reduce by two-thirds, then stir in the cream and reduce until the mixture coats the back of a spoon. Cut the cucumber lengthways into fine strips, then sauté in a little butter. Season with salt and pepper. When all is cooked, place a small nest of cucumber noodles in the centre of a serving plate, arrange the salmon on top and pour the sauce around the fish. Garnish with the tomato rose and fennel.

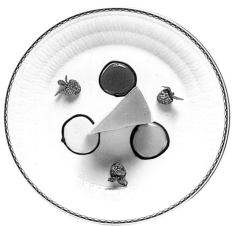

Panfried breast of guinea fowl with wild mushrooms in a ginger sauce

Serves 1
2 oz (¹/₂ stick/55 g) unsalted butter
1 x 6 oz (170 g) breast of guinea fowl
1 oz (30 g) finely-chopped shallots
1 oz (30 g) finely-chopped fresh root ginger
5 fl oz (140 ml) game stock
3 fl oz (85 ml) double cream
4 oz (110 g) wild mushrooms, e.g. cèpes, chanterelles, yellow pleurote, oyster, mousserons
salt and freshly-ground pepper
diced tomato
sprigs of fresh thyme

Preheat the oven to 190°C/375°F/Gas Mark 5. Melt 1 oz (2 tablespoons/30 g) of the butter in a sauté pan. Seal the breast on the presentation side first, then turn over and seal the second side. Transfer to the preheated oven and roast for 10 minutes, 5 minutes on each side. Remove from the oven and keep warm.
In the same pan, sweat the shallots and ginger until lightly browned. Add the stock, bring to the boil and reduce by two-thirds, then stir in the cream and simmer until thickened.
While the sauce is reducing, cook all the mushrooms separately in a clean sauté pan using the remaining butter. Season with salt and pepper.
Pass the sauce through a fine sieve. Arrange the mushrooms in neat bundles around the outside of a serving plate. Thinly slice the guinea fowl breast and fan in the centre. Pour the sauce around the breast and in between the mushrooms. Garnish each bundle of mushrooms with tomato and a small sprig of thyme.

A light passion fruit mousse with a dialogue of fruit purées

Serves 8
8 oz (225 g) sugar
3 egg whites, stiffly beaten
18 fl oz (510 ml) passion fruit purée (liquidize the fruit with 3 tablespoons stock syrup, then pass through a strainer)
1 lb 10 oz (750 g) crème fraîche
6 leaves gelatine
6 oz (170 g) raspberries, washed
1 mango, peeled and stone removed
3 tablespoons stock syrup
For the vanilla sauce:
10 fl oz (285 ml) milk
2 egg yolks
1 vanilla pod
For the decoration:
2 oz (55 g) dark chocolate, melted
24 fresh raspberries
24 sprigs chervil
icing sugar

Boil the sugar to the soft ball stage, 115°C/238°F, then pour onto the beaten egg whites in a thin stream, whisking all the time. Leave to cool, then gently fold into two-thirds of the passion fruit purée together with the crème fraîche. Heat the remainder of the purée and add 2 leaves of softened gelatine. Allow to cool but not set. Slowly add the remaining 4 leaves of softened gelatine to the passion fruit mousse and allow to chill but not set. Once chilled, divide equally between 8 individual cocotte moulds and allow to set firm. When set, pour over the passion fruit jelly and leave until set firm.

Purée the raspberries together with the stock syrup, then purée the mangoes. Pass each purée separately through a fine sieve and reserve. To make the vanilla sauce, boil the milk with the sugar, pour over the egg yolks and vanilla, stirring all the time, then return to the heat and cook until the sauce coats the back of a spoon. Leave until cool. To serve, unmould the mousses in the centre of the serving plates. Place the melted chocolate in a paper piping bag and pipe 3 equal-sized circles the same distance apart around the mousse. Place a spoonful of each of the 3 sauces into these circles and decorate with a raspberries and sprigs of chervil. Dust with icing sugar.

McCoy's

The Tontine, Staddlebridge, Nr Northallerton, North Yorkshire, DL6 3JB. On the edge of the Cleveland Hills, about 220 miles from London. Open Monday to Saturday, dinner only; closed Christmas and Bank Holidays. (Children welcome; pets welcome; air-conditioned.) Private parties: 40-120. Guest accommodation: 6 rooms all with bath/shower. To visit nearby: Mount Grace Priory; Cleveland Hills. Credit cards accepted: Access, AE, Diners, Visa. Tel: (060982) 671

French Guides tend to use symbols like * or a to denote "worthy of a detour", meaning that what is on offer at that location merits the tedium of extra driving time. McCoy's is such an establishment. It is said to be at Staddlebridge – which is unhelpful and infuriating, for the place only exists in italics on the 1-inch Ordnance Survey map, to des-

cribe some 50 yards of roadside. The confusion would amuse the owners, for orthodoxy does not rank high in their order of things.

McCoy's, then, is in the middle of hardly anywhere at all, but IS a sensational restaurant run by a trio of flamboyant and uniquely-talented brothers. To find it you drive along the A19 and where it is crossed by the A172 you see it standing back from the southern carriageway, which means that if you are driving north, you take a sliproad to the left, navigate across the bridge and find your way back, which would be harder were The Tontine not the only building for miles around.

It does not appear to have a front door, though you will find one by and by, through a garden and up some steps. Suddenly you are enveloped in a world of 1930s plush and kitsch and 78 rpm records featuring Duke Ellington and Jessie Matthews in her heyday. The sofas are low and comfortable, the lights leaded and so dim that you wonder whether they might have been a special purchase diverted from Scottish landladies (can there be 10 watt bulbs?) and there are mirrors and plants and aspidistras and antimacassars and when you get to the dining room there is much, much more: a black ceiling and stark-flowered wallpaper, mirrors and silver paper on some walls; pink slips over pink tablecloths and pink napkins, bone handles to the knives, plated spoons and forks, professional glasses made for serious drinking and menus that are dramatically large and black, with a red motif fashioned of sealing wax.

All this would only be of passing interest were the food of the runcible predictability that pertains in this part of England. In fact, the food is stunning.

There is duck's liver – foie gras of duck – that literally melts in your mouth, served on a slice of brioche, surrounded by a purée of potatoes sharpened with turnip, another purée of split peas. Homemade ravioli filled with a forcemeat of langoustine, spiked with truffle and served with a delicate lobster sauce. Partridge breasts with apricots stuffed with alcoholic currants and a herb mousse... it is breathtakingly original, served with precision – when they are good and ready and not before – and two or three minutes later they will ensure that all is to your liking, without making a drama of the enquiry. The baguettes are so authentically French that if you found their like in Paris, you would move across town to be close to the maker.

The restaurant seats about 40 and somewhere in the lower reaches of the building there is a bistro where the atmosphere is less formal, square footage per person less generous, but the food similarly inventive. Thomas McCoy cooks; brother Eugene buys the wine and runs the Bistro, Peter makes the puddings and commands the restaurant wearing a loose herringbone 1930s suit that looks like a snip from Oxfam until, on closer examination, it turns out to be handsomely bespoke. He is The Man; takes orders, makes bills, hires his staff and it is greatly to his credit that despite the isolation of the place the waitresses are very special: the one who served me had a Modigliani face on a Renoir body, spoke with a Jane Austen acent.

Before the meal you can have a drink in the drawing room, which is replete with polished mahogany and faded chintz, period candlesticks, many mirrors; yet despite the period feel to it, there are very contemporary drinks – like over-

proof single malt whisky. When you move, to the sound of a fox-trot, into the dining room, you note that the customers have entered into the spirit of the place, wear 30s finery, occasional cravats, a waxed moustache, and the flowers on the tables are in on the time-warp game : 1970s mimosa and only slightly more recent jonquils in vases that might have won their class in a pre-war Ideal Home Exhibition. Dim lights and parasols that turn tables into islands of subdued light provide an atmosphere that is uninhibited and intimate ; there is a feeling of harmony.

and not just amazing for an inn on an unfashionable crossroads on the Yorkshire Moors, amazing anywhere. They stock Cloudy Bay, a supreme Sauvignon from New Zealand – and with the foie gras offered a Pinot de Charentes.

McCoy's is unique and I just hope the brothers remain in situ, rather than spread themselves to London and Los Angeles, which must be a temptation. When the bill arrived it was not inexpensive... but then there is absolutely no reason why it should have been.

Everyone is having a terrific time and if you should fall off your perch before the end of the meal, there are six green bedrooms upstairs, each with private bath, each entitling the occupant to a breakfast that is spoken of with reverence across the county.

Peter's best pudding is "thin, thin, oh so very thin, layers of puff pastry, crème pâtissière and fresh strawberries". There is also – and I found this to be the most delicious confection – *Original Crêpe san Lorenzo at McCoy's*: it is a generous restaurateur who credits another with the invention of a dish. The pancakes were brilliant, the ratio of vanilla to Amaretto to Grand Marnier in the cream could not have been improved. On the menu it states "Cheese – please ask." I asked. They said they did not really have anything worthwhile. All that talent, and honesty as well. The wine list is long and carefully chosen

118

Fillet of beef, roasted shallot, a crêpe of girolles and tartlet of parsley purée, sauce vin rouge

Serves 2
2 large shallots
butter
2 trimmed fillets of beef, 4 oz (110 g) each
1 lb fresh parsley, picked over and washed
cream
salt and freshly-ground pepper
2 baked puff pastry tartlet cases
For the crêpes:
5 fl oz (140 ml) milk
1 whole egg
¹/₂ oz (15 g) plain flour
mixed fresh herbs, chopped
4 oz (110 g) girolles, washed
¹/₂ oz (1 tablespoon/15 g) butter
2 fl oz (55 ml) double cream
1 egg yolk
For the sauce:
10 fl oz (285 ml) red wine
1 stick celery, chopped
1 small carrot, chopped
¹/₄ onion
2 shallots, chopped
¹/₂ leek, white part only, chopped
5 fl oz (140 ml) veal stock
1 oz (2 tablespoons/30 g) unsalted butter

To make the crêpes, blend together the milk, egg, flour and herbs and leave to rest, then cook into 4 in (10 cm) diameter crêpes. Preheat the oven to 200°C/400°F/Gas Mark 6. Roast the shallots in their skins in the preheated oven for about 5 minutes until tender. Leave to cool, then remove skins and glaze in a little butter. Keep warm.
Increase the oven temperature to 240°C/475°F/Gas Mark 9. Seal the beef fillets in 1 oz (2 tablespoons/30 g) hot butter, then roast in the preheated oven for 4-6 minutes, according to taste. Leave to rest for 5 minutes and keep warm. Reserve the meat juices.
To make the sauce, place the wine and vegetables in a pan, bring to the boil and reduce by half, then pass through a fine sieve. Add the stock and reduce again by half. Whisk in the butter, add the meat juices and black pepper to taste.
To make the filling for the crêpes, cook the girolles in the butter until soft, then place in a food processor or liquidizer with the other ingredients and purée. Place 1 tablespoon of the mixture into each crêpe, fold over and seal. Brush with butter and bake in a hot oven for 3 minutes.
Blanch the parsley in boiling, salted water for 1¹/₂ minutes, drain, then liquidize with a little cream and salt and pepper to taste. Spoon into the puff pastry cases and place under a preheated grill to warm.
To serve, carve the fillet into 3 slices, place on the serving plate and pour on the sauce. Arrange the crêpe, parsley tartlet and roast shallot on top.

Diced scallop with lemon zest topped with a slice of foie gras and virgin olive oil, scallop juice and lemon juice

Serves 4
about 8 fresh scallops
salt and freshly-ground pepper
1 lemon
3 oz (85 g) foie gras
5 fl oz (140 ml) virgin olive oil
chopped fresh chervil to garnish

Remove the scallops from their shells with a soupspoon, separate the white from the coral and wash carefully. Dice the scallops – you will need about 7 oz (200 g) scallop meat – and place in four 2¹/₂ in (6 cm) rings. Season with salt and pepper and add a pinch of grated lemon peel to each. Steam in a pan with a little water until cooked, about 5 minutes. Keep warm.
Divide the foie gras into 4 pieces and season. Heat up a thick-bottomed sauté pan, add the foie gras and turn after 10 seconds. Cook for a further 30 seconds, then place on kitchen paper to drain.
Place a scallop ring in the centre of each serving plate and top with a slice of foie gras. Warm the olive oil and stir in the juice of ¹/₂ lemon. Pour round the scallops and garnish with chervil.

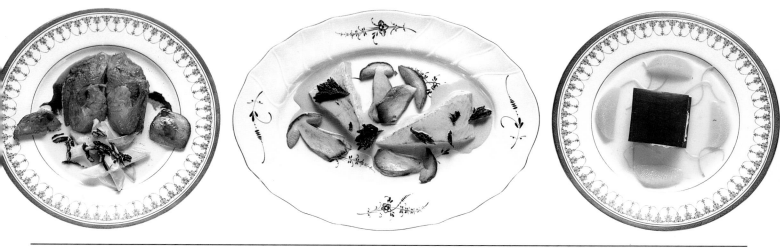

Norfolk pigeon roasted, sauce of baby leeks and truffle, slices of foie gras glazed with port

Serves 2
2 squab pigeons, 15 oz (425 g) each
melted butter
5 fl oz (140 ml) vegetable stock (made
 from equal quantities of dry white
 wine and cold water, with a selection
 of aromatic vegetables and herbs)
5 fl oz (140 ml) double cream
2 slices fresh truffle, cut into julienne
1 oz (2 tablespoons/30 g) unsalted
 butter
salt and freshly-ground pepper
10 small thin leeks, cooked (about
 1 ^{1}/$_2$ in (4 cm) in length)
4 small pieces of fresh foie gras
flour
6 tablespoons port

Preheat the oven to 240°C/475°F/Gas Mark 9. Brush the pigeons with a little melted butter and roast in the preheated oven for 10 minutes until crisp and rare. Remove from the oven, set aside and keep warm. Reserve the meat juices.
Reduce the vegetable stock and cream together to 5 fl oz (140 ml), add the truffle and whisk in the butter. Season to taste with salt and pepper, then add the reserved meat juices to thin the sauce slightly.
Gently reheat the leeks in the sauce, then transfer to warmed serving plates and pour round the sauce. Remove the legs from the pigeons and carve away the breasts. Arrange the breasts on each plate with the legs on either side.
Coat the pieces of foie gras lightly with flour, then fry in a dry hot pan until brown on both sides and tender. Place on either side of the pigeon. Reduce the port over a high heat until syrupy, about 1 tablespoon, then spoon over the foie gras and serve immediately.

Scotch salmon, paprika sauce with fried cèpes and celeriac leaves

Serves 4
4 salmon escalopes, 4 oz (110 g) each
salt and freshly-ground pepper
4 oz (110 g) cèpes
1 oz (2 tablespoons/30 g) butter
2 oz (55 g) celeriac leaves or celery
 flowers
vegetable oil for deep frying
For the sauce:
5 fl oz (140 ml) fish stock
5 fl oz (140 ml) white wine
10 fl oz (285 ml) double cream
1 teaspoon paprika

Preheat the oven to 140°C/275°F/Gas Mark 1. Place the salmon escalopes into a buttered ovenproof dish, season with salt and pepper and half fill with water. Cook gently in the preheated oven for 8 minutes until just cooked. Transfer to warmed serving plates.
To make the sauce, place the fish stock and wine in a pan, bring to the boil and reduce by half. Add the cream and reduce again until slightly thickened. Stir in the paprika. Clean and slice the cèpes, then sauté in the butter. Remove the leaves from the celeriac or celery, wash and dry, then drop into hot vegetable oil and fry until crisp.
To serve, arrange the mushrooms around the salmon, pour sauce over the fish and garnish with the celeriac leaves.

Chocolate strasse

Serves 4
4 oz (110 g) plain chocolate
For the mousse:
2 egg yolks
1 oz (30 g) sugar
^{1}/$_2$ teaspoon grated orange peel
10 fl oz (285 ml) double cream
2 ^{1}/$_2$ fl oz (70 ml) orange juice
2 tablespoons Grand Marnier
2 leaves gelatine
2 egg whites
For the honey sauce:
5 fl oz (140 ml) orange juice
1 tablespoon honey
Grand Marnier
For the garnish:
orange segments
julienne of orange peel, blanched

Melt the chocolate and spread onto 2 rectangles of greaseproof paper, 12 x 9 in (30 x 23 cm).
To make the mousse, mix the egg yolks, sugar and orange peel together. Boil half the cream, stir into the egg mixture, then return to the pan and cook until thick. Allow to cool a little, then stir in the orange juice and Grand Marnier.
Soak the gelatine, then melt in a little cold water. Stir into the egg mixture and allow to cool but not set. Whisk the ramainder of the cream to ribbon stage, then fold into the mixture. Whisk the egg whites until thick, fold into the mixture and leave to set.
To make the sauce, heat the orange juice with the honey and a little Grand Marnier to taste. Cut the chocolate into 16 equal squares and sandwich 4 squares together with the mousse. Repeat with the remaining squares. Arrange on serving plates, pour round the sauce and decorate with the orange segments and julienne.

Sharrow Bay Hotel

Howtown Road, Ullswater, Penrith, Cumbria, CA10 2LZ. Beside Lake Ullswater, south of Penrith, about 280 miles from London. Open all week; closed Dec. to Feb. (Vegetarian meals; no children under 13; no smoking in dining room; no dogs.) Private parties: 12 in private room. Guest accommodation: 30 rooms, 26 with bath/shower. (Lake swimming; trout fishing; fell walking.) To visit nearby: the Lake District; Standing stones; Beatrix Potter's cottage; Wordsworth's cottage. No credit cards; cheques accepted. Tel: (085 36) 301 and 483

In 1948 Francis Coulson went to the station of his home town of Bedford, bought a third class ticket to Penrith and called upon an estate agent who had advertised in the Manchester Guardian "Ullswater house; half a mile of lake frontage, 10 acres garden, gate house TO LET." Coulson made an offer,

waited four months, was accepted and moved north with wild optimism, £400 in the Post Office Savings Bank, a couple of saucepans and a determination to open a "country house" hotel.

Last year he – and his partner of almost equally long standing, Brian Sack – celebrated their 40th anniversary at Sharrow Bay. Francis cooks as accurately and lovingly as anyone in the land, Brian administers with quiet efficiency; and when you leave they are both there, at the front door, to bid farewell and thank you for being such good guests. With hosts of their calibre, it is actually almost impossible to be anything else.

I remember a hotel guide in which readers were asked to "report" on the places where they had been and a lady wrote of Sharrow Bay that she had cycled 70 miles to lunch there, arrived alone, elderly, shabby and sweaty and was treated like a Queen. It is the good manners of the pair which are so very impressive... and the beauty of the location and the quite astonishing precision with which all is done. It was Coulson's aim to make people feel like guests rather than customers and, as local-boy-made-good Hunter Davies wrote of it, "the place positively drips good taste; you get nothing so vulgar as a reception desk, a bar or any hotel-like notices; nothing is written down, no list shown, no prices mentioned and when the required drinks arrive silently and unobtrusively, no money is requested." For the record, they do not accept credit cards, you do not tip, must not smoke, and yes, of course, they will take your cheques and no, they do not want to see your banker's card.

The dining room has windows facing the lake and alcoves into which the most favoured guests are placed – and

given the choice of a view over the water or of the other diners. The tables are laid with care and artistry, there are vases of violets and bowls of grapes, slices of home-made bread and baskets of freshly-baked rolls (they bake twice each day) and one is sort of surprised to be served without having to rise to one's feet for the national anthem. The menu is printed in depth for each and every meal and lists many of the dramatis personae of the establishment, naming the two headchefs, four chefs, two pâtissières and restaurant manager. There are five courses. A choice of three soups and eight other starters including a terrine of venison, duck, foie gras and pistachio, served with Cumberland sauce; another of leeks with truffles; gravadlax with dill and a light mustard sauce; melon with curried cream. The obligatory fish course might be Aberdeen monkfish with borage cream sauce and cheese suissesses, then a fruit sorbet of rare quality while you await the main course amongst which the roast pork with abundant and perfectly-crisped crackling might persuade you to forgo the calves liver in puff pastry casing with Madeira sauce and lardons of bacon. Vegetables are crisp and fresh and genuine Roesti potatoes arrive on a separate plate. And all the time they bring you more hot rolls, and worry about your contentedness.

It may be because Sharrow Bay is such a very English hotel that great attention is paid to the puddings: there is *Sticky toffee sponge* with cream, "our speciality" it says on the menu; the bread and butter pudding is accompanied by apricot sauce, the *Brandy angel cream* is brilliant, the syllabub exceptional. And the English approach is shown in the seriousness with which they serve breakfasts and the shinyness of the sil-

ver trays upon which afternoon tea is produced in the lounges overlooking the lake.

Forty years ago the purchase of food was a nightmare; today it is merely difficult, for Ullswater is far from the beaten track, some 300 miles from Harrods delivery area. The fish and scallops come from northern lochs, the game from London – though it is probably shot locally and yo-yos back to Cumbria; cheeses are purchased from Keighley in Yorkshire, groceries in Keswick and it needs men of rare organi-sing ability and high principle to preserve the constant quality of ingredients that pertains.

The wine list runs to 22 pages, shows five mineral waters (three British) and is compiled in association with Youdell and Co of Kendal who have been suppliers to Sharrow Bay since 1955. It is particularly strong on clarets and has selections of bottles from all over the world, half a dozen malt whiskies, six vintage armagnacs, eight vintage ports including a Taylors 1963 at £70 which is a snip, though the 1960 Martinez at £40 could be snippier. House wines are chosen with care and the Mâcon Blanc Villages is particularly good.

Jeremy Thorpe maintained that when people shook elderly politicians' hands it was to ascertain the likelihood of a by-election. Well, I shook hands with both partners of the prestigious country house hotel as they saw me off on the road around the lake and they are in excellent heart; we for our part are astonishingly fortunate to have such principled ambassadors to fly our flag and seduce our appetites.

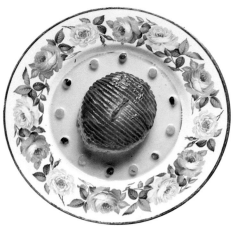

Chicken livers in a cream sauce with marjoram

Serves 6
1lb (455 g) very fresh chicken livers
vegetable oil
For the sauce:
1 oz (2 tablespoons/30 g) butter
½ onion, chopped
3 rashers bacon, thinly sliced
6-8 mushrooms, thinly sliced
¼ clove garlic, crushed
¾ oz (25 g) plain flour
20 fl oz (565 ml) single cream
1 tablespoon chicken jelly
2 tablespoons chopped fresh marjoram
salt and freshly-ground pepper
For the garnish:
12 turned button mushrooms, milk
24 lardons of bacon
courgettes
carrots

To make the sauce, melt the butter in a pan. Add the onion, bacon, mushrooms and garlic and cook for 3 to 4 minutes. Stir in the flour and cook out for 2 to 3 minutes. Stir in the cream, chicken flavouring and 1 tablespoon of the marjoram. Cook gently over a low heat for about 20 minutes or until the desired consistency is reached.

Meanwhile, gently poach the turned mushrooms in a little milk. Precook the lardons of bacon in boiling water. Refresh both under cold water and reserve.

Strain the sauce through a very fine sieve and liquidize. Add the rest of the marjoram and season with salt and pepper.

Next prepare the livers. Remove any sinew and green/yellow parts. Cut each liver into 2 or 3 pieces. Preheat a thick-bottomed frying pan over a high heat. Pour in a little vegetable oil, just to cover the bottom of the pan. Add the livers, season and toss for 2 to 3 minutes over a high heat. Remove any excess fat from the livers. Add the lardons of bacon and turned mushrooms and toss for about 1 minute. Add the sauce to the livers and gently infuse the livers with the sauce. Check seasoning and serve immediately, garnished with turned and cooked carrots and courgettes.

Fillet of halibut in puff pastry casing

Serves 6
3 oz (85 g) spinach
2 young carrots
2 courgettes
2 apples
6 halibut fillets
butter
white wine to poach fish
6 puff pastry casings, 3 in (7.5 cm)
  square x 1 in (2.5 cm) deep
salt and freshly-ground pepper
sprig of fresh dill
For the sauce:
3 shallots, chopped
4 ¾ oz (1 stick plus scant
  2 tablespoons/135 g) butter
20 cardamom pods
20 coriander seeds, crushed
a flavouring of root ginger, peeled and
  finely chopped
bay leaf
12 fl oz (340 ml) fish stock
12 fl oz (340 ml) white wine
about 20 fl oz (565 ml) double cream
lemon juice

Plunge the spinach into boiling, salted water for about 2 minutes. Drain, then place straightaway into iced water until cool. Leave to drain all the water away.

Scoop a small parisienne out of the carrots, courgettes and apples. Cook, then refresh.

To make the sauce, sweat the shallots in about ¾ oz (not quite 2 tablespoons/25 g) butter, then add the cardamom pods, coriander seeds, root ginger and bay leaf. Pour in the fish stock and white wine and reduce by two thirds. Add some double cream and continue to reduce, this time by half. Strain through a fine sieve and whisk in the remaining 4 oz (stick/110 g) butter, a knob at a time, over a medium heat. Season with salt, pepper and lemon juice. If required, a fine julienne of blanched root ginger can be added to the sauce.

Make sure there are no bones in the halibut fillets, then gently poach in a little butter and white wine with seasoning.

Cut the puff pastry casings in half horizon-

tally and place the lower halves on serving plates.

Warm the spinach in a little butter, salt and pepper, then place on top of the pastry casing. Warm the parisienne of vegetables in seasoned butter, to which the sprig of fresh dill has been added. Remove the halibut fillets using a slotted spoon and place on top of the spinach with a little of the sauce over and around the fish. Pour a little around the pastry casing also.

Top with the pastry lid and garnish with the parisienne of vegetables.

Variation
Fillets of lemon sole could be used instead of the halibut and the puff pastry casings could be cut in rounds.

Saddle of venison marinated in red wine

Serves 6
1 medium-sized saddle of venison –
  approximately 12 portions
approx. 1 lb (455 g) wild mushrooms
butter
fresh mixed herbs
salt and freshly-ground pepper
sprig of fresh redcurrants to garnish
watercress sprigs to garnish
For the marinade:
2 carrots, 2 sticks celery
2 shallots, 1 leek   } mirepoix
1 bay leaf
8 black peppercorns, crushed
6 juniper berries
6 sprigs fresh thyme
2 cloves garlic, cut in half
40 fl oz (1.1 litres) red wine
For the venison sauce:
20 fl oz (565 ml) demi glace
20 fl oz (565 ml) venison stock
1 tablespoon redcurrant jelly
6 oz (1 ½ sticks/170 g) butter

Preheat the oven to 190 – 200°C/375 –
400°F/Gas Mark 5-6.
Remove both fillets and both eyes from the
saddle. Trim off all the sinew and place in
the marinade for about 24 hours. Remove
from the marinade and reserve.
To make the sauce, place the demi glace,
venison stock, marinade and redcurrant
jelly in a pan and gently reduce by about two
thirds, skimming frequently. Pass through a
fine sieve, then whisk in the butter, a knob
at a time. Taste and adjust the seasoning.
Trim and thoroughly wash the wild mushrooms. Sauté them in a little butter and,
when cooked, sprinkle over some fresh
herbs and season.
Cut the venison into medallions and cook
with a little butter in the preheated oven for
8 to 10 minutes.
Press the wild mushrooms into dariole
moulds or similar and turn out in the
middle of each plate. Slice each medallion
into about 8 slices and arrange around the
wild mushrooms. Place the sauce around
the meat and garnish with the fresh redcurrants and watercress.

Iced hazelnut mousse with raspberries

Serves 6 – 8
2 oz (55 g) caster sugar
2 oz (55 g) hazelnuts, shelled and
  roasted
3 egg whites
4 ½ oz (125 g) icing sugar
9 fl oz (255 ml) double cream
For the sauce:
12 oz (340 g) raspberries
sugar
2 teaspoons lemon juice
For the decoration:
fresh raspberries
icing sugar
fresh mint

Gently heat the sugar until caramelized,
remove from the heat and stir in the hazelnuts. Allow to cool, then grind coarsely.
Whisk the egg whites with the icing sugar.
Whip the double cream until it softly peaks.
Fold the cream into the meringue mixture,
together with the ground hazelnuts. Pipe
into suitable moulds and freeze.
To make the sauce, liquidize the raspberries with sugar to taste and the lemon juice,
then pass through a fine sieve.
To serve, turn each mousse out on to a chilled plate. Pour a small amount of the sauce
to one side. Arrange a few raspberries
alongside the sauce and lightly dust with
some icing sugar. Garnish with a sprig of
fresh mint.
For a more elaborate presentation, the
raspberries can be arranged in coupelles.

"La stupenda" Joan Sutherland bavarois

Serves 6 – 8
4 egg yolks
4 oz (110 g) caster sugar
2 teaspoons powdered gelatine
2 tablespoons water
10 fl oz (285 ml) milk
10 fl oz (285 ml) double cream
apricot brandy
1 lb (455 g) fresh apricots
sugar to taste
pinch of cinnamon
grated peel and juice of 1 orange
For the decoration:
fresh apricots
pistachio nuts

Cream the egg yolks and sugar until white in
colour. Sprinkle the gelatine over the water
in a small bowl, place over a saucepan of hot
water and dissolve. Bring the milk to the
boil, then pour on to the egg and sugar mixture, stirring quickly and constantly. Pour
into a clean saucepan and heat slowly, stirring all the time until the mixture coats the
back of a spoon. Do not allow to boil. Stir in
the dissolved gelatine and strain. Leave to
cool.
Meanwhile, remove the stones from the
apricots, then place in a pan with the sugar,
cinnamon, orange peel and juice and cook
until tender and most of the liquid has evaporated. Check for sweetness, adding more
sugar if necessary, and allow to cool.
Lightly whip the cream and flavour with a
little apricot brandy, then fold into the
cooled egg and milk mixture.
Place about 2 tablespoons of the cooled
apricot compote into individual glass dishes and top with the bavarois mixture. Chill
until set, then turn out and decorate with
fresh apricots and pistachio nuts. Serve
with almond tuile biscuits.
For a more elegant presentation, serve on a
pool of crème anglaise and cover with a
caramel cage.

MILLER HOWE

Rayrigg Road, Windermere, LA23 1EY. In the heart of the English Lake District, about 250 miles from London. Open all week, dinner only; closed December to February. (Vegetarian meals by arrangement; no children under 12; no smoking in dining room; pets welcome; air-conditioned.) Private parties accepted. Guest accommodation: 13 rooms all with bath/shower. To visit nearby: the whole of the Lake District. Credit cards accepted: Access, AE, Diners, Visa.
Tel: (096 62) 2536

The Lake District is the largest expanse of manicured countryside in England; no mountain has the bad taste to be over-tall, or unapproachable; no lake is too wide or too wild to swim across, look where you will and the grass is green, the trees trim and the towns and villages exude rustic responsibility as if preening themselves for the "best kept"

award. Windermere is in the south of the district – best lake, best village: just like all the other places – but there is little doubt that when you discuss the place, the name John Tovey will come up in the first flush of conversation; his Miller Howe Hotel, set on a hill of that name with National Trust land separating him from the water below, is the most renowned hostelry in the area.

There is a temptation to lump together the two most famous Lakeland hotels – for they are within an hour's drive – but apart from the fact that they both please their customers, and Tovey in the distant past worked briefly for Coulson, there is no resemblance. Sharrow Bay (page 120) received its accolade for precision, for immaculate attention to detail and courtesy beyond the call of duty. Miller Howe got theirs for "theatrical brilliance and imaginative largesse".

John Tovey's thirteen bedroom hotel (rooms have binoculars, hair dryers, music centres with tapes of Beethoven, paintings of quality, antique furniture) was the home of a prosperous merchant. The present owner, who had been an actor, a diplomat but always a bon vivant and a Cumbrian, bought it in 1971 and runs it as the great actor/managers ran their theatres in the last century. Shakespeare wrote that one man in his time plays many parts. Tovey plays them all simultaneously: chef, manager, accountant, publicist – while he also writes most readable cookery books and has a television series. He is an original; not for him the diligent pursuit of classic receipts. Tovey is the no-nonsense master of all he surveys, knows the algebra of food, understands and empathises with the basic decency of the north country folk who make up his clientèle and has a flair for presenta-

tion. He runs what is quite simply the best boarding house in the land, has a staff who admire him and I doubt there is a place in England where fewer customers steal teaspoons than at Miller Howe – a sure sign of appreciation.

Dinner is at 7.30 for 8 p.m. You amble down to the lounge and sit at a table overlooking the lake beyond the terrace on which trees are illuminated by theatrical floodlights turning blue, then red, on a time switch; the Union Jack flutters from the lawn in its own spotlight. Drinks are served and you look at a menu, which seems to contain three first courses and wonder why no-one takes your order, asks whether you would like the chicken and veal terrine with fresh mangoes; the tomato, apple and celery soup with cream and croûtons, or the fillets of sea-trout served with caviar tartlet and hollandaise sauce... and when at 8 p.m. precisely you are moved to *your* designated table in the dining room, you realise why. You get one of each. This is a five course, no choice until you get to the puddings, set meal. There are seven vegetables with the main course. Salads are brilliant and have up to a dozen types of vegetation in one bowl. The Lakeland ham in a spiced peach sauce, sirloin in onion marmalade or pigeon comes as the base around which you receive your glazed carrots, mashed swede with horseradish, diced leeks in vermouth, sprouts with bacon, aubergine casserole, broccoli in raspberry vinegar and roast fanned potatoes. There is much "oohing" at the impressive food prepared by the chef – one Mr Galton Blackiston (well, you would not expect Tovey to employ someone called John Smith) – and his team deserve the praise they get. Then pudding. There is a choice of seven but if you speak nicely to the staff, you can

have a taste of most of them. Coffee in the lounge. No smoking in the dining room and it seems absolutely right that it should be they who take the decisions. Even on the menu there is a note "with this evening's meal I strongly recommend this or that wine from my private cellar". The cost is seldom in excess of £10 a bottle and the wine in question tends to be excellent. (Why the cellar should be "private" when it is listed and available is not clearly explained but "private cellar" has about it a nice ring.)

John Tovey's mission is to buy the best, freshest produce, lend to it his inventive culinary powers and make it fun to look at and delicious to eat. His approach is English, as are most of his customers and all of his recipes. Everyone gets the same handsome treatment, the same food, the same napkin rings ('well, I found them in Tahiti and thought they were fun') and everyone is very pleased. The wine list is admirable in that there is substantial choice at affordable prices, celebratory wine for those to whom money matters less and a well-balanced

selection of bottles from Australia and New Zealand, California, South Africa and the better vineyards of Spain and Italy.

Mr Tovey is branching out; there is now a Miller Howe Kaff and two other restaurant ventures, in 1988 he published two cookery books and if you watched afternoon TV in Britain he was constantly to be seen cooking with polished enthusiasm in the Cumbrian landscape that he loves so much.

Vegetable terrine on tomato basil sauce

Serves 15 – 20
8 large lettuce leaves
8 small radicchio leaves
salt
6 oz (170 g) French beans, topped and
  tailed
4 oz (110 g) carrots, cut into strips the
  size of your little finger
2 leeks, white end only, about ½ in
  (1.5 cm) in diameter, 6 in (15 cm) in
  length, peeled
2 oz (55 g) baby sweetcorn, thin ends
  removed
3 oz (85 g) red pepper, cut into thin
  strips
3 oz (85 g) courgettes, cut into strips
  the size of your little finger
12 oz (340 g) boned chicken breast,
  cubed
3 eggs
5 fl oz (140 ml) double cream
1 tablespoon mixed fresh herbs,
  chopped
freshly-ground black pepper
2 teaspoons caster sugar
For the garnish:
tomato sauce
cucumber quarters
parsley sprigs

Planning ahead
This terrine should be made the day before
you want to serve it. Cook in the normal terrine mould, which measures approximately
13 x 3 x 3 in (33 x 7.5 x 7.5 cm).

Prepare all the vegetables first. Remove any
thick stalks from the lettuce and radicchio
leaves, then quickly blanch them in boiling,
salted water. Remove immediately and put
in cold water. They will curl up tightly but
when cold they are relatively easy to unroll.
Use them to line the sides of the ungreased
terrine – lettuce all over first, followed by
radicchio – remembering to allow a little to
hang over the sides as this will eventually
cover the top.
All the remaining vegetables must be blanched in simmering, salted water as well and
the timings below are vital. Submerge each
vegetable separately in the saucepan inside
a metal strainer, cook for the specified time,
then immediately refresh under cold running water. Leave to one side to drain thoroughly.
Timings:
French beans: 2 min.; carrots: 2 min.;
leeks: 4 min.; baby sweetcorn: 1 min.; red
pepper: 1 min.: courgettes: 1 min.
  Put the cubed chicken into a food processor
with one of the eggs and whizz round on
high speed. Add the remaining eggs, one at a
time, then dribble in the cream and mixed
herbs. Season to taste with salt and pepper.
Preheat the oven to 180°C/350°F/Gas Mark
4. Sprinkle 1 teaspoon of the sugar over the
leaf-lined terrine, then spread a little of the
chicken mixture over the base (a spatula is
ideal for this job). Arrange half the cold
cooked French beans in close rows lengthways in the chicken mixture, then put in a
little more chicken. Push the carrot strips
lengthways in close rows down into this.
Add more chicken, then down the middle of
this place the leeks, end to end, the whole
length of the terrine. Arrange the sweetcorn on either side along the length of the
terrine. Add more chicken and follow this
with close rows of the red pepper strips.
After this the sequence is chicken, then
courgette strips, chicken, then the remainder of the French beans, arranged as before.
Top with the balance of the chicken.
Sprinkle on the remaining teaspoon of
sugar and fold over the lettuce and radicchio leaves to cover the outside. Place a
double layer of greaseproof paper on the
top, then the lid.
Place the terrine in a roasting tray and pour
in enough boiling water to come half-way
up the sides of the terrine. Bake in the preheated oven for 45 minutes. Remove the
terrine from the roasting tray and leave to
cool. Once cooled, refrigerate briefly.
Turn out the terrine. Slowly and carefully
slice using a long, sharp, serrated knife and
serve on a simple sauce of fresh tomatoes
and a little basil. Garnish with cucumber
quarters and parsley sprigs.

Chicken breast stuffed with banana and mango, baked in smoked bacon

Serves 6
butter
6 boned chicken breasts
1 medium fresh mango, peeled and cut
  into 6 wedges
1 ½ bananas, peeled, halved
  lengthways, then cut into two
6 large smoked bacon rashers, rinds
  removed
about 6 tablespoons white wine
dill sprigs to garnish

Preheat the oven to 180°C/350°F/Gas Mark
4. Butter 6 pieces of foil large enough to
enclose the chicken breasts. Do this on the
dull side of the foil.
Put the breasts, skin side down, on your
work surface and make an incision about 2
in (5 cm) long into the flesh underneath the
fillet. This must be big enough to take a
small wedge of mango and a piece of
banana. Insert the mango first, then the
banana on top. Fold the fillet over to close.
Lay the smoked bacon rashers down on
your work surface and place each chicken
breast, fillet side down, on the fat end of the
bacon. Wrap the thin tail bit of bacon round
the chicken.
Place each wrapped breast on a piece of
buttered foil. Start to bring the four edges of
the foil up, so that when you pour in about
1 tablespoon of white wine per parcel, it
does not run out over the work surface.
Place a knob of butter on each breast.
Secure the foil carefully all round to form
the shape of a Cornish pasty, making doubly
sure the wine won't be able to run out.
Place the parcels on a wire rack, placed in a
roasting tray. Fill the tray with some hot
water and place the whole thing in the preheated oven. Cook for 30 minutes. Serve
sliced and garnished with dill.

Chocolate orange gâteau

Makes 1 x 10 in (26 cm) gâteau, to serve
 8 – 12
3 fl oz (85 ml) liquid glucose
juice and finely-grated peel of 1 orange
2 ½ fl oz (70 ml) water
3 oz (85 g) caster sugar
1 lb (455 g) good chocolate, broken
 into pieces
8 tablespoons orange curaçao
15 fl oz (425 ml) double cream
1 egg white
cocoa powder, sieved, to finish

Lightly oil a 10 in (26 cm) round tin. Place
the glucose, orange juice and peel, water
and caster sugar together in a saucepan and
heat gently to melt the sugar, then bring to
the boil. Melt the chocolate with the orange
curaçao in a Christmas pudding type bowl
over a pan of simmering water. Combine the
glucose and chocolate mixture and leave to
cool slightly.
Beat up the cream until it forms soft peaks
and gently fold in the cooled chocolate mixture, followed by the stiffly-beaten egg
white. Turn this runny mixture out into the
prepared tin and leave in the refrigerator to
set.
Decorate with sieved cocoa and cut into
wedges to serve. The gâteau can be further
decorated with twirls of cream, piped, set
chocolate shapes and mint leaves.

Farmhouse pear and Stilton pie

Makes 1 x 8 – 11 in (20 – 28 cm) flan, to
 serve approx. 8
12 oz (340 g) self-raising flour
4 oz (110 g) Jordan's jungle oats or
 coarse oats
12 oz (3 sticks/340 g) soft butter,
 broken into walnut-sized pieces
4 oz (110 g) icing sugar
finely-grated peel of 2 oranges
3 egg yolks, lightly beaten
For the filling:
5 ripe pears
2 oz (55 g) Stilton, crumbled

I like to use a 14 in (35 cm) plastic bowl,
which is more or less a perfect half sphere,
as this means the butter and flour mixture
will not catch in any crevices.
Sieve the flour into the bowl and mix in the
oats. Add the soft butter pieces, spreading
them all over the dry mixture. Standing
quite relaxed, hold your hands spread out
in front of you, palms upwards and with left
and right hand fingers opposite each other.
Slowly go down into the mixture and lift up
as much as possible without the fingers clo-
sing up on one another. As you lift up, just
keep on flicking your thumbs across the
outline of your 4 fingers. The action at all
times is methodical – you must not force-
fully squeeze the butter into the flour as this
will result in heavy pastry. Once the butter
has been roughly absorbed, fold in the icing
sugar and the orange peel: do not overwork, as it will get wet and sticky.
Zig-zag the beaten egg yolks over the mixture, then, holding the bowl firmly at the
edges with both hands, shake it vigorously,
tossing the mixture up and down and
around. You will be amazed at how soon the
dough comes together. Divide the dough
into 2 parts and bring together into 2 balls
very gently. Wrap individually in foil and
leave overnight to chill.

Use 1 ball to line an 8-11 in (20-28 in) fluted
flan tin and return to the refrigerator to
chill for 30 minutes. Preheat the oven to
160°C/325°F/Gas Mark 3. Bake the case
blind for 30-35 minutes, then allow to cool.
Fill with the pears, peeled, cored and sliced.
Top with the cheese. Roll out the second
ball of pastry to fit the flan. Place over the
filled pie. Press your thumb gently around
the circumference to seal the pastry edges.
Use any leftover pieces to decorate the top
with roses and leaves.
Chill the pie again before baking. Preheat
the oven to 200°C/400°F/Gas Mark 6. Bake
for 20 minutes, then reduce the heat to
180°C/350°F/Gas Mark 4 and bake for a
further 25-35 minutes. If it is browning too
much, cover loosely with foil.
Serve with twirls of cream, decorated with
fresh raspberries.

THE BOX TREE RESTAURANT

Church Street, Ilkley, West Yorkshire, LS29 9DR. In the north west of England, about 200 miles from London. Open Tuesday to Saturday dinner and Sunday lunch; closed Christmas and New Years Day. (Children welcome; no pipes or cigars in dining room; no dogs.) Private parties: 30 in main room, 16 in private room. To visit nearby: Ilkley Moor; Bolton Abbey. Credit cards accepted: Access, AE, Diners, Visa. Tel: (0943) 608484

At the turn of the century Ilkley received a modicum of attention as a watering place. There was the River Wharfe and the mineral springs of the town; also good Yorkshire scenery, like the Ilkley Moors of 'Baht 'at' fame and nearby Bolton Abbey. Ilkley, in common with many other West Yorkshire towns, had a brass band to be reckoned with and there are few local men and women who did not spend some part of their youth blowing into a cornet or marching behind the drum. The fare on offer was plain fare: potato pies and Yorkshire pudding and you could have endless arguments about whether the latter should best be soggy from the drippings of the roast which was placed

on a tray above it or crisp by being baked in the meat tray in the top of the oven while the beef below rested, prior to being carved. As you can tell, Yorkshire was a busy place, with much to occupy the citizens.

In 1963 Malcolm Reid and Colin Long started a restaurant in a stone cottage in Church Street and within a few years it became quite simply the best dining room in the county. The Box Tree was what everyone had been waiting for: custom came from nearby Bradford, then Leeds – which is 16 miles away – got to hear of it and soon after that it took off; flourished, tables booked for weeks ahead and Mr Ronay, who was then a lad, put it into his Guide and gave it a star; folk travelled from the South and agreed that here was gastronomy to match the best in the land.

And it was not just gastronomy: the two men, having furnished their front room and bar to look like a Christmas cracker, with bows and ribbons and artefacts, lamps and candlesticks and mirrors and many paintings of the "I know what I like school of décor", furbished their dining room a little more seriously but still made it a relaxed, jolly place, in which one feels at ease with the world. They thrived, bought a castle up the road in which they held charismatic functions for celebratory occasions – weddings, anniversaries – and greatly to their credit, they recruited young chefs and taught them, in the Box Tree manner, to become ambassadors among the tall white hat brigade. The formula was best ingredients, classic preparation, stunning presentation.

At the end of 1986 Malcolm and Colin moved on to Harrogate to work in design, "they were always into design" said the waiter when I asked after them, and the place was purchased by Mr E Kyte,

who has very wisely allowed the successful enterprise to continue: new conductor, same excellent band. The Box Tree Restaurant continues to serve great food in unique surroundings via a staff who combine youth with wisdom, exude a natural courtesy and a commitment to ensuring that the customers have a good time. Edward Denny who was chef at the take-over remains chef; *vive* the absence of *différence*.

Enter the cottage and the front room is still like the lounge of an eccentric aunt in which every item has a history. The overall impression is cluttered, red, warm, informal, caring, welcoming. The frosted glass windows insulate you from the outside world and prepare you for the performance to come and it is a show of quality performed by professionals – every bit as sensitive to the feel of the audience as are actors who appear on stage.

The menu is written in French, with no translation; only the prices are in English. There are eight starters, four middle courses (one salad and three sorbets), eight main dishes and a choice of six or seven puddings. The cooking is very accurate, traditional rather than nouvelle, much alcoholic liquor in the sauces, a fair amount of fruit in the main dish garnishes, like figs in the *pigeon de Bresse*, and it all looks as pretty as a picture and they worry about you leaving any (which of course you do not). It is important to remember that among the puddings is *Grand dessert chocolatière*, which must not be missed unless the Doctor quite specifically forbade this confection. With it one may drink a glass of Robert Mondavi's Moscato d'Oro from California, which is one of the few dessert wines rich enough to stand up to the cocoa bean.

Wines are by Yorkshire Fine Wines, an

outstanding list that you would not expect to be inexpensive, which it is not, with a good selection of Californian growths.

What is unusual about the Box Tree is that without even a hint of grovelling or bowing, let alone scraping, they make you feel that you are special and they are quite exceptionally dedicated to making you a happier (and a fatter) person by the time you leave. They take credit cards which is a needless courtesy to customers, for they would be full if it were cash only... and to show their egregious decency, they add no gratuities to your bill and do not tell you that service is not included, posting the total in the bottom line of your credit-card receipt.

To sum up, not a place to miss, better to visit with friends or children than with a loved one who might expect total attention, for there is much to admire which would escape notice if one is involved in wooing. Their literature explains "smart dress preferred"; it seems the very least that one can contribute for all that is given in return.

Terrine de tetras à l'huile de noisettes

(Terrine of grouse with hazelnut oil)

Serves 4 (terrine makes 16 slices)
pig's caul to line terrine
12 oz (340 g) belly pork
12 oz (340 g) pork backfat
1 lb (455 g) boned and skinned grouse
  meat
2 fl oz (55 ml) port
2 fl oz (55 ml) Madeira
1 fl oz (30 ml) armagnac
1 ½ oz (3 tablespoons/40 g) butter
1 medium sized onion, chopped
½ teaspoon ground mace
8 juniper berries
2 teaspoons salt
1 teaspoon fresh chopped thyme
1 bay leaf
1 clove garlic
peel of 1 small orange
peel of 1 lime
¼ teaspoon green peppercorns
3 tablespoons double cream
1 egg white
For the vinaigrette:
2 fl oz (55 ml) Champagne vinegar
10 fl oz (285 ml) hazelnut oil
salt and freshly-ground pepper
selection of winter salad leaves as
  available
cherry tomatoes, halved

Planning ahead
Begin preparing the caul and the meat 2
days in advance and cook the terrine 1 day
ahead.

Soak the caul in water overnight to clean.
Trim the belly pork and dice with the backfat. Place all the meat in a bowl with the
port, Madeira and armagnac, cover and
leave to marinate for 24 hours.
Place the butter in a pan and gently sweat
the onion, mace and juniper berries
without allowing to colour, then pass all the
ingredients except the cream and egg white
through a fine mincer twice. Beat the mixture, then stir in the egg white and cream.

Line a 13 x 3 x 3 in (33 x 7.5 x 7.5 cm) terrine
dish with the pig's caul, so that it overlaps
the sides. Fill the terrine with the minced
mixture and fold over the caul to cover.
Cover the terrine with a lid. Preheat the
oven to 180°C/350°F/Gas Mark 4. Place the
terrine in a bain marie and cook in the preheated oven for 1 hour. To test the terrine,
place a skewer into the centre of the terrine
for 30 seconds, when it is ready the skewer
should feel warm on the bottom of your lip.
Place the terrine in the refrigerator and
keep for 24 hours.
To make the vinaigrette, place the vinegar
in a pan and boil over a high heat until reduced by half. Allow to cool slightly, then, drop
by drop, whisk in the hazelnut oil. Season to
taste with salt and pepper.
 To serve, cut eight ¼ in (0.5 cm) slices from
the terrine and place in the centre of 4 serving plates. Toss the salad leaves and cherry
tomatoes in the vinaigrette, then arrange
around the plate.

Sauté de pleurottes avec nouilles fraîches à la crème vin blanc à l'estragon et safran

(Sautéed oyster mushrooms with noodles in a white wine cream sauce flavoured with tarragon)

Serves 4
1 oz (2 tablespoons/30 g) unsalted
  butter
3 shallots, sliced
1 lb (455 g) oyster mushrooms
3 fl oz (85 ml) white wine
7 fl oz (200 ml) chicken stock
10 fl oz (285 ml) double cream
8 leaves fresh tarragon
salt and freshly-ground pepper
2 medium tomatoes, skinned, seeds
  removed and cut into strips
4 pinches of fresh saffron threads
4 sprigs fresh chervil

For the noodle paste:
8 oz (225 g) strong white flour
4 free range eggs
4 free range egg yolks
2 tablespoons olive oil
2 tablespoons peanut oil
3 teaspoons salt

To make the noodles, incorporate all the
ingredients in a food processor and blend
until fully amalgamated. Do not overwork.
Wrap in cling film to prevent oxidizing and
rest for 30 minutes. When rested, roll out
the paste very thinly either through a pasta
machine or by hand. Cut the pasta into very
fine strips (linguine) and place over a wooden rod to dry at room temperature.
To cook, bring a pan of water to a fast boil,
add some salt and a drop of olive oil to prevent sticking, add the pasta and cook until
al dente. Refresh the pasta under cold running water and reserve.
To cook the mushrooms, melt the butter in a
shallow pan, add the shallots and cook until
soft but not coloured. Add the oyster mushrooms and cook until lightly coloured, then
remove from the pan and reserve. Return
the pan to the high heat, add the white wine
and reduce until syrupy, then add the chicken stock and reduce by two-thirds. Add the
cream and reduce again by half. Return the
mushroom and shallot mixture to the sauce.
If the sauce is a little thick, stir in a couple of
tablespoons of hot water. Add the tarragon
leaves and allow to infuse.
To serve, reheat the pasta by plunging it into
boiling water. Place 1 oz (2 tablespoons/30
g) butter in a small pan and melt, add the
drained pasta and mix gently. Place the
pasta in the middle of 4 hot serving plates.
Check the mushroom mixture for seasoning, then spoon around the pasta. Add
some tomato strips. Sprinkle the top of each
plate with the saffron and garnish with a
sprig of chervil.

Emincé de chevreuil aux épinards sautés au porto

(Venison with sautéed spinach and port sauce)

Serves 4
1 lb 8 oz (680 g) venison cut from the saddle
2 oz (½ stick/55 g) clarified butter
salt and freshly-ground pepper
1 lb (455 g) spinach leaves
1 oz (2 tablespoons/30 g) unsalted butter
grated nutmeg
4 sprigs flat-leaved parsley
For the sauce:
10 fl oz (285 ml) best port
2 shallots, sliced
20 fl oz (565 ml) veal stock
1 sprig fresh thyme
1 oz (2 tablespoons/30 g) unsalted butter

Trim off all the fat and sinew from the venison, then cut into 4 even-sized portions of roughly 6 oz (170 g) each. Heat the clarified butter in a sauté pan. Season the venison on both sides with salt and seal in the hot butter for 2 minutes. Allow the meat to rest on a wire trivet.
To make the sauce, remove the excess butter from the pan, add the port and shallots, bring to the boil and cook over a high heat until reduced by half. Add the veal stock and thyme and reduce again by half. Pass the sauce through fine muslin twice and return to the heat. Whisk in the unsalted butter a knob at a time until fully blended. Remove from the heat and keep warm – do not allow to boil. Season to taste with salt and pepper. Place the venison in a hot oven to heat through. Blanch the spinach leaves in a pan of boiling, salted water for 30 seconds, then drain. Finish with the unsalted butter, salt and grated nutmeg.
Remove the venison from the oven and cut each portion into 9 even slices. Place the spinach leaves in the centre of 4 hot serving plates and arrange the venison fillets around. Spoon the sauce around the fillets and garnish with a sprig of parsley.

Médaillons de bœuf aux champignons sauvages et petits légumes au madère et salpicon de truffes

(Medallions of beef with wild mushrooms and vegetables in Madeira with a salpicon of truffles)

Serves 4
2 lb (900 g) fillet of beef cut from sirloin
8 oz (225 g) wild mushrooms in season, e.g. trompettes de mort, girolles
12 small new potatoes
1 large carrot
1 large courgette
salt and freshly-ground pepper
3 oz (6 tablespoons/85 g) clarified butter
2 oz (55 g) shallots, finely diced
1 clove garlic, finely chopped
2 oz (55 g) finely-chopped fresh parsley
4 sprigs fresh chervil
For the sauce:
2 shallots, sliced
7 fl oz (200 ml) Sercial or Bual Madeira
20 fl oz (565 ml) veal stock
1 bay leaf
1 oz (2 tablespoons/30 g) unsalted butter
1 oz (30 g) fresh truffle, peeled

Trim off all the fat and sinew from the beef fillet and cut into 8 medallions, each about 4 oz (110 g). Pick through the wild mushrooms, remove any grit or soil and trim. Reserve the trimmings.
Wash the potatoes and clean if necessary, then, with a small turning knife, take a slither from one end. At the other end, cut an even groove around the potato, ½ in (1 cm) from the top.

From the bottom end, turn the potato to create a stalk, so that the potato has a mushroom shape. Repeat with all the potatoes. Cut the carrot into 2 in (5 cm) lengths, then lengthways into quarters. Using the turning knife, trim each quarter into a slim barrel shape. Repeat this turning with the courgette.
Place the mushroom potatoes into a pan of cold, salted water and bring to the boil. Cook gently until *al dente*. Refresh under cold running water and reserve. Plunge the carrots into a pan of fast boiling, salted water and cook for 3-4 minutes until *al dente*. Refresh in the same manner as the potatoes and reserve.
Place 1 oz (2 tablespoons/30 g) of the clarified butter in a sauté pan. When hot sauté the wild mushrooms, shallots, garlic and 1 oz (30 g) of the parsley for 1-2 minutes. Season, remove from the pan and reserve.
Place the remaining clarified butter in a pan. Season the beef medallions on both sides with salt and seal in the hot pan for 1 minute on each side. Remove from the pan and allow the meat to rest on a wire trivet. To make the sauce, remove the excess butter from the pan and sauté the reserved mushroom trimmings with the shallots over a high heat until soft. Add the Madeira and reduce until syrupy. Add the veal stock and bay leaf and reduce by half. Whisk in the unsalted butter and remove from the heat. Pass the sauce twice through fine muslin cloth. Chop the truffle into very fine dice, add to the sauce, check the seasoning and reserve on the side of the cooker.
Bring a pan of salted water to the boil. Place the beef medallions and the wild mushroom mixture into a hot oven to heat through. Plunge the potatoes, carrots and courgettes into the boiling water for 2 minutes, then drain. Toss in a little butter and sprinkle with the remaining parsley and salt and pepper.
To serve, place 2 medallions of beef in the centre of 4 hot serving plates, spoon the wild mushroom mixture around the beef, then pour over the sauce. Arrange the mushroom potatoes and the turned vegetables in a circle round the meat and garnish with the chervil.

THE WALNUT TREE INN

Llandewi Skirrid, Abergavenny, Gwent, NP7 8AW, Wales. In south-east Wales, 2 ½ miles north-east of Abergavenny, 150 miles from London. Open Tuesday to Saturday (lunch in Bistro only, dinner in dining room and Bistro); closed Mondays and Tuesdays November to March, except for residents. (Vegetarian meals; children welcome; air-conditioned; dogs by arrangement.) Private parties: 45 in main room. Guest accommodation: 9 rooms all with bath/shower. (Fishing.) To visit nearby: Castles of the Marches; the Black Mountains and the Brecon Beacons; Offa's Dyke; Blaenavon Mining Museum; Llanthony Abbey. No credit cards.
Tel: (0873) 2797

Not at all easy to find; to get to this restaurant you need faith and a 1-inch Ordnance Survey map and even then... Forget about Llandewi Skirrid; no-one I met had heard of it but when you say "The Walnut Tree" recognition brightens the countenance. Up the hill at Abergavenny where it says "Hospital" and you should be on the B4521, which is no better than it sounds, and just under three miles from town, on the left hand side of the road, stands the Inn. Pub has about it a pejorative ring and country restaurant sounds grand and solemn. The Walnut Tree is neither: it is a hostelry in which you can eat at the bar or in a side room, sitting at small tables for which they accept no bookings. Or you can go through a door beside the counter and enter the only starred restaurant in the Principality with room for about 30 and uniquely, in a trade replete with practitioners who make a go of it and move on (or fall by the wayside and become insurance agents), it has been in the same hands for upwards of 25 years. The proprietors are Mr and Mrs Taruschio (the "ch" is pronounced as if it were a "k"); he is small, has not much hair and comes from Ancona in Italy; she is short and neat and efficient and comes from Derbyshire. They have a young daughter who comes from Thailand. I provide this background lest you should suppose this is some run-of-the-mill establishment. It is no such thing.

It is a plain, well-organised and honest eating-house with deceptively good food at prices that are fair. The staff is predominantly local and caring, though the remoteness of the place causes the Taruschios severe employment problems: likely chefs look at the social life on offer and tend to feel that a whist drive every other week compares unfavourably with what is on offer in London or Los Angeles – which is good news for the customers as the owner rather than an underling will prepare your food. He uses his Italian background to prepare the local food, much of it obtained from Vin Sullivan of Abergavenny, who is a Fortnum and Mason in the Welsh wilderness where mutton and Caerphilly cheese used to be the fare for highdays and holidays. Book for the restaurant and you will sit among a sprinkling of loyal locals to whom it is a culinary shrine, and meet some discriminating glitterati who can drink Château Grillet (both 1980 and 1983), a wine that is as rare as it is delicious as it is expensive, from an excellent wine list. There are about a dozen starters amongst which the Italian-esque trenette with pesto vies for attention with home-made tagliatelle in a hare sauce. Gravlax is excellent. They find samphire with which to garnish the garlicky racks of lamb and one can eat guinea-fowl in a cream sauce spiked with truffles, plates of fruits de mer, fillet of succulent brill with mustard relish and roasted woodcock with fresh cranberries braised in Madeira. Perhaps the chef's most famous dish is a suckling pig, expertly boned and rolled around an aromatic forcemeat before it is roasted to unparalleled crispness and carved in plate-sized slices. Ices are home-made, summer pudding is rated highly. Cheeses are exactly where an Italian Welshman shines and the board of local chèvres and dolcelatte and cheddar made with sheep's milk seemed to me the very best selection with which to finish the bottle of Amarone 1977, one of the star attractions from a handsomely-chosen score of Italian wines on the list. There is also claret for all tastes and most pockets and enter-

prising, un-obvious Burgundies, which will make me go back to sample those I have not previously encountered.

The atmosphere is intimate, the peace of the restaurant disturbed ever and anon by the door opening and letting in the noise and bustle of the bar where they eat pretty much the same as we eat, less formally. In our enclave, as new diners arrive, the old diners regard them as people in a railway compartment regard passengers who get on at a station half way up the line, yet unlike English travellers, they say good evening when they arrive, goodnight as they go and dinner takes on the air of a club function. The waitresses, the while, behave with the aplomb that a generation of satisfied punters has allowed them to attain. The admirable Drew Smith, former editor of "The Good Food Guide", writes of the place being run with magnificent, deceptively casual skill. That is it. There is no-one trying to prove anything at The Walnut Tree Inn; it looks as unpretentious as a boarding house dining room albeit they have a jewel of a cook, several wondrously-pleasant waitresses and an amazing cellar. If enjoying dinner entails being a linguist in order to decipher the menu, a fusspot to gauge whether or not they have given you all the right knives and forks and cruets, a master of etiquette to ensure that you receive the grovelling you feel is your right, you must go elsewhere. This is a place for appreciating the excellent food, marvelling at the fact that you can find it in such a remote part of the country, then buying the chef and his wife and the people at the next table several drinks because you have had such a good time. As befits an Italian Welshman with an English wife, Mr Franco Taruschio drinks Scotch.

Carpaccio with truffles

a selection of lettuces, e.g. radicchio,
  frisée, batavia, oak leaf, rocket,
  endive
vinaigrette
wafer-thin slices of raw beef fillet
thin slices of white and black truffle
thin slices of Parmesan cheese

The proportions of this dish can be varied according to taste and availability.
Dress the salad leaves with vinaigrette and arrange on a serving plate. Arrange the slices of beef, truffle and Parmesan cheese on top and serve immediately.

Panache of fish with warm balsamic vinaigrette

Serves 4
salt and freshly-ground pepper
2 ¼ lb (1 kg) mixed fillets of Dover
  sole, sea bass, red mullet and brill
4 well-cleaned scallops including coral
2 oz (55 g) tomato concassé
4 teaspoons mixed, finely-chopped
  fresh herbs, e.g. chervil, tarragon,
  basil, chives
For the balsamic vinaigrette:
1 clove garlic, crushed
2 ½ fl oz (70 ml) extra virgin olive oil
2 ½ fl oz (70 ml) balsamic vinegar

Season the fish fillets and place in a steamer with the scallops. Cook until lightly done. Meanwhile, mix together the ingredients for the vinaigrette with salt and pepper to taste and warm up in a saucepan.
When the fish is ready, transfer to warm serving plates and pour the vinaigrette over but do not be too generous. Decorate with the tomato concassé and fresh herbs. Serve immediately.

Fegato con cipolline agro dolce

(Calves' liver with sweet and sour onions)

Serves 4
8 thin slices calves' liver
seasoned flour for dusting
salt and freshly-ground pepper
extra virgin olive oil
2 fl oz (55 ml) balsamic vinegar
8 fl oz (225 ml) demi glace
butter
sprig of fresh sage to garnish
For the onions:
1 ¾ lb (800 g) pearl onions
2 oz (½ stick/55 g) butter
1 ¼ oz (35 g) sugar
2 ½ fl oz (70 ml) white wine vinegar

Dust the liver with the seasoned flour. Heat a little oil in a frying pan and cook the liver for 3 minutes on each side. Remove the liver and keep warm. Discard the oil, then add the balsamic vinegar to the pan and reduce to almost nothing. Add the demi glace and reduce again slightly, then add a small knob of butter. Remove from the heat and stir until the sauce has thickened.
Preheat the oven to 160°C/325°F/Gas Mark 3. Peel the onions and place in boiling water for 5 minutes, then drain. Melt the butter in a flame and ovenproof dish, add the sugar and stir over a medium heat for a few minutes. Add the wine vinegar and continue to stir until the sugar is dissolved. Add the onions and stir well, then cover the dish and place in the preheated oven for about 10 minutes or until the onions and golden and soft.
Arrange the liver and onions on serving plates. Pour the sauce over the liver and garnish with the sage.

Cockle and mussel pie

Serves 4
2 pints (1 litre) cockles
1 pint (0.5 litre) mussels
8 oz (225 g) streaky bacon, diced
oil
1 small clove garlic, finely chopped
6 tablespoons finely-sliced white part of leek
3 tablespoons finely-sliced spring onion
1 teaspoon chopped fresh thyme
2 teaspoons finely-chopped fresh parsley
salt and freshly-ground pepper
roux
prepared puff pastry
egg wash

Prepare the cockles and mussels and steam until shells open. Discard any that stay closed. Remove the cockles and mussels, strain and reserve the liquor given out during cooking. Take the cockles and mussels out of their shells.
Fry the bacon in a little oil until lightly crisp, add the garlic, then the leek and spring onion. Cook lightly, turning the vegetables regularly. Add the thyme, parsley and pepper to taste. Stir in 10 fl oz (285 ml) of the reserved cooking liquor and bring to the boil (if there is not enough natural juice, make up the quantity with water). Add a good pinch of roux to thicken slightly and blend in well. Add the cockles and mussels and bring back to the boil. Check the seasoning and add salt at this point if necessary. Remove from the heat immediately and pour the mixture onto trays to cool quickly.
Preheat the oven to 200°C/400°F/Gas Mark 6. Divide the mixture between 4 small deep pie dishes (large ramekins) and cover with a lid of puff pastry. Brush over a little egg wash and bake in the preheated oven for 30 minutes or until pastry is golden. Serve hot.

Toulouse chestnut pudding

Serve 6
3 ½ oz (¾ stick/100 g) unsalted butter
3 ½ oz (100 g) icing sugar, sifted
4 ½ oz (125 g) plain chocolate, melted
1 x 15 oz (425 g) can natural chestnut purée
3 ½ fl oz (100 ml) good quality brandy

Planning ahead
Make this pudding a day in advance.

Cream together the butter and icing sugar, then add the melted chocolate and beat well. Push the chestnut purée through a fine sieve, then add a little at a time to the creamed mixture, alternating with a little brandy until well amalgamated and all the purée and brandy have been incorporated. Transfer the mixture to a rectangular dish 7 x 3 ½ x 2 in (18 x 9 x 5 cm), smooth the surface to make it level and refrigerate for 24 hours. Turn out, slice and decorate with strawberries and fresh cream or crème anglaise.

MALLORY COURT

Harbury Lane, Tachbrook Mallory, Leamington Spa, Warwickshire, CV33 9QB. In the centre of England, 90 miles from London.
Open all year round. (Vegetarian meals; no children under 12; no pipes or cigars in dining room; no dogs.) Private parties: 50 in main room. Guest accommodation: 10 rooms all with bath/shower. (Swimming pool; squash and tennis courts; croquet lawn.) To visit nearby: Stratford-upon-Avon, Warwick Castle, The Cotswolds. Credit cards accepted: Access, AE, Diners, Visa.   Tel: (0926) 330214

Those who champion English food – and there are many and they have much to praise – tend to devise gastronomic tours that sweep from Cornwall's "Stargazey Pie" (which has heads of small fish peering through the pastry lid) via Devonshire cream, and Wiltshire bacon, straight across the land to Colchester oysters; not a lot seems worthy of praise in between. Move up a hundred miles and after Welsh lamb there is a gastro-void to Yarmouth bloaters, with only a small hurrah for the Pies of Melton Mowbray along the route. The Midlands is the most renowned wilderness when it comes to award-winning restaurants... perhaps because where one finds no indigenous ingredients of note, few expert practitioners are attracted to ply their trade. The exception is Tachbrook Mallory, which shines from the gazetteers' wasteland like a beacon. The village is near Leamington Spa, which is not far from Warwick, and it is there that you find Mallory Court – which has been discovered and rediscovered over the years: it stands up to scrutiny and maintains its reputation.

They do not build houses like Mallory Court any more – squat, comfortable, solid, grey-gabled; it is a pre-First World War construction, set in 10 acres of formal grounds among the green fields of Warwickshire. There you will find the obligatory lake, lawns, water garden, herb garden, kitchen garden, croquet lawn, pool, squash court and tennis court (also helicopter landing pad), all tastefully conceived and immaculately tended. Allan Holland, who cooks with rare skill, and Jeremy Mort, who designs with flair, bought the house in 1977 and made it into the oasis of well-mannered, understated excellence from which one can base visits to Warwick Castle, Stratford-upon-Avon, Oxford, the Cotswolds, Birmingham's National Exhibition Centre (Birmingham and good food seldom appear in one paragraph) and the whole panoply of life in the middle of the country.

They flourish deservedly even though the Hotel sign on the roundabout (the only cry for recognition) blends so effectively into the background that (a) I missed it the first time I tried to find it and (b) it was so mute that I could not discern the direction of the arrow without emerging from the car and doing my Mr Magoo imitation in front of the tree to which the notice is so tastefully attached.

Go through the doors of the entrance hall and you find yourself in a world of log fires, deep carpets, large sofas and easy chairs, satin drapes, great vases of fresh flowers – all in restrained Queen Mother pastel shades. The staff is young and helpful; the ten bedrooms are luxurious with four posters – you would expect no less – but also have about them all the amenities that a thoughtful host provides for an honoured guest: home-baked biscuits, interesting books and up-to-date magazines, a hairdryer, a clock beside the bed, oils and unguents in the bathroom, mending-kit, spot stain remover; there are comfortable velvety chairs, colour TV, pillowcases embroidered with satin-stitch, and many mirrors.

The restaurant is in two connecting rectangular rooms overlooking the gardens and the lake and exhibits "tangy" yellow cloths and napkins, handsome flower arrangements, impeccable silver and glass and beautiful china, with much attention paid to the presentation as well as the composition of the food on offer. Allan Holland is an English exponent of nouvelle cuisine and when he is there the food rises to substantial heights as in the goujons of salmon and turbot in a sauce of mustard and fish stock, cream and lobster coral. Bread is home baked and there is a good, imaginative array of canapés and petits fours and a sweet trolley upon which the *Diplomat pudding* – which is an upmarket bread and butter pudding of com-

mendable lightness – shines most brightly. Sorbets are excellent; there seemed to me to be too many cheeses of adequacy when there might have been two or three of genuine appeal, but that could be the way of the people of the region, who want a selection rather than to be bullied into eating this or that.

When it comes to choice they have done a fine job on the wine list which contains 170 wines from around the world – including Australia, California and Italy, and has a really comprehensive collection of half bottles. The list of Burgundies is especially good with wines from such excellent shippers as R Thévenin and Lupé-Cholet... and in each section there are bottles that make only miniscule holes in pockets.

Formal is the word that best describes the atmosphere; and one observes a consequent tendency on the part of guests to whisper when they might talk, smile when they could laugh. But they all enjoy it and come back and you must remember the location.

Veal sweetbreads with a leek and sorrel sauce

Serves 4
4 very white firm veal sweetbreads (from the heart), each 6 oz (170 g) in weight
30 fl oz (850 ml) good chicken stock
seasoned flour
2 eggs whisked with 1 teaspoon corn oil
fine fresh breadcrumbs
1 oz (2 tablespoons/30 g) butter
2 tablespoons oil
For the sauce:
3 shallots, chopped
1 teaspoon crushed black peppercorns
1 leek, white part only, roughly sliced
about 1 oz (2 tablespoons/30 g) butter
1 fl oz (30 ml) white wine vinegar
a handful of fresh sorrel
4 fl oz (110 ml) double cream
salt and freshly-ground pepper
½ teaspoon sugar
4 slender leeks, sliced into ¼ in (0.5 cm) rounds

Soak the sweetbreads in cold running water for at least an hour, then poach in the chicken stock for 10 minutes and allow to cool in the liquid. When cold, peel away the cartilage, fat and fibres carefully. Reserve the stock. Place the sweetbreads between 2 plates, place a 1-2 lb (½ – 1 kg) weight on top and refrigerate.
When ready to cook, slice the sweetbreads into ½ in (1 cm) thick pieces. Pass through the seasoned flour and egg mixture, then pat on the crumbs and place on a tray. Refrigerate while making the sauce.
Sweat the shallots, peppercorns and roughly-sliced leeks with a little butter in a saucepan over a gentle heat until tender. Add the wine vinegar and the stalks from the sorrel leaves, reduce a little, then add 5 fl oz (140 ml) of the reserved chicken stock. Reduce until the liquid is syrupy, then add the cream. Pass through a fine sieve into a small saucepan, check the seasoning and keep warm. Finely shred the sorrel (to make a chiffonade) and set aside.
In a shallow sauté pan melt ½ oz (1 table-

spoon/15 g) of the butter, add the sugar and salt and a little of the reserved chicken stock. Put in the sliced leeks and cook gently until just tender – they should still hold their shape. Set aside and keep warm.
To finish the sweetbreads, melt the 1 oz (2 tablespoons/30 g) butter and 2 tablespoons oil in a large sauté pan and when hot, sauté the sweetbreads for about 5 minutes, turning half way through, until they are crisp and golden. Drain on kitchen paper and keep warm. Add the chiffonade to the sauce and reheat briefly.
Arrange the leeks in the centre of each plate. Place the sweetbreads on top and surround with the sauce.

Sausage of smoked salmon with cucumber salad and dill vinaigrette

Serves 6
8 oz (225 g) smoked salmon trimmings
4 leaves gelatine
20 fl oz (565 ml) double cream
lemon juice
1 tablespoon horseradish sauce
cayenne pepper
6 long thin slices smoked salmon, each about 6 in (15 cm) long
For the dill vinaigrette:
10 fl oz (285 ml) olive oil
1 clove garlic, roughly chopped
1 large sprig fresh dill
½ medium-sized bulb fennel, finely diced
1 star anise, crushed
1 teaspoon salt
4 fl oz (110 ml) white wine vinegar
1 tablespoon caster sugar
freshly-ground black pepper
½ teaspoon Pernod
For the salad:
caviar (optional)
chopped fresh dill
cucumber strips

Purée the smoked salmon trimmings in a food processor and pass through a fine tamis (drum sieve) into a basin. Cover and

chill. Soak the gelatine in a little of the cream for 5 minutes. Warm over a very gentle heat until the gelatine is completely dissolved, then set aside. Set the basin of salmon purée over a larger basin of crushed ice and add the remaining cream gradually, beating well after each addition until the mousse is light and creamy. Season to taste with the lemon juice, horseradish sauce and cayenne, then stir in the dissolved gelatine. Cover and place in the refrigerator to firm.
Place each slice of salmon on a piece of cling film and spread the mousse along the centre of each slice. Fold the salmon over the mousse to form a sausage shape and wrap in the cling film. Refrigerate for 4-5 hours.
To make the dill vinaigrette, put the olive oil, garlic, dill, fennel, star anise and salt into a small saucepan and heat over a gentle heat until hot to the touch. Set aside and allow to cool and infuse. Put the vinegar, sugar and pepper into a basin. Strain the oil infusion, then gradually whisk into the vinegar mixture until well blended. Taste and adjust the seasoning, then finish with a little Pernod.
To serve, unwrap the smoked salmon sausages and place in the middle of the plate. Surround with the salad and spoon the dill vinaigrette around.

Roast partridge with fresh noodles, grapes, ginger and lime

Serves 4
1 fresh ginger root
2 limes
sugar
1 small bunch green grapes
4 fresh young partridge (preferably red-legged)
oil
4 shallots, chopped
wine or sherry vinegar
5 fl oz (140 ml) chicken stock
5 fl oz (140 ml) veal stock
5 fl oz (140 ml) dry white wine

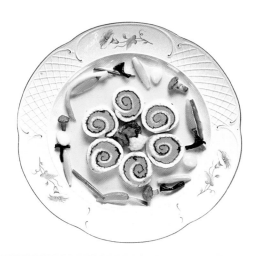

salt and freshly-ground pepper
6 oz (170 g) fresh noodles
2 oz (½ stick/55 g) chilled butter, cut
  into cubes

Peel the ginger root and cut into fine julienne. Reserve the trimmings. Place the julienne in a small saucepan and cover with cold water. Bring to the boil and boil for 2 minutes. Drain and repeat. Refresh under cold water and set aside.

Peel the zest carefully from the limes (without the pith) and cut half into fine julienne, reserving the other half. Blanch the julienne quickly in boiling water and refresh in cold water. Dissolve a little sugar in a small saucepan with a little water and add the blanched zest. Cook until tender and transparent. Set aside.

Blanch the grapes in boiling water for a moment and refresh under cold water. Peel, cut in half and remove seeds. Set aside.

Cut the wing tips off the partridge, chop and sauté in a little oil together with the chopped giblets (if available – but excluding the liver) and any other trimmings from the bird until golden brown. Add the shallots, ginger peelings and reserved lime zest and stir well over medium heat. Add a dash of wine vinegar and allow to evaporate. Add the stocks and wine. Bring to the boil, reduce the heat and simmer until the stock has reduced by half. Set aside.

Preheat the oven to 230°C/450°F/Gas Mark 8. Season the partridge with a little salt. Heat an ovenproof sauté pan or small roasting tin just large enough to hold the birds comfortably and quickly brown them all over in a little oil. Baste the birds with melted butter, turn the birds on their backs and place the pan in the preheated oven. Roast for 15 minutes. Remove and transfer the birds to a warm place to relax for 10 minutes. Drain the roasting tin of fat and set aside.

Meanwhile, cook the noodles, drain and season with a dash of wine or sherry vinegar, salt and pepper and finish with a knob of butter. Keep warm.

Remove the breasts and legs from the partridge and keep warm. Quickly chop up one of the carcases roughly and add to the roasting pan. Place over high heat and pour in the stock. Boil all together for a minute or so until well reduced. Strain through a fine strainer into a clean small pan and over a gentle heat, whisk in the 2 oz (½ stick/55 g) butter until incorporated. Add the grapes, ginger and lime julienne to the sauce and set aside.

Divide the noodles between 4 plates and arrange the partridge on top. Spoon over the sauce and serve at once.

Paupiette of Dover sole with a lobster mousseline

Serves 4
1 Dover sole
For the mousseline :
1 live lobster, about 1 lb (455 g) in
  weight
1 egg white
10 fl oz (285 ml) whipping cream
salt and freshly-ground white pepper
8 large spinach leaves, blanched,
  refreshed and spread out
For the sauce :
4 shallots, finely chopped
1 teaspoon crushed black peppercorns
butter for cooking shallots
1 fl oz (30 ml) white wine vinegar
3 fl oz (85 ml) white wine
3 fl oz (85 ml) fish stock (made from
  the sole bones)
2 sprigs fresh rosemary
½ clove garlic
8 oz (2 sticks/225 g) butter, diced
cayenne pepper
lemon juice
For the garnish :
a selection of baby or turned
  vegetables, e.g. carrots, button
  onions, courgettes, broccoli spears

Skin and fillet the sole. Trim the 4 fillets and lightly score the back of each one. Place the fillets between cling film and flatten out with the back of a heavy knife or cutlet bat. Cover and refrigerate.

To make the mousseline, plunge the lobster into boiling water for 2-3 minutes, then remove. Split in half and remove the flesh from the body and claws together with the coral and green meat from the head – you should have about 5 oz (140 g) lobster meat. Purée the flesh in a processor with the egg white and force the purée through a fine tamis (drum sieve) into a large basin. Set the basin over a bowl of crushed ice and, a little at a time, add the cream, mixing in thoroughly each time until the mousseline is shiny and just holds its shape. Season with salt and white pepper. Refrigerate.

Spread out the sole fillets on pieces of cling film, skin side down, season lightly with salt and white pepper, then cover each fillet with the spinach leaves. Spread the lobster mousseline on top and roll up the fillets. Wrap the cling film around each "paupiette" and refrigerate.

To make the sauce, sweat the shallots and peppercorns in a small saucepan in a little butter. Add the wine vinegar, white wine, fish stock, rosemary sprigs and garlic and reduce over medium heat until syrupy. Over a very gentle heat, whisk in the diced butter a little at a time until it is all incorporated and the sauce is creamy. Season to taste with salt, cayenne and lemon juice. Keep warm over hot water.

To cook the sole, place the sole in a steamer over gently boiling water and steam for approximately 15 minutes, until the mousseline has turned pink and is firm to the touch. Allow to rest in a warm place for a few minutes. Remove the cling film and cut each fillet into 4-6 slices. Arrange on a plate, surround with the warmed vegetables and pour the sauce around. Serve at once.

LE MANOIR AUX QUAT' SAISONS

Great Milton, Oxford, OX9 7PD. 10 miles from Oxford. Open : Hotel 7 days a week; restaurant closed Monday and Tuesday lunch, open for residents (limited menu) Monday evenings. Hotel and restaurant closed last week December, first 3 weeks January. (No children under 8; no smoking in restaurant; no dogs indoors, kennel in grounds.) Private parties : 10 in blue lounge, 45 in Cromwell room. Guest accommodation : 8 bedrooms and 2 suites all with bath/shower. (Swimming pool; tennis; croquet; horse riding.) To visit nearby : Blenheim Palace, Woodstock, Stonor Park in Henley, Waddesdon Manor near Aylesbury. Credit cards accepted : Access, AÉ, Diners, Visa. Tel : (0844) 278881.

Unlike spot-welding, which you have to learn, cookery is an art form and every now and then there comes to the attention of the public a practitioner who produces sensational food without formal training. Such a cook is Raymond Blanc, a Frenchman who came to England, worked in a kitchen, opened his own restaurant in a grotty premise – part of a shopping arcade in an unfashionable part of north Oxford – and was widely proclaimed a genius.

Five years ago he purchased a quite breathtakingly beautiful manor house in the rich water meadows of the Thames Valley, ten miles south east of the great spires of Oxford and has won every accolade that is available to people in the profession : Best Chef; Best Restaurateur; Best Hotel; Writer of the best cookery book and, if you were hellbent on looking around for further prizes with which to shower the young man (he is in his thirties), it might well be that he has the best herb garden, the smartest dove-cote, the richest fishpond and almost certainly the most elegant suites with the most gilded taps in the most marbled bathrooms. In a nutshell, in case I have not made this clear, Le Manoir is a good place to visit. It is also an expensive place to visit, but then M. Blanc would be certifiable if he did not make it so, for perfection such as he produces cannot be put into a traditional price range. Today the old Manor House of Great Milton, its history carefully charted since the early years of the 15th century, the sometime property of Knights of the Shire, Kings' favourites, Lord Mayors of London, Earls of Coventry, Barons Cromwell, is a hotel-restaurant with a French name and a French owner and a unique totally international approach to the serious business of cooking food – an approach that extends to making it look as wonderful as it tastes. Blanc is a man of astonishing industry, unlimited generosity when it comes to spending money on ingredients and a rare ability to blend foods, wines and spirits to create a tapestry of tastes and textures that is sensationally innovative.

Not for him the classic dishes of the great chefs. On a summer's day you might start with a cold soup – like *Essence de saumon sauvage en gelée*, which is a concentrated jelly of wild salmon garnished with Beluga Caviar, sour cream and paprika. His chicken bouillon is made of real farmyard chicken, such as it was Louis XIV's ambition to have every Frenchman able to afford to eat once a month. Chickens have gone down in the world since then – though not in south east Oxfordshire; the garnish for this broth is a handmade ravioli filled with parcels of gooseliver, and the waiter will come – and come back – with a variety of hot, freshly-baked bread rolls. If you should be able to stay the night, the brioches and croissants that accompany the breakfast are fashioned with the same expertise.

There is about Raymond Blanc's cooking a facility for marrying meat and fish and pastry and an ability to complement this with the most judiciously-selected herbs to bring out the individual flavours of, say, the John Dory in its pastry shell, the roasted scallops that surround it, and the rich reduction of veal stock spiked with rosemary on which the fish is placed; the velvety sauce is garnished with slices of truffle and a few golden chanterelles... and was that a hint of raspberry vinegar?

I have eaten at Le Manoir stunning mousses of Jerusalem artichoke interleaved with slivers of leek; baby courgettes from the garden of the manor house filled with a truffle mousse and a sabayon of wild mushrooms. His squabs come from Norfolk, are baked in a salt

crust and really have to be tasted rather than described; superlatives make for monotonous reading yet those pigeons were among the very best things I have ever eaten. If there is advice that I can give to prospective diners it is that the puddings are so splendid it is worth holding back in order to try the *Feuilleté tiède de Poire William rotie au gingembre et citron vert*; if this sounds unmanageable, try the sorbets which are brilliant and light or there is a caramelised apple tart in which thin slices of nougat take the place of the pastry.

Not unnaturally, there is little modesty about the place. The waiters are deeply aware of the rightness of all that occurs and serve with the gravitas that won the Establishment its many awards. If they appear rather grand, the splendour of the dining room, the excellence of the china, plate, glass and linen, the amazing length of the wine list (in which there is little choice for those wishing to contain expenditure to £20 a bottle) gives them the right to lord it a bit. You will see M. Blanc come into his restaurant, not to kiss and gossip with the

guests as do his fellow stars in the world of gastronomy, he appears to ensure that the clientèle is content, that nothing has befallen his food since it left his hi-tech kitchen; he perceives this as an act of courtesy from the host to his guests... then he is away to perform more artistry. What he does today might perhaps be imitated in the years to come but a bird in the hand – especially one cooked by Raymond Blanc – is worth an unlimited number of runcible meals in Shepherd's Bush.

Terrine de cœurs d'artichauts au coulis de tomates et Chantilly d'herbes

(Terrine of artichoke hearts served with a tomato coulis and herb chantilly)

Serves 12 – 15
<u>For the terrine:</u>
2 ¾ pints (1.5 litres) water
3 ½ fl oz (100 ml) white wine
salt
12 white peppercorns
juice of 1 lemon
1 onion, chopped
1 tablespoon sugar
12 coriander seeds
12 globe artichoke hearts
6 fine slices Parma ham
<u>For the tomato coulis:</u>
5 gelatine leaves
1 medium-sized onion, chopped
5 tablespoons olive oil
3 ¼ lb (1.5 kg) tomatoes
1 heaped teaspoon tomato purée
2 teaspoons sugar
2 cloves garlic, chopped
1 teaspoon freshly-ground white
   pepper
<u>For the chantilly d'herbes:</u>
8 basil leaves
20 chives
7 fl oz (200 ml) whipping cream
7 fl oz (200 ml) natural yogurt
pinch of salt and cayenne pepper
juice of ¼ lemon
<u>For the tomato vinaigrette:</u>
14 oz (400 g) ripe tomatoes
½ teaspoon salt
1 teaspoon sugar
1 tablespoon white wine vinegar
5 tablespoons olive oil
freshly-ground white pepper
<u>For the garnish:</u>
a handful of French beans
dash of white wine vinegar
olive oil

Planning ahead
The terrine must be prepared 1 day in advance. The tomato vinaigrette and herb chantilly can be made a few hours in advance. The garnishing, dressing and serving of the dish should be done at the last moment.

Mix together the water, white wine, salt, pepper, lemon juice, onion, sugar and coriander seeds in a saucepan and bring to simmering point. Add the artichoke hearts and cook for 30 minutes. Leave to cool in the cooking stock.

Meanwhile prepare the coulis. Soak the gelatine in warm water for 5 minutes until soft. Sweat the onion in a casserole with the olive oil for 2-3 minutes. Cut the tomatoes in half, squeeze to extract the seeds and juices, then chop the flesh roughly. Add the tomatoes and tomato purée to the pan, reduce over a strong heat, stirring continuously for 20-25 minutes, adding the garlic for the last 5 minutes. This should produce just over 10 fl oz (350 ml). Season with salt, sugar and pepper. Add the softened gelatine, which will melt, and stir. Force through a chinois (conical sieve) into a small bowl and allow to cool until just warm.

To assemble, line a terrine 11 in (28 cm) long x 3 in (8 cm) wide x 3 in (8 cm) deep with cling film, then with the Parma ham slices, leaving sufficient overlap of both, so that the terrine can be completely covered. Drain the cooked artichokes and pat dry with kitchen paper. Taste and adjust seasoning. Brush the inside of the terrine with 1 heaped teaspoon tomato coulis and line up a row of 3 artichoke hearts along the bottom, trimming them so that they fit snugly into the terrine. Line each side with a further 3 trimmed hearts, adding more tomato coulis. Add all the trimmings from the hearts, more coulis, finally covering with the last 3 artichoke hearts. Spoon over the remaining tomato coulis, cover with the overlapping Parma ham slices and seal with the cling film.

Pick up the terrine and tap the bottom on the work surface. Place a rectangular flat piece of wood the same size as the terrine on top, press down, then place a 2 lb (1 kg) weight on top. Refrigerate for a minimum of 24 hours.

To make the chantilly d'herbes, wash, roll and shred the basil leaves. Wash, roll and finely chop the chives. Mix the herbs, cream, yogurt, salt and pepper together. Leave to infuse for 10 minutes to allow the flavour of the herbs to develop. Pass through a chinois, then add lemon juice. If the sauce is too thick, loosen with 1 tablespoon water. Taste and adjust seasoning.

To make the tomato vinaigrette, halve the tomatoes and remove the seeds using a teaspoon. Chop the flesh roughly, then purée finely. Force through a chinois into a mixing bowl, using a ladle. Season with salt and sugar, add the vinegar, then whisk in the olive oil until well emulsified. Finally season with pepper.

To make the garnish, blanch the French beans in boiling salted water for 3-4 minutes. Refresh under cold water, then pat dry with kitchen paper. Cut in two lengthways to expose the beautiful beans inside. Season with salt and white pepper. Add a dash of vinegar and olive oil. Set aside.

To serve, remove the weight and the piece of wood from the terrine. Open up the cling film and turn the terrine upside down onto a chopping board. Remove the cling film. Using a sharp serrated knife, carve the terrine into ½ in (1.5 cm) thick slices. Do not apply too much pressure, as this would disturb the terrine's fragile layout. Arrange the slices in the middle of the plates and place the tomato vinaigrette on each side of the terrine, with herb chantilly at the top and bottom. Tap the plates lightly so that the sauces merge. Arrange the French beans around the plates. Brush each slice with a thin film of olive oil and add a pinch of white pepper.

Duo de millefeuille de chocolat amer et framboises

(Duet of white and dark chocolate layered with chocolate and raspberry mousse)

Serves 4

<u>For the raspberry mousse:</u>
17 oz (500 g) raspberries
2 gelatine leaves
3 ½ fl oz (100 ml) whipping cream
2 egg whites
2 oz (55 g) caster sugar

<u>For the chocolate mousse:</u>
3 oz (85 g) bitter chocolate (Grande if possible)
1 oz (2 tablespoons/30 g) unsalted butter
3 ½ fl oz (100 ml) whipping cream
6 egg whites
⅓ oz (10 g) caster sugar

<u>For the chocolate leaves:</u>
3 ½ oz (100 g) cooking couverture chocolate
3 ½ oz (100 g) white chocolate

<u>For the sauces:</u>
3 ½ fl oz (100 ml) prepared raspberry coulis, made with 7 oz (200 g) raspberries, 2 oz (55 g) sugar and a dash of lemon juice
3 ½ fl oz (100 ml) chocolate sauce, made with 3 1/2 oz (100 g) cooking chocolate, melted with 3 ½ fl oz (100 ml) water, brought to the boil, then ¾ oz (scant 2 tablespoons/20 g) butter whisked in
2 oz (55 g) melted plain chocolate, for piping

<u>For the garnish:</u>
12 raspberries
4 mint sprigs
julienne of blanched orange peel

Planning ahead
Make the raspberry and chocolate mousse at least 4 hours in advance. Prepare the chocolate leaves a minimum of 2-3 hours in advance (they can be prepared 1-2 days in advance). Prepare the sauces in advance, so that they have time to cool.

To make the raspberry mousse, purée the raspberries, strain into a saucepan and reduce until 7 fl oz (200 ml) remains. Add the gelatine leaves and allow to cool. Whip the cream and set aside. Whip the egg whites until firm, then add the caster sugar. Combine the cream and beaten egg whites, then fold into the cooled raspberry mixture. Spread evenly onto a tray to make a layer about ¾ in (2 cm) high. Refrigerate for at least 3 hours.

To make the chocolate mousse, melt the bitter chocolate and whisk in the butter in pieces. Whip the cream and set aside. Whip the egg whites until firm, then add the caster sugar. Combine the cream and the beaten egg whites, then fold into the prepared chocolate sauce. Spread evenly onto a tray to make a layer about ¾ in (2 cm) high. Refrigerate for at least 3 hours.

To prepare the leaves of dark and white chocolate, temperate both chocolate types and, using a brush, create a thin layer of dark chocolate over a smooth plastic sheet. Refrigerate for 15 minutes, then make another layer of chocolate. Fold back the plastic carefully, so that the large chocolate leaf peels off without breaking. Warm up a 2 ¾ in (7 cm) diameter round cutter by placing under a grill and cut circles out of the dark chocolate.

Repeat this process with the white chocolate but instead of using a round cutter, cut the leaf into triangles using a knife which has been dipped into hot water and wiped dry. After the first one has been cut, use this as a guide for cutting the remainder, so that they are all the same shape.

Assemble the millefeuille by cutting 4 circles of raspberry mousse using the round cutter and 4 triangles of chocolate mousse using the knife and template. Sandwich each raspberry mousse between two dark chocolate rounds and each chocolate mousse between two white chocolate triangles. Refrigerate until needed.

Take 4 oval plates and, by filling a piping bag with the melted plain chocolate, design a large triangle outline on one side of each plate. On the other side make a large circle. Place the raspberry coulis into the circle and the bitter chocolate sauce into the triangle. Place the raspberry mousse into the centre of the circle and the chocolate mousse into the triangle. Arrange a little mound of fresh raspberries on each plate and top with a sprig of mint and some strands of orange peel.

L'ORTOLAN

The Old Vicarage, Church Lane, Shinfield, Nr Reading, Berkshire, RG2 9BY. 3 miles from Reading, 35 miles from London, 20 miles from Heathrow airport. Open Tuesday to Sunday, except Sunday dinner; closed last week February, first week March, last week August, first week September. (Vegetarian meals; no dogs.) Private parties: 35 in main room; 30 in private room. To visit nearby: Windsor Castle; Windsor Great Park. Credit cards accepted: Access, AE, Visa. Tel: (0734) 883783

In 1985, the great and angry Nico Ladenis, having scaled the gastronomic heights at his eponymous Queenstown Road restaurant in London, took the step successfully executed by Raymond Blanc and moved to the countryside. Blanc had found a manor house in Great Milton (see page 148); Ladenis discovered a vicarage in Shinfield.

Blanc remains in situ, bedecked with honours; Ladenis is back in town. His erstwhile vicarage was sold to Mr and Mrs Burton Race who previously managed the Oxford establishments of Raymond Blanc... to show that it is a small world and that the pedigrees of both the location and the current proprietors are faultless.

Shinfield is a small village that now finds itself beneath the M4 motorway, from which you emerge at Exit 11 and snake back for a few miles along minor roads. It is a substantial house set in three acres of quince and apple trees (the relative size of village to vicarage has less to do with population than random endowments by wealthy spinsters of the parish). As you come through the front door, there is a bar on one side, on the other a sizeable room, probably the cleric's dining and drawing room, made into a comfortable restaurant seating 32 with a most generous provision of space per cover. A conservatory seats another 30 people.

The name "Ortolan" is not one that is instantly recognised by gourmets – not like "The Entrecôte" or "The Peking Duck". Ortolan is a brown and greyish green European bunting and if, like me, you thought that bunting was just something you hung from the flagpole of a marquee on feastdays, you would be wrong. This bunting is any one of a variety of birds that have short strong beaks and are related to the finch family. There.

The ceiling is pink with Concorde spotlights providing pools of light on the tables bedecked with pale yellow cloths; the motif is starched white and polished silver. Fresh flowers provide discreet colour. Glasses are excellent and plates so large that each individual component of even the most complica-ted of dishes has room to breathe: my lobster ravioli with fresh langoustines in a thin glaze garnished with asparagus tips came on an oval that was 15 inches long.

Mr Ladenis had a reputation as a man of passion. "The place where the owner throws you out if you don't eat what he tells you to" is how the restaurant is remembered by the county – there is nothing like that now: the present régime radiates sympathetic anonymity. Mr Burton Race remains in his kitchen, Mrs Burton Race runs the restaurant with quiet consideration for the well-being of the customers and there is a sufficiency of well-trained waiters and waitresses, who are so genuinely French that you feel a bit inhibited about being "foreign". My long-held theory that the Frencher the accent, the closer to Stockport the provenance of the waiter, does not apply here.

With the drinks you receive three canapés per person, to signal that here is a place of importance. As you sit at your table, along come appetisers of a slice of duck liver on brioche and a tartelette of fruits de mer, "with compliments", and they bring the menu and the wine list. The set dinner is a four course meal on which absolutely no expense is spared, in which the food is prepared by a chef of substantial talent and imagination as befits one who spent some years of his life under M. Blanc. There is a choice of a double handful of hors d'oeuvres and each day there are some "specials", like the impressive foie gras marbled with breast of poussin set upon a startlingly clear vinous jelly, which attracts a surcharge but which comes with a glass of excellent Sauternes presented "with the compliments of the chef". In passing, you note that the baguettes are impeccable, the butter is farmhouse

butter and comes in a decent sized slab at the perfect temperature and the atmosphere exudes confidence, which is the way of things when the chef is an artist and the customers manifest appreciation.

On a single day, for the maximum 65 diners there would be a dozen main courses from which to choose: duck, wild duck, chicken, rabbit, lamb, tournedos, and half a dozen kinds of fish – all classically complicated and stunningly beautiful and prepared by a man who clearly has a love affair with strong flavours to achieve what he describes as "contemporary classic cuisine". He stuffs a leg of poussin with a purée of snails, serves it on a glaze of Burgundy. The quality and varieties of cheese that come your way after the main course are breathtaking (and amazingly debonair when you consider that he has more kinds of cheese than he has customers in an evening). The care that is bestowed upon the puddings is comprehensive and richly rewarding to the consumer: a sandwich of banana parfait with sliced caramelized bananas

and a mousse flavoured with rum between layers of crisp pastry upon a sauce that zings of lemon zest, the whole confection bedecked by a dome of spun sugar. There is an *Assiette chocolatière*, which has eight different examples of the chocolatier's art – black and white chocolate, crisp and soft, iced and at room temperature, placed upon a plate with such artistry that you look at it for some time before making inroads.

The wine list is complete and at the rich end of the market there are many bottles of remarkable quality. At the worker's end a sound collection of regional wines among which a 1982 Cahors was exceptionally good. There is also upon the liqueur trolley, a Vieux Marc de Bourgogne which was the most perfect digestif and cheered me all the way back along the restricted carriageways of the M4.

Langoustines et ris de veau en friture

(Little parcels of langoustine and fried sweetbreads)

Serves 15
10 lb (4.5 kg) medium size langoustines
2 lb (1 kg) veal sweetbreads
clarified butter
45 small spinach leaves, washed
rice paper
oil for deep frying
For the court bouillon:
1 large onion
trimmings from 3 bulbs fennel
1 large carrot
2 teaspoons olive oil
2 oz (½ stick/55 g) butter
½ cup white wine vinegar
½ cup dry white wine
½ bay leaf
1 sprig fresh thyme
parsley stalks
2 sticks celery
2 leeks
1 teaspoon fennel seeds
crushed white peppercorns
salt
2 cloves garlic
3 pints (1.7 litres) water
For the lobster mousse:
2 x 1 lb (455 g) live lobsters
5 fl oz (155 ml) lobster coulis
1 pinch cayenne pepper
juice of ½ lemon
blanched fresh tarragon leaves
salt
1 egg
1 egg yolk
9 fl oz (255 ml) cream
4 oz (1 stick/110 g) butter
For the tomato sauce:
3 tablespoons olive oil
3 generous tablespoons cognac
Mirepoix: 1 onion, 1 carrot
2 sticks celery, 2 leeks, fennel trimmings
4 heaped teaspoons tomato puree
12 ripe tomatoes, seeds removed
3 cloves garlic, chopped
2 sprigs basil

1 sprig fresh tarragon
1 bay leaf
1 sprig fresh thyme
1 star anise
1 teaspoon crushed peppercorns
3 pints (1.7 litres) chicken stock
For the garnish: 2 tomatoes, 2 carrots
2 leeks, 2 celery sticks, 2 bulbs fennel
2 courgettes, fish stock
sprigs of fresh chervil
For the beurre blanc:
2 large shallots, chopped
1 clove garlic, chopped
1 small sprig fresh thyme
1 small sprig fresh tarragon
⅛ bay leaf
5 peppercorns, crushed
2 ½ fl oz (70 ml) white wine vinegar
2 ½ fl oz (70 ml) white wine
2 tablespoons double cream
8 oz (2 sticks/225 g) butter
cayenne pepper, lemon juice

Break the langoustines in half separating the head from the tail. Remove the entrails and reserve the heads.
To make the court bouillon, wash and peel the vegetables, then wash again. Heat the olive oil and butter in a pan, add the vegetables and stir often ensuring they do not colour. Deglaze the pan with vinegar and reduce the liquid by half. Add the white wine and repeat the process. Add the herbs, aromats and garlic and cover with the water. Bring to the boil and skim off the surfacing scum.
Plunge the langoustine tails into the boiling court bouillon and cook for approximately 3 minutes. Lift them out with a slotted spoon and plunge into the iced water to cool them as quickly as possible. When cold, strain off the water and peel, leaving the flesh whole.
To make the lobster mousse, first kill the lobsters with the point of a knife through the brain. After 10 minutes break off the claws and tails. Crack the claws by smashing them with a hammer. Plunge them into the boiling court bouillon for 1 minute and add the tails for just 30 seconds. Cool as for the langoustines, then peel the shell from the claws and cut the tail out of its shell. Cut the tail down the middle lengthways to remove the entrails.

Reduce the lobster coulis until syrupy, then leave to cool. When cold, place in a food processor with the lobster meat, cayenne pepper and lemon juice. Process until completely puréed, then add the tarragon and purée again. Place in the refrigerator to chill. Meanwhile whisk the butter in a bowl until soft and white (not runny). Return the lobster purée to the food processor and add a large pinch of salt: this will tighten the mixture. Next add the egg and egg yolk, then the cream. Finally add the softened butter, ensuring it is cold and approximately the same consistency as the lobster cream. When combined, gently pass the finished mousse through a fine tamis.
Bring a pan with plenty of salted water to the boil, add the veal sweetbreads and cook until firm to the touch, approximately 3 minutes, then cool in cold running water. Now peel off the outside skin with your fingers. Dry them in a cloth and cut into slices, approximately ¼ in (0.5 cm) thick. Season with salt and pepper and sauté in a little clarified butter until golden brown. Place on a tray and leave to cool.
Plunge the spinach into boiling, salted water, cook for 5 seconds, then refresh in iced water. Lift out the leaves individually and lay them down opened out onto a dry tea towel.
Cut the spinach into 3 x 2 in (7.5 x 5 cm) rectangles and lay out. Pipe a little lobster mousse lengthways down the middle of the spinach but not right up to the edges. Next place a langoustine tail directly on top of the mousse and season with a pinch of salt. Cut the sweetbreads again and place some on either side of the langoustine tail. Now pipe more mousse on top. Wrap the excess spinach over the top. Dip the rice papers into warm water to soften them and make them pliable. Place them on the work surface and put the spinach packet slightly off centre on top. Wrap the paper around the packet tightly. Repeat with the remaining spinach rectangles.
To make the sauce, heat the olive oil in a pan until it starts to smoke. Throw in the reserved langoustine heads and seal them, then cook until well-coloured. Add the cognac and flambé. Add the mirepoix and continue cooking for another 10 minutes. Add the

tomato purée and cook for 5 minutes, then add the tomatoes, garlic, herbs and spices. Cover with the chicken stock and bring to a rapid boil. Skim off all the surfacing fat and scum, then reduce to a gentle simmer and cook out slowly, skimming regularly, for approximately 2 hours.

To prepare the garnish, blanch the tomatoes in boiling salted water for 8 seconds then refresh. Skin, cut into 4 segments, remove seeds, then cut into small dice. Cut the rest of the vegetables into a fine julienne ensuring each is kept separate. Cook the vegetables in a little fish stock which has been reduced with butter, garlic, salt and pepper. Place the carrot in first, then the leeks followed by the celery and fennel and finally, at the last minute, the courgettes. Reheat the tomatoes in an emulsion of butter water flavoured with basil, salt and pepper. When the sauce has cooked pass it through a colander and crush with a wooden spoon to extract as much flavour as possible. Pour the liquid into another pan and bring to a rapid boil, again skimming the surface. Pass through a fine chinois (conical sieve), check seasoning and flavour. If it is a little weak, reduce it to the desired level.

To make the beurre blanc, sweat the shallots, garlic, thyme, tarragon, bay leaf and peppercorns in a little butter. Add the vinegar and reduce until dry. Add the wine and reduce until dry, then add the cream and a little water. Lower the heat to a gentle simmer and mix in the butter, a knob at a time, keeping the sauce warm but not letting it boil. Season with salt, cayenne and lemon juice.

Cook the langoustine parcels in a deep fat fryer until golden brown all over, turning half way through cooking. They take 2-3 minutes. When ready, remove from the fat and place on a tray in a hot oven to expel any excess fat.

To serve, sprinkle the parcels with salt and a squeeze of lemon juice. Place 3 piles of julienne on a plate and arrange some tomato concasse in between, Sieve the sauce into the centre of the plate to just cover the base. Put a small spoonful of beurre blanc on the tomatoes and finally place the parcels on top of the julienne. Garnish with chervil and serve straightaway.

Assiette chocolatière

(Chocolate assortment)

Serve 15

For the granite :
10 passion fruit, peeled, halved and passed through a sieve
3 ½ fl oz (100 ml) orange juice
3 ½ fl oz (100 ml) water
3 ½ fl oz (100 ml) white wine
2 ½ oz (70 g) sugar
juice and peel of 1 lemon

For the terrine
9 oz (255 g) each white, milk and plain chocolate
3 egg yolks for each type of chocolate
18 fl oz (510 ml) double cream, whipped to ribbon stage, for each type of chocolate
7 fl oz (200 ml) each of Grand Marnier, Cointreau and Eau de Framboise
3 gelatine leaves for each type of chocolate

For the chocolate gâteau :
9 oz (255 mg) white, plain or milk chocolate
9 oz (2 sticks plus 2 tablespoon/255 g) butter, creamed
6 egg whites
4 oz (100 g) sugar
3 egg yolks
thin sponge soaked in coffee
melted chocolate
cocoa butter

For the millefeuille :
approx. 1 tablespoon melted plain couverture
7 fl oz (200 ml) cream
2 fl oz (55 ml) milk
9 oz (255 g) plain couverture
cocoa powder

For the garnish :
fresh strawberries
mint sprigs

To make the granité, bring all the ingredients to the boil, then leave to cool. Sieve, pour into a stainless steel container and freeze.

To make the terrine, melt each chocolate separately to about 40°C/104°C. For each batch of chocolate, beat the egg yolks and add to the cream. Warm up the alcohol with the gelatine leaves until dissolved, the add to the chocolate, the Cointreau to the milk and the Eau de Framboise to the plain. Fold the chocolate gently into the cream. Pour into a terrine mould. Leaves to set before repeating the process with the second type of chocolate and when this, too, has set, repeat with the third type.

To make the cake, melt the chocolate, then mix in the butter. Whip the egg whites with the sugar to a ribbon consistency and quickly add the egg yolks. Fold the egg mixture into the chocolate. Pour into a round tin. Cover with the sponge and freeze overnight.

To make the chocolate millefeuille, spread a thin layer of the melted chocolate on a sheet of graseproof paper. Just before it sets cut into small rounds or squares and leaves to set completely. Boil the cream with the milk, then remove from the heat. Add the chocolate in small pieces, whisking thoroughly after each addition. Leave until cool. Sandwich 3 pieces of chocolate millefeuille together with this cream and dust with cocoa poweder.

To serve, slice the terrine and place one slice on each serving plate. Remove the granité and the chocolate cake from the freezer. Turn out the cakes sponge side down and glaze with melted chocolate mixed with cocoa butter, then cut into portions. Place one portion of each plate. Add a chocolate millefeuille and arrange scoops of the granité in between. Decorate with fresh strawberries and mint sprigs.

This dish could also be accompanied by an orange or passion fruit butter sauce.

WATERSIDE INN

Upstream from its disappointing exit at Southend, the River Thames meanders through some pretty humble territory like Tilbury and Woolwich but west of London it acquires a new elegance. After Richmond, there is no town or village through which it passes that does not have its clutch of waterfront million-aires, its double garages of Jaguar and BMW with a Mercedes runabout as backstop. Bray is such a village, hard by Maidenhead and as inadequately sign-posted as is most of England... but the Waterside Inn has been there long enough for friendly natives to direct you. It is, not unnaturally, on the river down a looping lane and you notice first the Rolls Royces and Bentleys that become denser as you get closer. It looks like a white pub that has fallen on good times.

It is much more than that: a luxurious restaurant in a romantic location; floor to ceiling windows overlooking the

water which – at this end – has a fair representation of up-market rowing eights rather than Port of London tug-boats that crash into London bridges, which is the scene further east. A large old willow tree is illuminated at night and there hangs about the place an air of well-kept orderliness maintained by young professionals working under the guiding hand of a man who knows exactly what he is at.

Michel Roux is the quieter, more orga-nised, more diplomatic of the two Bro-thers (see also page 22). He is the plan-ner, the instigator of the "Meilleur Ouvrier de Grande Bretagne" award scheme for young chefs, the encourager of people setting up on their own. Spea-king of the Brothers, a French col-league said "C'est Michel qui est le businessman". Mrs Thatcher should be proud of him – an honorary honour should have come his way (honorary because Michel is French and will remain French; as his restaurant, his staff and his philosophy are overtly French). It is also elegant and stylish: there are little summer houses in the garden in which you can have a drink before a meal – with canapés that may be better here than anywhere. Like his brother, Michel also made his reputa-tion as a pastry cook, and his *foie gras en mille feuilles* has a special qua-lity; lobster mousse on slices of brioche is brilliant; rusks topped with cream cheese and chives memorable.

There is, when you come into the Inn, a withdrawing room in which you can sit and drink and browse in comfort – before moving to the spacious restau-rant which seems steadily orderly: even when the place is humming with 80 customers (as it does most evenings), you would think the scene had been prepared for a colour supplement pho-

tograph. Chaos has no place in the Roux way of life. The tables are round and parties of four or more have a better view than do couples. The menu is very pretty, shows on the cover an Edwar-dian lady punting a moustachioed dandy in a white suit, he with a carna-tion the colour of the damsel's blouse. As at Le Gavroche, there is a Menu Exceptionel (a touch, well 50p, cheaper than in London) and every bit as sophisticated: at the Waterside the cof-fee is included – and you have *either* sweet or cheese – cheese coming from M. Olivier of Boulogne, who is one of the very best purveyors. The notices on the menu give you a good indication of the establishment's philosophy:

"We have no specialities as such in our menu as we have created the great majority of our dishes."

"The few classical dishes which figure have also the hallmark of our interpre-tation."

"The temperature of these dishes depends on their content and varies from tepid to hot, never very hot."

"Our crayfish and trout are kept in a fish-tank and are taken out and prepa-red when ordered."

"Although a cigar can be satisfying after a meal, it can be disturbing to other diners. We would therefore appreciate it if you would retire to the lounge or to one of our summer houses to enjoy your coffee and cigar."

The *à la carte* menu lists twelve main courses, nine starters and a similar *Œufs brouillés aux œufs*, scrambled eggs in which you find beautifully soft-boiled quails' eggs, are as delectable as they sound. His soufflés, from which the waiters lift the lid to spoon in a cou-lis of raspberries, and his *Tarte au citron* are especially well regarded.

Where Michel Roux is consistently

outstanding is in the high quality of and disregard for economies in the ingredients he uses: the very best, freshest wild mushrooms; caviar that is steadily Beluga; smoked salmon of rare deliciousness; peerless foie gras; wonderful lamb and beef and deeply-concentrated sauces enriched with the richest cream; oysters that are Colchester No 1s, served warm in a feuilleté.

The wine list is, as you would expect, voluminous and expensive and there are quite a lot of half bottles and an exceptional collection of digestifs and

Eaux de Vie and vintage ports. His petits fours are sensational.

It might be best to come here in the summer, by boat, landing at the private jetty, and after canapés of lobster, sit and watch the life on the river and be grateful that fortune has spared you from witnessing it from a disco boat that comes by every now and then bearing raucous customers who are, well, less totally *comme il faut* than the excellent clientèle that gathers in the premises of the statesman-like M Roux.

Ferry Road, Bray, Berkshire, SL6 2AT. Beside the River Thames, 30 miles from London. Open Tuesday to Sunday except Tuesday lunch and Sunday dinner in winter; closed 25 December after lunch for 7 weeks. (Children welcome; no smoking of cigars in dining room; air-conditioned; no dogs.) Private parties: up to 80 by arrangement. To visit nearby: Windsor Castle; Cliveden; Henley-on-Thames; Ascot. Credit cards accepted: Access, AE, Carte Blanche, Diners, Visa. Tel: (0628) 20691 & 22941

Arc-en-ciel de crudités

(A rainbow of crudites)

Serves 12
9 oz (250 g) carrot, washed and peeled
12 oz (350 g) celeriac, washed and
  peeled
1 medium-size cucumber, washed and
  peeled
11 oz (310 g) cauliflower florets, washed
  and drained
9 oz (250 g) button mushrooms,
  washed and patted dry
2 lemons
3 large uncooked Britanny artichoke
  hearts
3 ½ fl oz (100 ml) olive oil
5 ½ fl oz (155 ml) white wine
15 coriander seeds, crushed
20 x 5 oz (140 g) firm, ripe tomatoes,
  skinned
16 small fresh basil leaves
salt and freshly-ground pepper
For the tomato sorbet:
18 fl oz (500 ml) fresh tomato coulis
2 teaspoons stock syrup
juice of ½ lemon
Tabasco sauce, to taste
For the crudités:
9 oz (250 g) mayonnaise
12 mint leaves, snipped
hazelnut oil-based vinaigrette
lemon juice-based vinaigrette
4 teaspoons snipped chives
pinch of paprika
4 tablespoons double cream
12 sprigs fresh chervil
1 tablespoon olive oil

Planning ahead
The sorbet can be made 2-3 hours before
needed but do not make it any earlier as it
will lose flavour and become hard. It is best
made in an ice cream machine: it can be
made without but the texture is not as good.

First prepare the vegetables. Cut the carrot
and celeriac separately into julienne. Put in
bowls, cover and reserve in the refrigerator.
Cut the cucumber in half lengthways and
remove the inner pips. Cut into 1 ½ in (4 cm)
pieces, slice finely lengthways, then cut into
fine julienne. Put in a bowl, cover and
reserve in the refrigerator. Cut the cauliflower into very small florets, taking just the
tops and discarding any stalk. Put in a bowl,
cover and reserve in the refrigerator. Slice
the mushrooms finely. Squeeze a little
lemon juice on top to keep them white. Put
in a bowl, cover and reserve in the refrigerator.
Slice the artichoke hearts into ⅛ in (¼ cm)
strips. Heat the olive oil in a frying pan until
very hot. Sauté the artichoke strips off in
the hot oil quickly, add the juice from one of
the lemons, white wine and coriander
seeds. Cook until the artichoke is just tender. Deseed 4 of the tomatoes and dice. Add
to the mixture. Snip 4 of the basil leaves and
add. Bring to the boil, season with salt and
pepper, then transfer to a bowl and reserve.
From the remaining tomatoes, choose 6 of
the best. Cut in half across the middle,
remove the seeds and reserve. Put the halves
on a tray and reserve in the refrigerator.
To make the sorbet, take the remaining 10
tomatoes plus any trimmings from the other
tomatoes and liquidize. Pass the coulis
through a fine sieve into a bowl, add the
stock syrup, lemon juice and Tabasco sauce
to taste. Season well with salt and pepper.
Put into an ice cream making machine.
When firm, remove the sorbet and keep in
the freezer until needed. (Alternatively,
freeze the tomato mixture until semi-
frozen, then beat and return to the freezer
until firm.)
To assemble the crudités, mix the cauliflower florets with 5 oz (140 g) of the mayonnaise and season with salt and pepper.
Divide equally between 12 plates, placing
the mixture at the top of the plate. Sprinkle
a little paprika over the top of each portion.
Mix the carrot with the snipped mint leaves,
toss in a good, hazelnut-flavoured vinaigrette and season with salt and pepper.
Divide equally between the 12 plates, placing the mixture to the right of the cauliflower.
Toss the mushrooms in a good lemon vinaigrette and add the snipped chives. Season
with salt and pepper. Divide equally between the 12 plates, placing the mixture
next to the carrot.
Mix the remaining mayonnaise with the
cream, pour over the celeriac, season and
mix well. Divide equally between the 12
plates, placing the mixture next to the
mushrooms. Place a nice sprig of chervil on
top.
Season the cucumber with a good olive oil,
salt and pepper. Divide equally into 12 and
place next to the celeriac.
Taste and adjust the salt and pepper seasoning on the artichokes. Divide equally into
12 and place between the cucumber and the
cauliflower.
Place a half tomato in the middle of each
plate and season the inside with a little salt.
Place a scoop of tomato sorbet in the centre
of each half and finish by placing a small
leaf of fresh basil on top of the sorbet. Serve
immediately.

Tronçonettes de homard poêlées minutes

(Medallions of lobster with white port)

Serves 4
4 x 1 lb (455 g) live lobsters
1 leek
1 carrot
¾ oz (20 g) fresh root ginger
5 ½ oz (1 stick plus 3 tablespoons/
  155 g) butter
2 teaspoons redcurrant jelly
¾ oz (20 g) salt
¼ oz (8 g) cayenne pepper
3 ½ fl oz (100 ml) extra virgin olive oil
7 fl oz (200 ml) white port
10 ½ fl oz (300 ml) veal stock
14 fl oz (400 ml) fish stock
⅓ oz (10 g) sprigs fresh chervil

Blanch the lobsters in boiling water for 45
seconds, then leave to cool.

Cut the leek, carrot and ginger into
julienne strips and sweat in 1 oz (2 table-
spoons/30 g) of the butter, until just cooked
and still crisp. Moisten with the redcurrant
jelly, set aside and keep warm.
Mix together the salt and cayenne pepper.
Cut the lobsters into pieces. Cut the tail into
approximately 3 medallions and crack the
claws and elbows using the back of a knife.

Reserve the tail and the top of the head. Season all the pieces well with the salt and cayenne pepper.

Heat up the olive oil in a large, flat-bottomed sauté pan until very hot. Sauté the lobster pieces quickly on all sides until three-quarters cooked. Remove from the pan and set aside in a warm place. Deglaze the pan with the white port and cook until reduced. Add the veal and fish stocks and reduce until syrupy. Whisk in the rest of the butter and season to taste.

Preheat the oven to 230°C/450°F/Gas Mark 8. Place the lobster pieces in the oven for 3-4 minutes. Arrange the julienne on 4 hot plates, dress the lobster pieces and place on top of the julienne, then return to the oven for 30 seconds. Pass the sauce through a fine sieve, then use to coat the lobster. Garnish with plenty of chervil leaves.

Tournedos et petit mille-feuille de champignons

(Tournedos with a millefeuille of wild mushrooms and a truffle sauce)

Serves 4
salt and freshly-ground pepper
1 ¼ – 1 ½ lb (600-700 g) best fillet of
  beef, cut into 4 equal portions
2 fl oz (4 tablespoons/50 ml) clarified
  butter
3 ½ oz (100 g) each carrots, celeriac
  and French beans, cut in small dice
10 fl oz (300 ml) double cream
9 oz (250 g) mixed wild mushrooms,
  cooked in butter
1 oz (30 g) chopped fresh parsley
12 x 2 in (5 cm) squares of already-
  baked puff pastry
¾ oz (scant 2 tablespoons/25 g) butter
3 ½ fl oz (100 ml) veal stock, reduced
  until syrupy
For the sauce:
2 oz (50 g) veal or beef trimmings
7 oz (200 g) chopped shallots and
  carrots (mirepoix)
1 clove of garlic

1 ½ tablespoons Madeira
1 ½ tablespoons dark port
sprigs of fresh thyme
1 bay leaf
17 fl oz (500 ml) veal stock
¾ oz (25 g) chopped truffles
¾ oz (scant 2 tablespoons/25 g)
  unsalted butter

First make the sauce. Brown the trimmings in a pan, then add the mirepoix and garlic with a little butter and cook until golden brown. Add the alcohol and the herbs, bring to the boil and reduce by half. Add the stock, bring to the boil, skimming well and simmer until reduced by approximately half or until the sauce is a good consistency. Pass through a chinois (conical sieve) and pass again through a muslin. Add the chopped truffles and unsalted butter at the last moment. Season with salt and pepper.

Season the tournedos and cook in a hot pan with a little clarified butter until rare or as preferred. Leave to rest before carving 3 slices from the side of each tournedos. Keep warm.

Cook the carrots, celeriac and French beans in boiling, salted water for 2-3 minutes, until very lightly crisp.

Reduce the cream by half, take out 4 tablespoons and reserve. Add the wild mushrooms and the parsley to the rest of the reduced cream and season to taste.

To assemble the millefeuilles, place 4 squares of puff pastry on a tray, cover these with half the mushroom mixture, top with a second piece of pastry and spread over the remainder of the mushrooms. Cover with a final layer of pastry.

Bring the reserved cream to the boil and whisk in ¾ oz (not quite 2 tablespoons/25 g) butter. Do not reboil. Put the veal glaze into a small piping bag fitted with a 1 mm size nozzle. Spread an even layer of cream over the top of the millefeuilles, then pipe the veal glaze around in a spiral and feather using a cocktail stick.

To serve, arrange the tournedos on large hot plates and sprinkle around the diced vegetables. Place the millefeuilles at the top of the plates and pour the sauce around each tournedos. Serve immediately.

Pêches rôties au caramel noisettine

(Peaches in nutty caramel)

Serves 4
2 oz (50 g) sugar
3 oz (¾ stick/75 g) butter
juice of ½ lemon, strained
few drops of grenadine (optional)
4 white or yellow peaches
2 oz (60 g) flaked hazelnuts
¾ oz (20 g) unsalted shelled pistachios

To make the caramel, place the sugar and butter in a shallow pan over a low heat and cook, stirring continually with a spatula, until the mixture becomes pale golden. Remove from the heat, stir in the lemon juice and a drop or two of grenadine, if using. Set aside and keep warm.

Preheat the oven to 240°C/475°F/Gas Mark 9. Bring a saucepan of water to the boil. Plunge in the peaches for a few seconds, then skin them. Arrange them in a roasting tin. Pour over the reserved caramel and scatter over the hazelnuts. Cook in the preheated oven for about 10 minutes. (If the peaches are very ripe, they will only need 7-8 minutes.) Baste them with the caramel 3-4 times during cooking to glaze as they cook. Split the pistachios in half. Two minutes before the peaches are cooked, add half the pistachios to the caramel and hazelnut mixture and reserve the rest.

To serve, place each peach in a shallow dish. Divide the caramel-nut mixture equally between the dishes, spooning it generously over the peaches. Stud the top of the peaches with the remaining pistachios. Serve either hot or warm.

HINTLESHAM HALL

In my East Anglian youth, wondrous rumours swept our county of Suffolk about the "goings on" at Hintlesham Hall. The master, it was said, invited ladies from London, harnessed them to a chariot and had them race around the circular drive of his mansion. They were naked, said some; the mistress was among their number, said others. He carried a whip, it was alleged. When, at the end of the swinging Sixties, Robert Carrier bought the beautiful 16th century house four miles west of Ipswich, locals said "mark my words – there'll be more happenings" and they were right: no chariot races, but the anglophile American foodwriter/restaurateur used his good taste to restore the hall to its former glories and cooked therein such meals as the populace had only read about in the Sunday Times Colour Supplement – of which Carrier was food and beverage editor.

His days were pre-nouvelle cuisine and he combined a composite knowledge of the algebra of cookery with traditional respect for establishment food. His *Coq au vin* (serves four) told you exactly how many sculpted button mushrooms, glazed onions, lardons of green bacon and heart-shaped croûtons of fried

bread should accompany the ensemble. He wrote "Great Dishes of the World", lending authority to the practice of the great chefs for whom he had admiration. In an age of angry young men, he was the traditionalist and at Hintlesham he combined his gastronomic talents with a flair for presentation. Carrier sold Hintlesham in the early 1980s, went to live in Marrakesh and has recently published the very readable "Taste of Morocco".

Now there is absolutely no reason why a place that was once the treasure trove of a master-chef should continue to enjoy a high reputation for food when the motivating spirit has taken the money and left the country. I can name palaces that have become pizza parlours in similar circumstances, but not Hintlesham Hall. It was bought by David and Ruth Watson – after he had sold his computer company in London. He has a love for wine, she loves people and between them they turned Hintlesham into one of the most beautiful country houses in East Anglia, possibly the most luxurious country house hotel in the land.

The pale yellow Georgian façade that was added to the Elizabethan manor house overlooks the 175 acres of flat Constable country parklands and cornfields; the gardens are lovingly maintained; there is a pool, a tennis court, fishing adjacent and the 34 bedrooms have all the modern amenities that one could wish for. There is an air of gracious unstuffiness about the place: among the impressive pictures that adorn the walls, there are some that are engaging without having artistic merit; an Adam fireplace burns "logs" that are efficiently gas-motivated; the vases on the restaurant tables contain fruit... and there are ripe kumquats in the

fruit-bowls on the upstairs landing. The staff are dressed for the precise job that they do and each performs with skill and tact – be it the white-coated commis in the dining room, the dinner-jacketed waiter, the formally lounge-suited manager, the uniformed porter. One reads of non-catering people who purchase hotels and try to do everything themselves – often with disastrous consequences. The Watsons have employed the very best team and are there to direct, to encourage, not to interfere. In Tim Sunderland they have a general manager with an encyclopaedic knowledge of the trade – one whom you would trust right down to the last glass of Trockenbeerenauslese, which he rightly recommends as being better value at £26 a half bottle than the Beerenauslese at £13.80.

The wine list contains four pages of recommendations', which are written with wit and understanding and plug a house champagne as "mirthful and marvellously high-spirited". There you will find the house claret, a contribution each from Spain and Italy, a page of Country Wines at around £10 a bottle... whereafter it becomes serious and more expensive but very complete with a real showing of wines from North America, Australia and New Zealand and a substantial choice of half bottles including three first growth clarets of 1961.

The restaurant consists of two intercommunicating rooms, each with open fires and soft carpets, round tables which are a boon and chairs that allow you to lounge at leisure and in great comfort, while you spend a happy evening being a gourmet. There is an air of contented orderliness about the place: appetisers arrive as one picks *à la carte* listing eight starters, eight main courses and half a dozen puddings: a choco-

Hintlesham, near Ipswich, Suffolk, IP8 3NS. Amidst the cornfields of Suffolk, 60 miles from London. Open all year, Saturday lunch excepted. (Children by arrangement; no smoking in dining room; pets by arrangement.) Private parties: 40 in main room, 100 in private room. Guest accommodation: 34 room all with bath/shower. (All-weather tennis; croquet; billiards; horse-riding.) To visit nearby: Long Melford; Lavenham; Dedham Vale. Credit cards accepted: Access, AE, Diners, Visa.   Tel: (047 387) 268

late *Fetishist's fantasy* might make most appeal : it has the word "Fetishist" writ in white chocolate on a base of black. Alan Ford, who is the head chef, prepares food with a fine flourish, makes sauces of deep flavour and prepares his own good ricotta and spinach cannelloni for vegetarians. A seascape of salmon, monkfish and scallops served with a saffron sauce was especially admirable. A nice touch here is called "A Fillip Between Courses", being a choice of small or large portions of excellent smoked salmon and "a con-sommé according to chef's whim", with which you toy after the feuilleté, before the noisette of English lamb. Petits fours come at room temperature, but a really warm feeling of being a cossetted guest makes up for that.

Hintlesham does just what it sets out to do : in a spectacularly luxurious setting it provides excellent food – and drink of the very highest quality – brought to you by staff who appear to enjoy the work that they do. The price you pay includes service, there is a helicopter landing pad, spinach is grown in the kit-chen garden, they don't let people smoke in the dining room, which I applaud, and when the bill comes it is computerised, bears the name of the diner and lists every item that was consumed – right down to the *Passionfruit soufflé glacée.* I seriously doubt that a successful hotelier could sell out and run a computer company with a fraction of the expertise shown by Mr Watson.

Guineafowl and pheasant terrine

Serves 10
10 oz (285 g) pork fat
12 oz (340 g) boneless leg meat from
  guineafowl and pheasant, trimmed of
  all fat
¼ teaspoon chopped garlic
1 shallot
2 oz (55 g) pistachio nuts, blanched
  and skinned
2 tablespoons reduced game stock
salt and freshly-ground pepper
mixed salad leaves
For the marinade:
8 oz (225 g) diced lean leg meat from
  guineafowl and pheasant
4 fl oz (110 ml) Madeira
1 fl oz (30 ml) brandy
1 shallot, halved
1 sprig fresh thyme
4 juniper berries
a few white peppercorns
For the sauce:
10 fl oz (285 ml) plain yogurt
1 teaspoon grain mustard
cream

Planning ahead
Make this terrine 1 day in advance.

Mix all the marinade ingredients together
in a bowl and leave aside for 4 hours.
Meanwhile, mince 6 oz (170 g) of the pork
fat together with the guineafowl and pheasant meat, the garlic and shallot. Blanch the
remaining pork fat and dice. Remove the
meat from the marinade and add to the
minced mixture together with the diced
pork fat and the pistachio nuts. Strain the
marinade juices and stir in. Mix in the reduced game stock and season with salt and
pepper. Place in a terrine mould, 10 x 3 x 3
in (25 x 8 x 8 cm), ensuring that there are no
gaps. Cover with foil, then the lid.
Preheat the oven to 180°C/350°F/Gas Mark
4. Place the terrine in a bain marie and cook
in the preheated oven for about 1 ¼ hours.
Allow to cool to room temperature, then
remove the lid and place weights on top.
Leave overnight.

To make the sauce, mix together the yogurt
and mustard and add cream to give a pouring consistency. Season to taste. To serve,
unmould the terrine and serve in slices with
the sauce and a mixed salad.

Seized escalopes of salmon, monkfish and red mullet

Serves 1
1 oz (30 g) salmon ⎫
½ oz (40 g) monkfish ⎬ cut into neat
1 oz (30 g) red mullet ⎭ shapes
butter
salt and freshly-ground pepper
1 ½ oz (40 g) mixed salad leaves, e.g.
  radicchio, lollo rosso, frisée, iceberg
walnut oil-based vinaigrette
chopped fresh chives

Preheat a cast iron shallow pan. Brush the
fish on both sides with butter and season
with salt and pepper. Place in the pan and
cook quickly on both sides. Toss the salad
leaves in the vinaigrette and arrange on a
serving plate. Arrange the fish neatly on top
and brush with the vinaigrette. Sprinkle
with chives and serve immediately.

Breast of pheasant with whisky and wild mushroom ragoût

Serves 1
1 breast of pheasant, 6 oz (170 g)
salt and freshly-ground pepper
butter
2 oz (55 g) wild mushrooms
1 tablespoon whisky
chopped fresh parsley
2 fl oz (55 ml) pheasant juice
1 oz (2 tablespoons/30 g) unsalted
  butter

Season the pheasant breast with salt and
pepper. Pan-fry in butter, ensuring that it is
still pink in the centre. Remove and keep
warm.
Sauté the mushrooms in the same pan,
deglaze with the whisky, then stir in the
parsley. Taste and adjust the seasoning.
Heat up the pheasant juice, then whisk in
the unsalted butter.
Arrange the mushroom ragoût in the
middle of a serving plate. Slice the pheasant
breast in half and arrange on top of the
mushrooms. Spoon the sauce over the meat
and serve.

Hot hazelnut soufflé with chocolate sauce

Serves 4
For the chocolate sauce:
12 fl oz (340 ml) water
7 oz (200 g) sugar
1 oz (30 g) dark chocolate
1 ½ oz (40 g) cocoa powder
For the soufflé:
1 ½ oz (40 g) roasted hazelnuts,
crushed
6 tablespoons crème pâtissière
3 egg yolks
12 egg whites
2 oz (55 g) sugar
icing sugar

To make the chocolate sauce, place 10 fl oz
(285 ml) of the water, 4 oz (110 g) of the
sugar and the chocolate in a pan and bring
to the boil. Mix the remaining sugar and
water together with the cocoa powder. Once
the chocolate mixture is boiling, add the
cocoa mixture and bring back to the boil,
whisking all the time. Keep warm.
Preheat the oven to 190°C/375°F/Gas Mark
5. Line individual soufflé dishes first with
butter, then with sugar. Mix the hazelnuts
with the crème pâtissière, then beat in the
egg yolks. Whisk the egg white and sugar
together until firm, then fold into the egg
yolk mixture. Divide this mixture between
the soufflé dishes and bake in the preheated
oven for 7 minutes. Sprinkle with icing
sugar and serve immediately with the chocolate sauce.

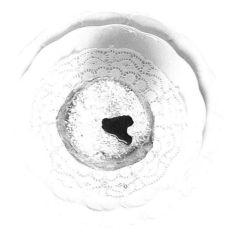

Apple tart with caramel

Serves 1
1 circle of thin puff pastry, 6 in (15 cm) in diameter
2 apples, peeled, cored and finely sliced
1 teaspoon caster sugar
½ oz (1 tablespoon/15 g) butter
icing sugar
For the caramel sauce:
4 oz (110 g) caster sugar
5 fl oz (140 ml) water
5 fl oz (140 ml) double cream

Preheat the oven to 200°C/400°F/Gas Mark 6. Prick the pastry circle with a fork and bake in the preheated oven for about 7 minutes.
Arrange the apple slices in circles on the pastry, starting from the outside and working in to the centre. Sprinkle the sugar over the apples and dot with the butter. Reduce the oven temperature to 180°C/350°F/Gas Mark 4 and bake for 10 minutes. Sprinkle with icing sugar and brown under the grill.
To make the caramel sauce, cook the sugar and water together until a dark, golden brown, then remove from the heat and carefully add the cream until the required colour and consistency is obtained. Be cautious when doing this as the sugar can easily boil over.
Pour the caramel sauce onto a serving plate and place the apple tart on top.

Chocolate fetishist's fantasy

Serves 6
For the chocolate parfait:
8 oz (225 g) dark chocolate
4 oz (1 stick/110 g) unsalted butter
2 large eggs, separated
3 oz (85 g) sugar
For the white chocolate tart:
white marzipan
4 oz (110 g) white chocolate
2 fl oz (55 ml) double cream
1 oz (30 g) dark chocolate
For the tuile basket:
5 oz (140 g) egg whites
5 oz (140 g) caster sugar
2 oz (55 g) flour
2 oz (½ stick/55 g) warm melted butter
For the ice cream:
20 fl oz (565 ml) double cream
8 oz (225 g) caster sugar
8 egg yolks
2 oz (55 g) cocoa powder
2 fl oz (55 ml) milk
½ oz (15 g) chopped white and dark chocolate
For the raspberry coulis:
8 oz (225 g) raspberries
4 oz (110 g) sugar
lemon juice to taste
5 fl oz (140 ml) water
For the decoration:
plain unsweetened yogurt
grated white and dark chocolate
a little melted chocolate

To make the chocolate parfait, line a small loaf tin 6 x 3 x 3 in (15 x 8 x 8 cm), with cling film. Melt the chocolate and butter together, then beat until smooth. Beat the egg yolks and sugar over a bain marie to a sabayon. Whisk the egg white lightly. Fold the sabayon into the melted chocolate, then fold in the egg white. Place in the terrine and freeze.
To make the white chocolate tart, thinly roll out the marzipan and use to line individual tart tins. Leave to dry overnight. Melt the white chocolate over a bain marie, add the cream and beat until smooth and glossy. Place in the marzipan lined tins. Melt the

dark chocolate, place in a paper piping bag, snip the end and decorate the tarts. Place in the freezer.
To make the tuile baskets, preheat the oven to 160°C/325°F/Gas Mark 3. Whisk the egg whites and sugar together until combined. Add the flour and mix to a smooth paste, then slowly add the warm butter. Place 1 teaspoon of the mixture onto a buttered and floured baking sheet and spread the mixture out until it is a 2½ – 3 in (6-7.5 cm) circle. Bake in the preheated oven for 5 minutes until just pale golden, then remove from the tray immediately and place inside a small cup to shape. Leave to set for about 1 minute, then remove from the cup and store in an airtight container. Repeat with the remaining mixture.
To make the ice cream, boil the cream. Cream the sugar and egg yolks together until thick, then slowly pour on the boiling cream, stirring continually. Return to the heat and stir until the mixture coats the back of a spoon. Pass through a fine sieve, then leave until cold. Bring the cocoa powder and milk to the boil and cook for 1-2 minutes. Cool slightly, then add to the crème anglaise. Turn into an ice cream machine until firm, then mix in the chopped chocolate. Alternatively, place in a freezer container and freeze until mushy, then beat well and add the chopped chocolate. Freeze until firm.
To make the raspberry coulis, boil all the ingredients together until soft, then purée in a liquidizer. Strain through a fine chinois (conical sieve). Refrigerate until needed.
To assemble, place the coulis in a pool in the centre of the serving plates. Pipe the word "fetish" on top in yogurt. Unmould the parfait, remove the cling film and slice. Cut each slice diagonally in two, then place both portions on each plate. Sprinkle with a little grated white chocolate. Remove the marzipan tarts from the moulds (straight from the freezer) and place on the plates. Using dessertspoons, take quenelle-shaped scoops of the ice cream and place one in each tuile basket, having secured the basket to the plate with a little melted chocolate. Decorate with grated dark chocolate.

Recipe Index

Turbot	Turbot escalope with a scallop and ginger tian	61
Witch	Witch with crab and ginger and a Champagne butter sauce	90

Poultry

Chicken	Breast of chicken wrapped in Savoy cabbage and pancetta	19
	Chicken breast stuffed with banana and mango, baked in smoked bacon	132
	Chicken gruyère	80
Duck	Marinated grilled duck breast	61
Grouse	Roast grouse on a bed of cabbage	87
Guinea fowl	Panfried breast of guinea fowl with wild mushrooms in a ginger sauce	115
Partridge	Roast partridge with fresh noodles, grapes, ginger and lime	148
	Roast young partridge on a bed of cabbage with its juices	102
Pheasant	Breast of pheasant with whisky and wild mushroom ragoût	172
Pigeon	A ragoût of wood pigeon and wild Scottish mushrooms	102
	Breast of pigeon with red chard, sauce Beaujolais	85
	Emincé of Bresse pigeon with wild mushrooms, foie gras and maize	23
	Grilled breast of woodpigeon with warm Cumberland sauce	96
	Norfolk pigeon roasted, sauce of baby leeks and truffle, slices of foie gras glazed with port	121
	Pigeon in a parcel with ravioli and its tartare	40
	Roast pigeon breast with lentil and lambs lettuce	60
	Stuffed breast of woodpigeon in a trellis of puff pastry with a marsala sauce	114
Quail	Roast smoked quail with a potato galette	60
Teal	Roast teal with braised red cabbage	46

Meat

Beef	Fillet of beef, roasted shallot, a crêpe of girolles and parsley purée	120
	Medallions of beef with wild mushrooms and vegetables in Madeira	139
	Tournedos with a millefeuille of wild mushrooms and a truffle sauce	167
Calves' liver	Calves' liver with sweet and onions	143
	Sauté of calves' liver	80
Lamb	Lamb fillet with a parsley cream sauce and garlic fritters	35
	Rosette of lamb with pistou	13
Mixed meats	A meat assortment	28
Rabbit	Saddle of rabbit stuffed with grapes	69
Veal	Fillet of veal with lime sabayon	56
Venison	Medallions of roedeer with a sauce of its own juices, grapes, juniper and dill flambéed in armagnac	90
	Roast saddle of roedeer with apple purée and rosemary sauce	96
	Saddle of venison marinated in red wine with thyme and vegetables	127
	Saddle of venison with beetroot mousse	57
	Venison with sautéed spinach and port sauce	139

Desserts

Apples	Apple and blackberry pie	47
	Apple hat pudding	47
	Apple tart with caramel	173
	Vol-au-vents with apples	81
Apricot	Joan Sutherland bavarois	127
Cake	Chocolate orange gâteau	133
	Norwegian cream cake with a cloud berry filling and a marzipan topping	91
	Salzburger nockerln	61
Chocolate	Chocolate assortment	161
	Chocolate fetishist's fancy	173
	Chocolate strasse	121
	Dark and white chocolate millefeuille	65
	Duet of dark chocolate layered with chocolate and raspberry mousse	155
	Tears of dark chocolate filled with whisky mousse	97
	Thin chocolate wafers filled with bitter chocolate mousse	41
Cream cheese	Fresh cream cheese with rose petal jelly and wild strawberries	69
Figs	Hot figs with pine nuts and honey sauce	35
Fruit	A feuilleté of fruits	103
Ices	Iced hazelnut mousse with raspberries	127
	Iced passion fruit soufflé with a strawberry sauce	41
	Krumkaker filled with pistachio ice cream and spun sugar	91
	Mango parfait with mango coulis	13
	Mixed sorbets in "tulip" biscuits with raspberry sauce	57
	Praline ice cream	81
Mousses	A light passion fruit mousse served with a dialogue of fruit purées	115
	Charlotte of white coffee mousse with an orange and Grand Marnier sauce	109
Oranges	Nectarine and caramel tart	75
Peaches	Peaches in nutty caramel	167
Pears	Farmhouse pear and Stilton pie	133
Prune	Prune and almond tart	19
	Prune, armagnac and mascarpone tart	53
Pudding	Toulouse chestnut pudding	143
Soufflé	Hot hazelnut soufflé with chocolate sauce	172
Strawberry	Roasted strawberries with pink grapefruit sorbet	97
	Shortbread with strawberries	29

The measurements: All quantities have been given in imperial and metric measurements (in this order), except for butter and margarine quantities, which have also been given in American measures. Imperial measures (cups, tablespoons, etc.) are not always equivalent to American and Canadian measures. For further explanation and for other American measures, consult the note to readers and the conversion table. When following the recipes, use one set of measures throughout since metric and imperial have been calculated separately and are not necessarily direct equivalents.

The photographs: Claude Pataut photographed all the restaurants except for the recipes from Le Soufflé. These photographs were taken by Tim Ridley.

The restaurants: Hours of business and credit cards accepted may change without notice. The publishers would advise calling ahead to confirm details.

Abreviations for credit cards accepted in the restaurants are as follows:
AE   American Express
Diners   Diners Club

Artistic Director:
Eric Tschumi

Photographers:
Claude Pataut
Tim Ridley

Editing:
Rosemary Wilkinson

Composition:
Jacques Audebert, SCG, PARIS
Printing:
Grafiche A. Pizzi, Milan